Temporal and Spatio-Temporal Data Mining

Wynne Hsu
National University of Singapore, Singapore

Mong Li Lee
National University of Singapore, Singapore

Junmei Wang
National University of Singapore, Singapore

IGI PUBLISHING

Hershey • New York

Acquisitions Editor:	Krisitn Klinger
Development Editor:	Kristin Roth
Senior Managing Editor:	Jennifer Neidig
Managing Editor:	Sara Reed
Copy Editor:	Amanda Appicello
Typesetter:	Amanda Appicello
Cover Design:	Lisa Tosheff
Printed at:	Yurchak Printing Inc.

Published in the United States of America by
    IGI Publishing (an imprint of IGI Global)
    701 E. Chocolate Avenue, Suite 200
    Hershey PA 17033-1240
    Tel: 717-533-8845
    Fax: 717-533-8661
    E-mail: cust@igi-pub.com
    Web site: http://www.igi-pub.com

and in the United Kingdom by
    IGI Publishing (an imprint of IGI Global)
    3 Henrietta Street
    Covent Garden
    London WC2E 8LU
    Tel: 44 20 7240 0856
    Fax: 44 20 7379 0609
    Web site: http://www.eurospanonline.com

Library of Congress Cataloging-in-Publication Data

Hsu, Wynne, 1966-
  Temporal and spatio-temporal data mining / Wynne Hsu, Mong Li Lee, and Junmei Wang.
    p. cm.
  Summary: "This book presents probable solutions when discovering the spatial sequence patterns by incorporating the information into the sequence of patterns, and introduces new classes of spatial sequence patterns, called flow and generalized spatio-temporal patterns, addressing different scenarios in spatio-temporal data by modeling them as graphs, providing a comprehensive synopsis on two successful partition-based algorithms designed by the authors"--Provided by publisher.
  Includes bibliographical references and index.
  ISBN 978-1-59904-387-6 (hardcover) -- ISBN 978-1-59904-389-0 (ebook)
  1. Data mining. 2. Temporal databases. I. Lee, Mong Li. II. Wang, Junmei, 1975- III. Title.
  QA76.9.D343H78 2008
  005.74--dc22
                 2006102335

British Cataloguing in Publication Data
A Cataloguing in Publication record for this book is available from the British Library.

Temporal and Spatio-Temporal Data Mining

Table of Contents

Preface

Data mining has been an active area of research since the early 1990s. Data mining has evolved from relational data to include time and space constraints. More recently, advances in positioning technology and location-based services have led to a growth of spatio-temporal databases that require advanced data mining capabilities.

Temporal data mining is complex due to the existence of time which imposes an ordering on the temporal events. However, temporal data mining is able to discover the behavioral aspects of objects as opposed to simple mining rules that describe their states at a point in time. Spatio-temporal mining has several challenges due to the complexity of geographical domains, the mapping of data in spatial and temporal frameworks, and the spatial and temporal correlation. Mining in spatio-temporal databases needs to consider the multi-states of the data, and integrate spatial and temporal information together to find meaningful spatio-temporal patterns.

The target audience of this book is students, researchers, and professionals who are interested to work in the area of data mining, data analysis, machine learning, and knowledge discovery in spatial and/or temporal databases. More specifically, the book will be a useful companion for graduate students studying the issues of data mining in spatio-temporal databases, and for instructors who can use the book as a reference for advanced topics in spatio-temporal databases.

To the Data Mining Researchers

This book is designed to give an in-depth discussion on the issues and challenges facing pattern discovery in temporal and spatio-temporal databases. The book consists of two parts: the first, comprising of chapters II to V, is focused on temporal data mining. The second part, comprising of chapters VI to XI, concentrates on spatial-temporal mining. Each chapter is self-contained so that you will be able to focus directly on those chapters that interest you.

To the Graduate Students

This book will provide the necessary background information and the latest research in the area of temporal and spatio-temporal data mining. The materials are presented in a clear and easy to understand manner. The emphasis of the book is on the design and implementation of novel algorithms and techniques used for patterns discovery in temporal and spatio-temporal databases. To enable you to better appreciate these algorithms and techniques, two chapters, namely Chapter II and Chapter VI, are included to introduce the necessary background information and related work in time series mining and spatio-temporal mining respectively.

Organization of the Book

The book is organized as follows. Chapter I provides an overview of the various types of patterns that could be discovered in temporal and spatio-temporal databases. Chapters II to XI can be divided into two parts. The first part, comprising of chapters II to V, is focused on temporal data mining. The second part, comprising of chapters VI to XI, concentrates on spatial-temporal mining. Chapter XII summarizes the book and suggests possible future research directions for researchers and graduate students who would like to explore into this exciting field.

In Chapter II, two types of temporal data are dominant in the development of temporal data mining. They are time-series data and sequence data. Interesting temporal patterns that could be discovered from these two types of data include periodic patterns and sequential patterns, respectively. We will first discuss several issues in time series mining such as similarity measures, dimension reduction, and data discretization. Then we will examine the existing techniques for mining periodic patterns and sequential patterns in temporal databases.

Periodic patterns are patterns that occur regularly over time in a time series database. Periodic patterns could be full, partial, asynchronous, and surprising. A full periodic pattern such as season cycles for every year requires that every event in the database contributes to part of the pattern. Discovering periodic patterns from an entire time series may not be suitable in applications where the periodic patterns occur only within small segments of the time series. Chapter III presents a class of periodic patterns called dense periodic patterns, and describes an algorithm that efficiently discovers short period patterns that may exist in part of a time series.

Sequence patterns aim to show precedence relationships and ordered associations among events in the sequence. Sequential pattern mining has been a well-studied problem and has become an important in applications such as market and customer analysis. Many techniques have been developed for general sequence pattern mining, constraint-based sequence pattern mining, frequent episode mining, sequence pattern mining in noisy environment, and closed sequence pattern mining. Chapter IV analyzes the I/O cost of one of the state-of-the-art sequence mining techniques called GSP and discusses an I/O conscious algorithm called MFS as well as the incremental versions of GSP and MFS for mining sequence patterns in evolving databases.

We observe that many real-world objects have states that change over time. By tracking the state sequences of these objects, we can study their behavior and take preventive measures before they reach some undesirable states. Chapter V introduces a new kind of pattern called progressive confident rules. This class of pattern captures sequences of states with an increasing confidence that leads to a particular end state. In order to reduce the search space, we devise new pruning strategies and employ the concise set analysis of rules in the mining of progressive confident rules. We also demonstrate how progressive confident rules can be incorporated in existing classifiers to improve their accuracy.

Besides techniques to discover time-varying patterns, there has been increasing interest to extract patterns from spatio-temporal databases. While there has been much research on association rule mining on transactional, spatial, and temporal data, there is little literature on finding interesting associations in spatio-temporal data. Chapter VI first examines the early works in spatio-temporal mining which have been concentrated on finding evolution patterns of natural phenomena, frequent movements of objects over time, and space-time clusters. Then we give a review of the traditional association rules mining algorithms and their variants on transactional data, temporal data, and spatial data.

Chapters VII, VIII, and IX describe new classes of patterns that can be found in spatial-temporal data and algorithms to efficiently mine these patterns. We investigate the discovery of interesting spatio-temporal patterns from two aspects. First, we impose temporal constraints on the mining of spatial col-location patterns to discover topological patterns. Such patterns can reveal the intra-relationships of events in a time period. These events may relate to each other in a star, clique, or star-clique manner within the given time window. Chapter VII deals with topological patterns discovery.

Next, we search for spatial sequence patterns by incorporating spatial information into the process for mining sequence patterns. We will introduce two classes of spatial sequence patterns, called flow patterns and generalized spatio-temporal patterns. These two classes of spatial sequence patterns are useful to the understanding of many real-life applications. Such patterns can disclose the inter-relationships of events in different time windows, for example, how the observation of one event in some location implies the occurrence of another event in a second location, or how changes of events in one location can affect the events in another location. The discovery of spatial sequence patterns is challenging because of the potentially large search space and the large number of candidates. Chapters VIII and IX will describe efficient methods to discover flow patterns and generalized spatio-temporal patterns, respectively.

With appropriate models, a spatio-temporal database can be transformed into a tree or graph database, and the problem of mining frequent spatio-temporal patterns then becomes the problem of finding frequent trees or subgraphs. Chapter X and XI present efficient and scalable methods for mining arbitrary complex spatio-temporal association patterns, in the form of tree patterns and graph patterns, respectively. We note that changes in spatio-temporal databases can cause changes to the graph structures that model the relationships in the spatio-temporal data. Re-execution of the mining algorithm each time the graphs are updated is costly, and may result in an explosion in the demand for computational and I/O resources. Chapter XI also describes an incremental algorithm to handle such situations.

Finally, we conclude in Chapter XII with a summary of the contributions in each chapter and provide directions for future research.

Acknowledgments

We would like to express our special thanks to all those who have worked or are currently working with us on the mining of spatio-temporal databases. These include our invited chapter authors: Minghua Zhang, Chang Sheng, Ben Kao, Chi-Lap Yip, and David W. Cheung. We are also grateful to the Center for Remote Imaging Signal Processing for providing us the data for analyzing the forest fire hot spots. We also wish to thank Irene Woon for her many invaluable feedbacks and comments as we prepare this manuscript. Finally, we thank our families for their wonderful supports throughout this project.

Wynne Hsu, Mong Li Lee, & Junmei Wang

Chapter I

Introduction

Data mining, a major advance in the area of computing, has been applied in almost all possible fields in science, engineering, and business. The objective of data mining is to discover useful information and knowledge from a large collection of data, in particular, relational databases. One important class of regularities that exist in data is association rules. An example of an association rule is as follows

$$cheese \rightarrow beer \ [\text{sup} = 10\%, \text{conf} = 80\%]$$

This rule says that 10% of customers buy *cheese* and *beer* together, and those who buy *cheese* also buy *beer* 80% of the time. Although association rule mining was first designed for relational database/transactional systems, it has proven to be a general data mining technique. It can be and has been applied to almost every possible application domains including new applications which involve temporal and spatial data.

Temporal databases capture time-related attributes whose values change with time, for example, stock exchange data. Temporal data mining is an important extension of data mining as it can be used to mine the activity rather than just states, and thus, infer relationships of contextual and temporal proximity, some of which may also indicate a cause-effect association.

Two types of temporal data are dominant in the development of temporal data mining. They are time-series data and sequence data. Time-series data is a sequence of real numbers that vary with time, for example, stock prices, exchange rates, biomedical measurements data, and so forth. Sequence data is a list of transactions, and a transaction time is associated with each transaction, for example, Web page traversal sequences.

Mining patterns from temporal databases is complex due to the existence of time. Time implies an ordering, and this ordering affects the statistical properties of the data and the semantics of the rules being extracted from them. In particular, the incorporation of time into mining techniques provides an ordering on the temporal events and thus, an ability to suggest cause and effect that are overlooked when the temporal component is ignored. Moreover, temporal data mining has the ability to mine the behavioral aspects of objects as opposed to simply mining rules that describes their states at a point in time, that is there is the promise of understanding why rather than what.

Recent advances in positioning technology and location-based services have led to a rapid accumulation of spatial-temporal data. Spatio-temporal databases have become a very active area of research. New techniques have been developed for modeling, indexing, and querying of moving objects (Cai & Ng, 2004; Güting, Böhlen, & Erwig, 2000; Saltenis, Jensen, & Leutenegger, 2000; Sun, Papadias, & Tao, 2004; Tao, Papadias, & Shen, 2002; Tao, Taloutsos, & Papadias, 2004). Even as database technologies play a central role in the development and deployment of spatio-temporal applications, data mining capabilities will become increasingly important to discover and extract information from spatio-temporal databases.

Spatio-temporal data mining can be regarded as a generalization of temporal data mining or spatial data mining in the three-dimensional space. While mining techniques for temporal data and spatial data can be adapted for spatio-temporal data, however, spatio-temporal data contains complex relationships that cannot be discovered simply by looking at the spatial dimension or the temporal dimension independently.

Compared to temporal data mining and spatial data mining, spatio-temporal data mining is more complicated and presents a number of challenges due to the complexity of geographical domains, the mapping of data in spatial and temporal frameworks, and spatial and temporal autocorrelation (Miller & Han, 2001). In spatio-temporal databases, each object is related to other objects in complex interactions which are captured in the form of past, present, and future states in the modeled environment.

Data mining in spatio-temporal databases should consider the multi-states of spatio-temporal data. Techniques that integrate spatial information and temporal information together in order to find meaningful spatio-temporal patterns are needed. The spatio-temporal patterns can further be used to disclose insightful knowledge embedded in spatio-temporal phenomena and enable decision makers to understand the underlying process that controls changes and patterns of changes.

In this book, we will examine techniques for mining association patterns in temporal databases and spatio-temporal databases.

Temporal Data Mining

Time is one of the essential natures of data. Many real-life data describes the property or status of some object at a particular time instant. For example, a supermarket transaction database records the items purchased by customers at some time point. In this database, every transaction has a time stamp in which the transaction is conducted. In a telecommunication database, every signal is also associated with a time. As a third example, the price of a stock is not a constant, but changes with time as well.

Temporal data mining refers to data mining performed on the temporal data. The primary objective is to discover interesting patterns hidden in the data. For example, an interesting pattern in a stock database may be that when the price of stock A increases, the price of stock B will increase in the next two days.

The diversity of applications has led to the development of many data models in temporal data mining. Some of the representative temporal data mining problems include time series mining, temporal association rule mining, and periodic pattern mining. There are two criteria to classify temporal data mining problems. The first criterion is based on the extent that time participates in the mining process. The second criterion is based on the domain of data.

There are three levels in which time can participate in the mining process. The first level is the order or sequence of data. In this level, researchers are only interested in the order of data points, regardless of their concrete time stamp. This is the simplest usage of time. One example is sequence mining which considers only the order in which data points occur, and not their concrete time stamp.

The second level is focused on the real-time instant. For example, in a pattern which states that Mr. White leaves home around 8 a.m. every weekday, the actual time 8 a.m. plays a role in the mining result.

The third level examines not only the real time, but also the time hierarchies in the real-time represent. For example, a time stamp of 2 p.m. on May 1, 2006, implies that it is in the afternoon of a summer and falls on Monday. Here the information of *afternoon, summer,* and *Monday* are implied in the time stamp. Algorithms that deal with the time hierarchies are more complicated than algorithms for the first two levels, that is, order of data and actual time stamp.

The second criterion to classify temporal data mining problems is based on the input data type, whether it is numerical data or categorical data. If the data consists of numerical values, such as the stock price, we usually say that the data is time series. On the other hand, when the data take on categorical values, it is typically called sequence data. One example is the items purchased by customers in a supermarket, such as milk, bread, and so forth.

To date, there are three types of analysis of temporal data.

Temporal Association Rules

This type of rules treats the temporal information as a natural extension to the existing association rules semantics. For example, the rule: "Beachside flooding only occurs during Spring high tides" is a temporal association rule.

Sequence Patterns

These patterns aim to detect precedence relationships and ordered associations among events in the sequence. An example of a sequence pattern is as follows: "90% of students borrow the book 'Learning Java', then the book 'Java Server Pages', and then 'Enterprise Java Beans'."

Periodic Patterns

Periodic patterns are primarily considered as temporal regularity. For example, a periodic pattern may state that: "Lisa reads the Straits Times newspaper from 7:00 a.m. to 7:30 a.m. every week day morning."

Spatio-Temporal Data Mining

Besides techniques to discover time-varying patterns (Agrawal & Srikant, 1996; Pei, Han, & Mortazavi-Asl, 2001; Wang & Han, 2004; Zaki, 1998), the works in Han, Koperski, and Stefanovic (1997), Shekhar and Huang (2001), Morimoto (2001), and Zhang, Mamoulis, and Cheung (2004) develop spatial data mining methods to extract spatial patterns.

Spatial data exhibits a unique property in that *"Everything is related to everything else but nearby things are more related than distant things"*, which is also known as Tobler's first law of geography (Tobler, 1979). Hence, the goal of spatial data mining is to discover relationships between spatial data and non-spatial data by using spatial proximity relationships, such as topological relationships like *intersects, overlap, disjoint*; spatial orientation, such as *left_of, east_of*; and distance information, such as *close_to, far_away*.

Spatial data mining covers a wide spectrum of paradigms for knowledge discovery. The patterns discovered from spatial data includes characteristic and discriminant rules, spatial association rules, extraction and description of prominent structures or clusters, and so forth (see Han & Kamber, 2001).

A *spatial characteristic rule* is a general description of a set of spatial-related data. For example, the description of general weather patterns in geographic regions is a spatial characteristic rule. A *spatial discriminant rule* is the general description of contrasting or discriminating features of a class of spatial-related data from other classes. For example, the comparison of the weather patterns in two geographic regions is a spatial discriminant rule.

The spatial characteristic and discriminant rules describe the spatial and non-spatial relationships at a general concept level, where spatial objects are expressed as merged spatial regions or clustered spatial points. However, they do not reflect the relationships of spatial/spatial data or spatial/non-spatial data, compared to spatial association rules.

A *spatial association rule* is a rule which describes the implication of one set of features by another set of features in spatial databases. A spatial association rule has the form $X{\rightarrow}Y$, where X and Y are sets of predicates and some of which are spatial predicates. A rule such as *"large towns in British Columbia are close to the sea"* is a spatial association rule.

Applying association rule mining to spatial data can be problematic. One main issue is that while non-spatial association rule mining seeks to determine associations among transactions that are encoded explicitly in a database, spatial data mining aims to discover patterns in spatial relationships that are typically not encoded in a database but are rather encoded within the spatial framework of the geo-referenced data. These spatial relationships must be extracted from the data prior to the actual association rule mining. Hence, there is a trade-off between pre-processing spatial relationships among geo-graphical objects and computing those relationships on-the-fly.

To date, two association rules in spatial databases which find correlation among spatial data have been introduced (see the following sub-sections).

Spatial Association Rules

These rules are a natural extension of the classic association rules in the spatial databases by incorporating the spatial predicates into either the antecedent or the consequent. For example, the following rule finds the association re-lationships between schools and parks, that is, 80% of schools are close to parks: $is\_a(x, \text{school}) \rightarrow close\_to(x, \text{park})$ (80%).

Spatial Collocation Patterns

Such patterns seek to find the feature sets with instances that are located in the same neighborhood. For example, a collocation rule can be described as: "76% of the occurrences of smoke aerosols imply the occurrence of rainfall in a nearby region."

While both time varying and spatial patterns can reveal interesting informa-tion from data, these patterns either focus on the temporal dimension or the spatial dimension. As spatio-temporal data becomes more prevalent, research-ers (Mamoulis, Cao, & Kollios, 2004; Mesrobian, Muntz, & Shek, 1995; Peng & Chen, 2003; Steinbach, Tan, & Kumar, 2001; Stolorz, Nakamura, & Mesrobian, 1995; Tan, Steinbach, & Kumar, 2001; Tsoukatos & Gunopulos, 2001) have re-focused their attention to the discovery of interesting patterns in spatio-temporal databases.

Initially, most of the works in spatio-temporal data mining are simply adap-tations of techniques from the spatial or temporal data mining field for use on spatio-temporal data. However, spatio-temporal data contains complex relationships that cannot be discovered simply by looking at the spatial dimension or the temporal dimension independently. We illustrate this with a simple example.

Suppose that we have a spatio-temporal database of the weather system in Southeast Asia. The information stored in the database includes events, such as atmospheric pressure, forest fire, haze, rainfall, earthquake, tsunami, and so forth, locations of the events, and time of the events. Figure 1.1 shows an example of the spatio-temporal database. With this spatio-temporal database, we want to study the interaction relationships of these events in different areas in Southeast Asia.

Using existing spatial data mining techniques, we can discover the following spatial association patterns:

Figure 1.1. Example of a spatio-temporal database

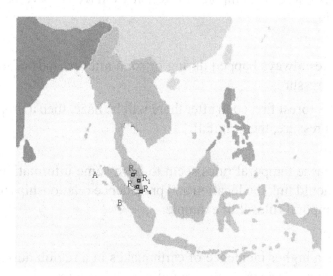

ID	Time	Location	Event
xxx	July 26, 1965	R2	forest fire
xxx	July 28, 1965	R1	haze
xxx	July 30, 1965	R3	atmospheric pressure ↓
xxx	August 2, 1965	R4	rainfall
xxx	February 26, 2005	A	earthquake
xxx	February 26, 2005	A	tsunami
xxx	March 28, 2005	B	earthquake

S1: If an earthquake occurs in the place close to sea, there is high probability of the occurrence of tsunami.

S2: There is a higher confidence of earthquakes in a region if there is high atmospheric pressure in the nearby regions.

S3: There is high probability of haze in region R_1 if there is forest fire occurring in the nearby region R_2.

S4: If there is a drop in atmospheric pressure in region R_3, rainfall will always occur in the nearby region R_4.

S5: There is high probability of a drop in atmospheric pressure in region R_3 if there is haze in the nearby region R_2.

However, these spatial rules (S1 to S5) do not reveal any information about the temporal relationships of the events. In order to discover the temporal relationships among these events, we have to use temporal data mining techniques. Examples of temporal rules that we have discovered are listed in the following:

T_1: Earthquakes always happen during or soon after periods of high atmospheric pressure.

T_2: If there is a forest fire, soon after there will be haze, then a drop in atmospheric pressure, then rainfall.

Once again, these temporal rules seem to have some information missing. Ideally, we should link the location and precedence relationships together in our spatio-temporal rules. For example:

ST_1: There is a higher incidence of earthquakes in a region during or soon after high atmospheric pressure in the nearby region.

ST_2: Forest fire always occurs at region R_1 prior to the occurrence of haze in the nearby region R_2, then a drop in atmospheric pressure at region R_3, then rainfall at region R_4.

ST_3: From March to April, if there is forest fire in a region in South Asia, haze and rainfall will subsequently occur in its Southeastern neighbors.

Clearly, the patterns ST_1, ST_2, and ST_3 are much more informative compared to spatial patterns and temporal patterns. These spatio-temporal patterns not only link events in different locations, but they also establish the sequence of changes of events in these locations. Hence, spatio-temporal patterns are more useful and helpful for decision makers in understanding the evolving process and making accurate predictions.

We investigate the discovery of interesting spatio-temporal patterns from two aspects. First, we impose temporal constraints on the mining of spatial collocation patterns to discover topological patterns such as: "There is higher incidence of earthquakes in a region during or soon after periods of high atmospheric pressure in the near by regions." The purpose of topological patterns is to discover the intra-relationships of events in a time period.

Next, we search for spatial sequence patterns by incorporating spatial information into the process for mining sequence patterns. Examples of spatial sequence patterns include: "Forest fire always occurs at region R_1 prior to the occurrence of haze in the nearby region R_2."; "A drop in atmospheric pressure at a region always precedes rainfall in the nearby regions."

In this book, we will describe two classes of spatial sequence patterns called flow patterns and generalized spatio-temporal patterns. These two classes of spatial sequence patterns are useful to the understanding of many real-life applications. Algorithms designed to discover these two classes of spatial sequence patterns have shown to be efficient and scalable.

Some complex relationships among spatio-temporal data cannot be captured with these two simple approaches. To further discover complex relationships in spatio-temporal data, we model data as trees or graphs. Each vertex in a tree/graph represents a variable labeled by an attribute or event, and each edge represents the spatial relationship, the temporal relationship, or both. With this, we transform the problem of mining arbitrary spatio-temporal patterns into the problem of finding frequent trees/sub-graphs. Figure 1.2 shows the possible graph structures representing the spatio-temporal patterns ST_1, ST_2, and ST_3.

Extending existing algorithms to find these spatio-temporal patterns is not feasible due to the large search space of both the spatial and temporal dimensions. To find these patterns, we instead design and develop a partition-based graph mining algorithm. These algorithms work by discovering frequent sub-graphs in the graph database. The proposed algorithm is effective and scalable in finding frequent sub-graphs, and outperforms existing algorithms in the presence of updates.

Figure 1.2. Graph representation of spatio-temporal patterns

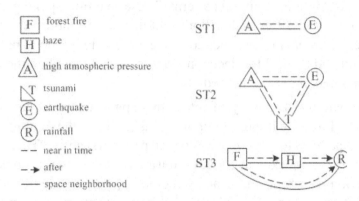

Organization of the Book

The rest of the book is organized as follows. Chapter II gives the background and related work in temporal mining. This is followed by discussions of mining period patterns in Chapter III, mining of sequence patterns in evolving temporal databases in Chapter IV, and mining of a special class of sequence patterns called the progressive confident rules in Chapter V. Starting from Chapter VI onward, we focus on mining in spatio-temporal databases. Early works in this area are presented in Chapter VI. Chapter VII deals with topological patterns discovery. In Chapter VIII and Chapter IX, we introduce two new classes of spatial sequence patterns and illustrate the algorithms designed for mining these two classes of spatial sequence patterns in detail. The work for mining arbitrary spatio-temporal association patterns in the form of tree patterns and graph patterns are described in Chapter X and Chapter XI, respectively. Finally, we conclude the book with future directions in Chapter XII.

References

Agrawal, R., & Srikant, R. (1996). Mining sequential patterns: Generalizations and performance improvements. In *Proceedings of the International Conference on Extending Database Technology,* Avignion, France, March 25-29 (pp. 3-17). Berlin/Heidelberg: Springer.

Cai, Y., & Ng, R. (2004). Indexing spatio-temporal trajectories with Cheby-shev polynomials. In *Proceedings of the ACM SIGMOD International Conference on Management of Data,* Paris, France, June 13-18 (pp. 599-610). New York: ACM Press.

Güting, R. H., Böhlen, M. H., & Erwig, M. (2000). A foundation for repre-senting and querying moving objects. *ACM Transactions on Database Systems, 25*(1), 1-42.

Han, J., & Kamber, M. (2001). *Data mining: Concepts and techniques.* San Francisco, CA: Morgan Kaufmann Publishers.

Han, J., Koperski, K., & Stefanovic, N. (1997). GeoMiner: A system pro-totype for spatial data mining. In *Proceedings of the ACM SIGMOD International Conference on Management of Data,* Tucson, Arizona, USA, May 13-15 (pp. 553-556). New York: ACM Press.

Mamoulis, N., Cao, H., & Kollios, G. (2004). Mining, indexing, and query-ing historical spatiotemporal data. In *Proceedings of the ACM SIGKDD Knowledge Discovery and Data Mining,* Seattle, Washington, USA, August 22-25 (pp. 236-245). New York: ACM Press.

Mesrobian, E., Muntz, R., & Shek, E. C. (1995). Exploratory data mining and analysis using CONQUEST. In *IEEE Pacific Conference on Com-munications, Computers, Visualization, and Signal Processing,* Victoria, May 17-19 (pp. 281-286). Los Alamitos, CA: IEEE Computer Society Press.

Miller, H. J., & Han, J. (Eds.) (2001). Geographic data mining and knowledge discovery: An overview. In *Geographic Data Mining and Knowledge Discovery* (pp. 3-32). Boca Raton, FL: CRC Press.

Morimoto, Y. (2001). Mining frequent neighboring class sets in spatial data-bases. In *Proceedings of the ACM SIGKDD International Conference on Knowledge Discovery and Data Mining,* San Francisco, California, USA, August 26-29 (pp. 353-358). New York: ACM Press.

Pei, J., Han, J., & Mortazavi-Asl, B. (2001). PrefixSpan: Mining sequential patterns efficiently by prefix-projected pattern growth. In *Proceedings of the IEEE International Conference on Data Engineering,* Heidelberg, Germany, April 2-6 (pp. 215-224). Los Alamitos, CA: IEEE Computer Society Press.

Peng, W. C., & Chen, M. S. (2003). Developing data allocation schemes by incremental mining of user moving patterns in a mobile computing system. *IEEE Transactions on Knowledge and Data Engineering, 15*(1), 70-85.

Saltenis, S., Jensen, C., & Leutenegger, S. (2000). Indexing the positions of continuously moving objects. In *Proceedings of the ACM SIGMOD Conference on Management of Data,* Dallas, Texas, USA, May 16-18 (pp. 331-342). New York: ACM Press.

Shekhar, S., & Huang, Y. (2001). Discovery of spatial co-location patterns. In *Proceedings of the International Symposium on Advances in Spatial and Temporal Databases,* Redondo Beach, California, USA, July 12-15 (pp. 236-256). Berlin/Heidelberg: Springer.

Steinbach, M., Tan, P. N., & Kumar, V. (2001). Clustering Earth science data: Goals, issues and results. In *ACM SIGKDD Workshop on Mining Scientific Dataset,* San Francisco, California, USA, August 26. New York: ACM Press.

Stolorz, P., Nakamura, H., & Mesrobian, E. (1995). Fast spatio-temporal data mining of large geophysical datasets. In *Proceedings of the International Conference on Knowledge Discovery and Data Mining,* Montreal, Canada, August 20-21 (pp. 300-305). Menlo Park, CA: AAAI Press.

Sun, J., Papadias, D., & Tao, Y. (2004). Querying about the past, the present and the future in spatio-temporal databases. In *Proceedings of the 20th IEEE International Conference on Data Engineering,* Boston, Massachusetts, USA, March 30-April 2 (pp. 202-213). Los Alamitos, CA: IEEE Computer Society Press.

Tan, P. N., Steinbach, M., & Kumar, V. (2001). Finding spatio-temporal patterns in Earth science data. In *ACM SIGKDD Workshop on Temporal Data Mining,* San Francisco, California, USA, August 26. New York: ACM Press.

Tao, Y., Papadias, D., & Shen, Q. (2002). Continuous nearest neighbor search. In *Proceedings of the International Conference on Very Large Data Bases,* Hong Kong, China, August 20-23 (pp. 287-298). San Francisco, CA: Morgan Kaufmann Publishers.

Tao, Y., Taloutsos, C., & Papadias, D. (2004). Prediction and indexing of moving objects with unknown motion patterns. In *Proceedings of the ACM SIGMOD International Conference on Management of Data,* Paris, France, June 13-18 (pp. 611-622). New York: ACM Press.

Tobler, W. R. (1979). Cellular geography. In S. Gale, & G. Olssen (Eds.), *Philosophy in geography* (pp. 379-386). Dordrecht, Holland: D. Reidel Publishing Company.

Tsoukatos, I., & Gunopulos, D. (2001). Efficient mining of spatiotemporal patterns. In *Proceedings of the International Symposium on Advances in Spatial and Temporal Databases,* Redondo Beach, California, USA, July 12-15 (pp. 425-443). Berlin/Heidelberg: Springer.

Wang, J., & Han, J. (2004). BIDE: Efficient mining of frequent closed sequences. In *Proceedings of the International Conference on Data Engineering,* Boston, Massachusetts, USA, March 30-April 2 (pp. 79-90). Los Alamitos, CA: IEEE Computer Society Press.

Zaki, M. (1998). Efficient enumeration of frequent sequences. In *Proceedings of the International Conference on Information and Knowledge Management,* Bethesda, Maryland, USA, November 3-7 (pp. 68-75). New York: ACM Press.

Zhang, X., Mamoulis, N., & Cheung, D. W. (2004). Fast mining of spatial collocations. In *Proceedings of ACM SIGKDD International Conference on Knowledge Discovery and Data Mining,* Seattle, Washington, USA, August 22-25 (pp. 384-393). New York: ACM Press.

Chapter II

Time Series Mining:
Background and
Related Work

co-authored with

Minghua Zhang, National University of Singapore, Singapore

A time series is a sequence of real numbers over time. Time series data occurs nearly everywhere. For example, the closing price of stock A over a week could be represented by a time series of *{23.80, 22.95, 21.87, 22.45, 23.32}*. A time series database contains a set of time series. Current work on time series databases mainly focuses on indexing and querying, clustering and classification.

In this chapter, we will first give the background and review existing works in time series mining. The background material will include commonly used similarity measures and techniques for dimension reduction and data discretization. Then we will examine techniques to discover periodic and sequential patterns. This will lay the groundwork for the subsequent three chapters on mining dense periodic patterns, incremental sequence mining, and mining progressive patterns.

Issues in Time Series Mining

Similarity Measures

Time series mining problems are based on similarity computation, that is, to determine some numerical number that represents how similar two time series are. Therefore, it is important to choose a suitable similarity measure. Two similarity measures are commonly used: one is Euclidean distance, and the other is dynamic time warping (DTW).

Euclidean Distance

Euclidean distance is a simple yet widely used similarity measure. Given two time series ts_1 and ts_2 of length L, where

$$ts_1 = \{d_{11}, d_{12}, \ldots, d_{1L}\} \text{ and } ts_2 = \{d_{21}, d_{22}, \ldots, d_{2L}\},$$

the Euclidean distance between ts_1 and ts_2 is calculated as

$$d = [(d_{11}\text{-}d_{21})^2 + (d_{12}\text{-}d_{22})^2 + \ldots + (d_{1L}\text{-}d_{2L})^2]^{1/2}$$

The smaller the value of d, the closer is ts_1 and ts_2.

The Euclidean distance measure is easy to understand and can be efficiently computed. It has a time complexity of $O(n)$. However, in cases where phase shift in time axis exists, the Euclidean distance is not a suitable measure. For example, consider the following two time series

$$ts_1 = \sin(t)$$
$$ts_2 = \sin(t+10)$$

These two time series have similar shapes and differ only in the phase. Unfortunately, if we were to utilize the Euclidean distance as the similarity measure, we would conclude that ts_1 and ts_2 are quite different. This leads to the design of another similarity measure dynamic time warping (DTW).

Dynamic Time Warping

For several decades, dynamic time warping (DTW) has been used in speech recognition to solve the problem caused by time axis distortion (Rabiner & Juang, 1993; Sakoe & Chiba, 1978). Berndt and Clifford (1994) first introduce the DTW technique to the data mining community. Subsequently, researchers examine how DTW can be applied to time series (Chan & Fu, 1999; Keogh, 2002; Ratanamahatana & Keogh, 2004; Zhu & Shasha, 2003).

The basic idea of DTW is to allow a point in a time series to be mapped to many points in the other time series and vice versa. Thus, small phase shift in time axis would not influence the similarity between the two time series.

We will briefly discuss how the DTW between two time series can be calculated. Given two time series ts_1 and ts_2, where

$$ts_1 = \{d_{11}, d_{12}, \ldots, d_{1n}\}$$
$$ts_2 = \{d_{21}, d_{22}, \ldots, d_{2m}\}.$$

In order to compute DTW between ts_1 and ts_2, we first generate a matrix M[n, m] with n rows and m columns. The matrix element m(i, j) is the Euclidean distance between d_{1i} (the ith element in ts_1) and d_{2j} (the jth element in ts_2).

A warping path W is a set of matrix elements which is represented by W = $w_1 w_2 \ldots w_k$, where max (n,m) $\leq$ k $\leq$ m+n-1. Each w_s = m(i, j) is a matrix element, which indicates that the ith element in ts_1 is mapped to the jth element in ts_2, or d_{1i} is mapped to d_{2j}. A warping path W has three requirements:

1. w_1 should be equal to m(1,1) and w_k should be equal to m(n,m). This ensures that the first element in ts_1 (d_{11}) is mapped to the first element in ts_2 (d_{21}), and that the last element in ts_1 (d_{1n}) is mapped to the last element in ts_2 (d_{2m}).

2.   **Monotonic property:** For every pair of w_i = m(x, y) and w_{i-1} = (x', y'), we have x $\geq$ x' and y $\geq$ y'. It implies that the order of the elements in the time series should not be inverted.

3.   **Continuous property:** For every pair of w_i = m(x, y) and w_{i-1} = (x', y'), we have x - x'$\leq$1 and y - y'$\leq$1. That is, the step length in the warping path should be no more than 1, or every data point in a time series should be mapped to some point(s) in the other time series.

The warping cost of a warping path W is C(W) which is given by $(w_1 + w_2 + \ldots + w_k)^{1/2}/k$. Here the denominator k is used for the compensation of the warping path length, since different warping path could have different length.

The DTW between two time series ts_1 and ts_2, denoted by $DTW(ts_1, ts_2)$, is the minimum warping cost, that is,

$$DTW \ (ts_1, ts_2) = \min C(W).$$

The value of DTW and its corresponding warping path could be obtained by dynamic programming. For more details of DTW, we refer readers to Kruskall and Liberman (1983) and Rabiner and Juang (1993).

In addition to these three requirements for a warping path, global constraints are often utilized when calculating DTW. The global constraints specify how far the matrix elements in a path could stray away from the diagonal. These constraints actually provide a subset of matrix which a warping path must fall in. The primary objective of global constraints is to avoid pathological warping, where a data point in one time series matches to too many data points in the other time series.

Two frequently used global constraints are Sakoe-Chiba Band (Sakoe & Chiba, 1978) and Itakura Parallelogram (Itakura, 1975; Rabiner & Juang, 1993). Sakoe-Chiba Band requires that all the $m(i,j)$ in the warping path satisfy the requirement that $i-r \leq j \leq i+r$, where r is a constant (see Figure 2.1). In Itakura Parallelogram, r is not a constant. Instead, r is a function of i and j (see Figure 2.2).

A similarity measure that is based on DTW is more suitable for cases where time axis distortion exists. However, DTW requires $O(n^2)$ computation time compared to the Euclidean distance which only needs $O(n)$ time. Some works have studied how to reduce the computational cost of DTW. For example, Keogh and Pazzani (2000) propose a modification of DTW that works on a high-level representation of time series. The new high level abstraction is based on piecewise aggregate approximation (PAA). Experiment results show that the proposed approach is able to achieve a speedup of one to two orders of magnitude without loss of accuracy.

Another drawback of DTW is that it does not obey the triangular inequality, which makes exact indexing difficult. As a result, studies on time series indexing typically consider the Euclidean distance (Chan, Fu, & Yu, 2003;

Figure 2.1. Sakoe-Chiba Band

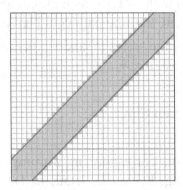

Figure 2.2. Itakura Parallelogram

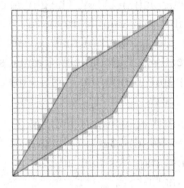

Faloutsos, Ranganathan, & Manolopoulos, 1994; Keogh, Chakrabarti, & Pazzani, 2001a; Korn, Jagadish, & Faloutsos, 1997; Yi & Faloutsos, 2000).

Yi, Jagadish, and Faloutsos (1998) propose a method for approximately indexing DTW. Subsequently, Kim, Park, and Chu (2001) develop a technique for the exact indexing of DTW. This is accomplished by extracting the four features from each time series, that is, the first data point, the last data point, the maximum data point, and the minimum data point. A lower bound of DTW between two time series is then calculated as the maximum absolute difference of corresponding four pair of features. The proposed index is constructed with the help of the lower bound. Keogh (2002) improved the efficiency of the indexing method put forward in Kim, Park, and Chu (2001) by introducing a tighter lower bound for DTW and devising a method with better pruning power and no false dismissals. However, the algorithm, in Keogh (2002), works only in the case when DTW is calculated with certain global constraints.

In one sense, DTW could be regarded as a type of local warping. In some applications, a global scaling factor is also necessary for sequence matching (Keogh, Palpanas, & Zordan, 2004). Fu, Keogh, and Lau (2005) propose to combine DTW and uniform scaling (US) to support more accurate time series querying. In applications with natural variability such as query by humming, both DTW and US should be taken into consideration. This is because DTW provides local flexibility in time axis while US allows global scaling along the time axis. In order to handle DTW and US simultaneously, Fu, Keogh, and Lau (2005) propose a method to compute SWM (scaled and warped matching). Since the computation of SWM is very costly, the work in Fu, Keogh, and Lau (2005) suggests calculating a lower bound of SWM instead. With the help of the lower bound, a large amount of search space could be pruned.

Dimension Reduction

Another concern in time series data mining is dimension reduction. For a time series of length L, we can regard it as a point in an L-dimensional space. When L is large, the "curse of dimensionality" appears.

Many techniques have been applied to reduce dimensionality. These techniques include discrete fourier transform (Faloutsos, Ranganathan, & Manolopoulos, 1994), discrete wavelet transform (Chan & Fu, 1999; Gilbert, Kotidis, & Muthukrishnan, 2001), perpetually important points (Fu, Chung, & Ng, 2001), piecewise aggregate approximation (Keogh, Chakrabarti, & Pazzani, 2001b), singular value decomposition (Korn, Jagadish, & Faloutsos, 1997), adaptive piecewise constant approximation (Keogh, Chakrabarti, & Pazzani, 2001a), and so forth.

Discrete fourier transform (DFT) transforms the original time series into the frequency domain. A length-L time series is converted to L numerical values in the frequency domain. We call the L numbers in the frequency domain the DFT co-efficients. In order to achieve dimension reduction, we simply keep the first k (k<L) co-efficients. The effect is that the number of dimensions is reduced from L to k. One advantage of DFT is that the co-efficients are invariable with respect to time shifts (Faloutsos, Ranganathan, & Manolopoulos,

1994). Therefore, DFT is able to find similar time series with different phases (Faloutsos, Ranganathan, & Manolopoulos, 1994).

Discrete wavelet transform (DWT) transforms a time series into the time-frequency domain. It is a linear transformation. Similar to DFT, dimensionality could be reduced by selecting a subset of the resulting coefficients (Chan & Fu, 1999; Gilbert, Kotidis, & Muthukrishnan, 2001).

Perpetually important points (PIP) represents a time series by its highly fluctuated points. Thus, points which do not fluctuate greatly are omitted (Fu, Chung, & Ng, 2001).

Piecewise aggregate approximation (PAA) segments a time series into several pieces, and represents the time series by the mean value of every piece (Keogh, Chakrabarti, & Pazzani, 2001b).

Zhao and Zhang (2006) design a general dimension-reduction framework that gives a bias to recent data. The proposed framework first divides the time series into equal length segments or various length segments. Then it applies dimension reduction technique on each segment. By keeping more co-efficients for recent data and fewer co-efficients for old data, a bias on recent data is achieved. The dimension reduction technique applied in the framework could be any of DFT, DWT, SVD, PIP, PAA, and so forth.

Data Discretization

Before performing the mining task on time series data, a discretization on numerical values is necessary. During the process of data discretization, an original real-valued data point in a time series is converted to a symbol in an alphabet. Note that according to the second classification criteria of temporal data mining, the time series is transformed to sequence data.

An example of such conversion is the usage of the Shape Definition Language (Agrawal, Giuseppe, & Edward, 1995). Shape Definition Language is applicable in cases when users are interested only in the overall shape of the time series, but not the specific details. Given a time series, by comparing the value of a data point with its immediate next one, we replace the original numerical value with a pre-defined symbol in the Shape Definition Language. After this transformation, the mining process is then performed on the newly constructed symbol sequence.

Lin, Keogh, and Lonardi (2003) put forward the symbolic approximation for symbolic representation of time series. The basic idea of symbolic approximation is similar to equal frequency histogram. It makes use of an approximate distance function to lower bound the Euclidean distance. The temporal information is only considered in its preprocessing step when performing piecewise aggregate aggregation.

Morchen and Ultsch (2005) investigate how temporal information can be incorporated into the discretization process. They propose an unsupervised method based on the Kullback-Leibler divergence between the marginal and the self-transition probability distributions of the discretization symbols. The symbols generated correspond to persisting states. Therefore, meaningful mining results in subsequent knowledge discovery steps are likely to be obtained. Experiment results show that the algorithm achieves an obvious improvement in accuracy compared to the commonly-used discretization methods. In addition, the algorithm is robust against noise.

Time Series Mining Techniques

Periodic Pattern Mining

Periodic patterns are patterns that occur regularly over time in a time series (events) database. Two kinds of periodical patterns have been studied: full periodic pattern and partial periodical pattern. For full periodicity, every event in the database contributes to part of the pattern—for example, season cycles for every year. This requirement is often too rigid in real life. For example, Mr. White has breakfast at 7:30 a.m. every weekday. However, on weekends, he usually has breakfast after 8 a.m. Here, the weekends do not contribute to the periodicity of breakfast time.

Partial periodicity, on the contrary, allows only part of events to participate in the pattern. In the earlier example, the eating breakfast at 7:30 a.m. is a partial periodic pattern. Compared to full periodic pattern, partial periodic pattern is more common in practice. Many algorithms have been designed to find the partial periodic patterns in time series databases.

Given a feature set Z and a temporal database D, let D_i be the set of features occurring at time instant i. A sequence of D_i over n time instances forms a time series $S = D_1D_2...D_n$, where n is the length of S, denoted by $|S|$. For example, if $S = \{abc\}d\{ag\}$, then $D_i = \{abc\}$, $D_2 = \{d\}$, $D_3 = \{ag\}$, and $|S| = 3$.

A pattern s is a sequence of feature set, i.e., $s = s_1 s_2 \ldots s_p$, where each s_i is either a feature set or *. p is called the *length* or *period* of s. If $s_i = *$, then s_i could match any feature set. The number of feature set in s which is not * is called the Z-length of s. If the Z-length of s is k, we say s is a k-pattern. For example, if s = {ab}*d, then the length of s is 3, and its Z-length is 2, that is, s is a 2-pattern.

Given a time series of length n, and a period value |s|, let m be the integer such that $m|s| \le n < (m+1)\,|s|$. The frequency count of a pattern s in time series S is defined as frequency_count $(s) = |\{\, i \mid 0 \le i < m,\ s\ \text{is true in } D_{i|s|+1} \ldots D_{i|s|+|s|} \}|$. The confidence of a pattern s in time series S is defined as conf(s) = frequency_count (s) /m. If conf (s) is no less than a user specified confidence threshold min_conf, we say s is a frequent periodic pattern.

Given a time series S, a period or a set of periods, and a confidence threshold min_conf, the problem of mining periodic pattern is defined as discovering all frequent periodic patterns from S. Note that in periodic pattern mining, the input is one time series, and not a set of time series. Further, the data in the time series takes on categorical values instead of numeric ones.

Partial Periodic Patterns

Han, Gong, and Yin (1998) first propose the problem of mining partial periodic patterns. Given a specified period, they mine partial periodic patterns with an Apriori-based algorithm. The algorithm consists of two steps. The first step computes the set of frequent 1-patterns of period p. This is done by accumulating the frequency count for each 1-pattern in each whole period segment and then select among them those frequency count is no less than min-conf * m, where m is the maximum number of periods. In the second step, all frequent i-patterns of period p are found and the process is terminated when the candidate frequent i-pattern set is empty. While this approach is effective for association rule mining, however, in periodicity mining, the number of frequent i-patterns shrinks slowly as i increases. This slow reduction of the set of frequent i-pattern makes the Apriori pruning less attractive.

To address this issue, Han, Dong, and Yin (1999) introduce the notions of maximal pattern and hit set to mine partial periodic patterns more efficiently. Unlike the Apriori-based algorithm which mines patterns level by level, the max-subpattern hit set property allows an algorithm to perform a top-down mining.

The rough definition of max-subpattern hit set is as follows: If F_1 is the set of frequent-1 patterns, then a candidate frequent max-pattern, C_{max}, is the maximal pattern which could be generated from F_1. For example, if $F_1 = \{a***, b***, ***c\}$, then $C_{max} = \{ab\}**c$.

Given a period segment D_i of S, the maximal subpattern of C_{max} that matches D_i is said to be the hit of D_i. The set of hits in all D_i ($0 \le i < m$) forms the hit set. One property of the hit set is that one can derive all frequent partial periodic patterns from the frequency_count of patterns in the hit set.

The algorithm first obtains the set of frequent 1-patterns of period p as before. Next, it scans the time series to determine for each period segment, whether its hit set is non-empty. If it is, it adds the max-subpattern into the hit set buffer, and increases the count of the max-subpattern by one. In order to accomplish this step efficiently, the algorithm makes use of the max-subpattern tree. The root node of the max-subpattern tree is the candidate max-pattern C_{max}. At each level, an additional * is introduced if there is a hit with the node. Each node has a count field to register the number of hits of the current node, a pointer to the parent, and pointers to the children.

Once the tree has been generated, the frequent k-patterns can be obtained by joining the frequent patterns with length k-1 by (k+1)-way join and scan the tree to find the frequency counts of these candidate patterns. The non-frequent ones are eliminated.

With this top-down mining process, the number of scans required on the time series is only two. Therefore, it improves the performance greatly. In addition to discovering patterns of a single period, the algorithm could also deal with a range of periods by a shared mining of multiple periods.

Yang, Wang, and Yu (2000) addresses the problem of mining the error tolerance periodic patterns in time series. They find the longest valid sub-sequence for every 1-pattern and employ a bottom-up level-wise approach to generate the sub-sequences for k-patterns (k> 1). The drawback of this algorithm is that it has to scan the data multiple times for mining the long period patterns. In Wang, Yang, and Yu (2001), they propose a meta-pattern model which encapsulates periodic patterns and meta-patterns together through a hierarchical organization. Although this approach is flexible to capture the hierarchical periodic patterns, it suffers from the exponential growth of candidate meta-patterns.

Aref, Elfeky, and Elmagarmid (2004) study the problem of incremental mining of periodic patterns when the underlying time series changes with time.

Since the max-pattern is dynamically updated in incremental time series, the authors also use the max-subpattern tree and further tune it to guarantee its coherence to the whole time series. The algorithm also provides some interaction of users by allowing online alteration of mining threshold.

Yang and Lee (2004) observe that many partial periodic patterns are redundant. For example, suppose pattern A states that "we need to stock with milk every 2 days", and pattern B states that "we need to stock with milk every 4 days", then obviously pattern B is redundant. The authors propose an approach to avoid generating such redundant periodic patterns. This is accomplished by transforming the original time series into a bit vector and storing the bit vector in the main memory. Experiment results show that filtering out redundant patterns leads to an improvement in the performance of the mining algorithm.

Asynchronous Periodic Patterns

The works in mining partial period pattern assume that there is no disturbance in the input time series. If there does exist such disturbance, it only causes missing occurrence of patterns, but not the misalignment of them. In other words, the patterns they are looking for are synchronous periodic patterns.

Yang, Wang, and Yu (2000) address the problem of mining asynchronous periodic patterns. In their model, misaligned patterns caused by some intervention of random noise could be discovered. Two parameters min_rep and max_dis are introduced to control the level of allowed disturbance. min_rep specifies the minimum number of continuous repetitions of the pattern in order to form a valid segmentation. max_dis is the maximum allowed disturbance between two successive valid segments. The longest sub-sequence that satisfying these two requirements is returned. In Yang, Wang, and Yu (2001), they propose to use information metrics as a measure of the importance of a periodic pattern. The information metrics is calculated based on the probability of the occurrence of events. This measurement provides for the seamless handling of patterns with highly different occurrence probabilities. Based on the bounded information gain property, they design an efficient algorithm for mining surprising periodic patterns.

Huang and Chang (2005) also works on mining asynchronous periodic patterns in temporal databases. The authors find that the method proposed in Yang, Wang, and Yu (2000) could only work on a sequence of events, and not on a sequence of event sets. In addition, Yang, Wang, and Yu (2000) only returns the longest sub-sequence, which may result in information loss. To solve the problem, Huang and Chang (2005) propose a more general model of mining asynchronous periodic patterns. Besides the parameters min_rep and max_dis used in Yang, Wang, and Yu (2000), the work in Huang and Chang (2005) put forward an extra parameter, global_rep, to specify the total repetitions required for a valid sub-sequence. The algorithm would discover and output all sub-sequences meet the three requirements.

Unknown Period Patterns

All of the work (Aref, Elfeky, & Elmagarmid, 2004; Han, Gong, & Yin, 1998; Wang, Yang, & Yu, 2001; Yang, Wang, & Yu, 2000) assume that the periods of the patterns are known in advance, and the algorithms are correspondingly designed to find the periodic patterns with the given periods. For applications where the periods are not available, these algorithms have to iterate themselves for all of the possible periods to discover the patterns. This approach is very expensive.

To deal with this problem, Ma and Hellerstein (2001) devise a linear distance-based algorithm for discovering the possible periods. It mines partially periodic events by taking the following situations into consideration. First, the period length is unknown. Second, the time information is imprecise. Third, noise disrupts periodicities. Two sub-tasks are investigated. The first sub-task is to determine the periods. The second task is to mine temporal associations. The period is estimated based on chi-square test. Ma and Hellerstein (2001) design two algorithms based on the order in which the two sub-tasks are performed, that is, the period-first algorithm and the association-first algorithm. Experiment results show that the association-first algorithm has better noise tolerance, while the period-first algorithm is more efficient in computation cost.

The works in Berberidis, Aref, and Atallah (2002), and Elfeky, Aref, and Elmagarmid (2004, 2005) employ a convolution-like formula to validate all the periods from 2 to n/2 in a time series of length n. Although this approach can discover all the periodic patterns, it does not take advantage of the fact that short periods are preferred since they are more accurate and informative compared to the longer one.

Periodic Patterns with Gap Requirement

In many applications, particularly those related to bio-informatics, interesting patterns are *periodic* with a *gap requirement*. That is to say, the characters in P should match sub-sequences of S in such a way that the matching characters in S are separated by gaps of more or less the same size.

Zhang, Kao, and Cheung (2005) study the problem of mining frequently occurring periodic patterns with a gap requirement from sequences. Given a character sequence $S=s_1 s_2 \ldots s_L$ of length L and a pattern $P = p_1 p_2 \ldots p_l$ of length l, the authors consider P a frequently occurring pattern in S if the probability of *observing* P given a randomly picked length-l subsequence of S exceeds a certain threshold. They examine the complexity of the mining problem and discuss why traditional mining algorithms are computationally infeasible. They propose practical algorithms for solving the problem, and study their characteristics. They also present a case study in which the algorithms are applied on some DNA sequences to reveal some interesting patterns.

Sequential Pattern Mining

One well-studied temporal data mining problem is the extraction of frequent sequences from transactional databases. The goal is to discover frequent sequences of events and infer relationships of contextual and temporal proximity in the data. Agrawal and Srikant (1995) first introduce sequence mining to discover all sequential patterns with a user-specified minimum support. Sequence mining has become an essential data mining task with broad applications, such as in market and customer analysis, and so forth.

For example, an online bookstore may find that most customers who have purchased the book, *The Gunslinger*, are likely to come back again in the future to buy, *The Gunslinger II*, in another transaction. Knowledge of this sort enables the store manager to conduct promotional activities and to come up with good marketing strategies. As another example, applying sequence mining on a medical database may reveal that the occurrence of a sequence of events would likely lead to the occurrence of certain illness or symptoms. As a third example, a Web site manager may mine the Web-log sequences to find the visitors' access patterns so as to improve the site design.

In sequence mining, the input data is a set of sequences called data sequences. Each data sequence is a list of transactions consisting of items. Each transaction is associated with a transaction time to provide the ordering information. The data sequences are ordered by increasing transaction time.

The support count for a sequence is defined as the fraction of total data sequences that contain this sequence. Briefly, a sequence s is contained in a data sequences if s is a sub-sequence of the data sequence. Given a database D of data sequences, a taxonomy T, and a user-specified sliding-window size, the problem of mining sequential patterns is to find all sequences whose support is greater than the user-specified minimum support. Each such sequence is called a frequent sequence.

Efficient mining methods have been studied extensively, including general sequence pattern mining (Agrawal & Srikant, 1996; Ayres, Gehrke, & Yiu, 2002; Pei, Han, & Mortazavi-Asl, 2001; Zaki, 1998), constraint-based sequence pattern mining (Garofalakis, Rastogi, & Shim, 1999; Pei, Han, & Wang, 2002), frequent episode mining (Mannila, Toivonen, & Verkamo, 1995), long sequence pattern mining in noisy environment (Yang, Wang, & Yu, 2002a), and closed sequence pattern mining (Wang & Han, 2004).

General Sequence Mining

Agrawal and Srikant (1995) first study the problem of mining frequent sequences and propose an algorithm called AprioriAll. Later, they improve AprioriAll and design a more efficient breadth-first disk-based algorithm called GSP which follows the candidate maintenance and test paradigm to discover frequent sequence patterns.

GSP is a multi-phase iterative algorithm that finds all frequent sequential pattern given a taxonomy T and the user-specified sliding window size. The algorithm makes multiple passes over the data.

In the first pass, the support of each item is determined. The frequent items will form the 1-element frequent sequence. For each subsequent pass, the frequent sequences that are found in the previous pass are used to generate new potentially frequent sequences. This is the candidate sequence generation phase. The phase is made up of two steps: the join step and the prune step. A sequence s1 joins with s2 if the sub-sequence obtained by dropping the first item of s1 is the same as the sub-sequence obtained by dropping the last item of s2.

GSP uses a function GGen to generate candidate sequences of length $k+1$, given the set of all frequent length-k sequences. The candidate generation function GGen works as follows. Given the set of all frequent length-k sequences, L_k, as input, GGen considers every pair of sequences s_1 and s_2 in L_k. If the sequence obtained by deleting the first item of s_1 is equal to the sequence obtained by deleting the last item of s_2, then a candidate is generated by appending the last item of s_2 to the end of s_1.

For example, consider $s_1 = <\{A,B\}, \{C\}>$ and $s_2 = <\{B\}, \{C,D\}>$. Since removing the leading item A from s_1 gives the same sequence ($<\{B\}, \{C\}>$) as that obtained by removing the trailing item D from s_2, a candidate sequence $<\{A,B\}, \{C,D\}>$ is generated by GGen. After a candidate sequence s is generated, GGen checks whether all sub-sequences of s are frequent. If not, the candidate is pruned. The supports of these new potentially frequent sequences are determined via a separate pass over the data. The algorithm terminates when no more frequent sequences are discovered during a database scan.

For example, consider the database shown in Table 2.1. If the support threshold is 75%, then a sequence is frequent if it is contained in at least three customer sequences. In this case, the candidates (C_i's) generated by GGen

Table 2.1. Example database

Customer ID	Sequence
1	$<\{A,B,C\}, \{E,G\}, \{C,D\}>$
2	$<\{A,B\}, \{A,D,E\}>$
3	$<\{A,F\}, \{B,E\}>$
4	$<\{A,B,F\}, \{C,E\}>$

Table 2.2. Mining process of GSP

C_1	$\{<\{A\}>, <\{B\}>, <\{C\}>, <\{D\}>, <\{E\}>, <\{F\}>, <\{G\}>\}$
L_1	$\{<\{A\}>, <\{B\}>, <\{E\}>\}$
C_2	$\{<\{A,B\}>, <\{A,E\}>, <\{B,E\}>, <\{A\},\{A\}>, <\{A\},\{B\}>, <\{A\},\{E\}>, <\{B\},\{A\}>, <\{B\},\{B\}>, <\{B\},\{E\}>, <\{E\},\{A\}>, <\{E\},\{B\}>, <\{E\},\{E\}>\}$
L_2	$\{<\{A,B\}>, <\{A\}, \{E\}>, <\{B\}, \{E\}>\}$
C_3	$\{<\{A,B\}, \{E\}>\}$
L_3	$\{<\{A,B\}, \{E\}>\}$
C_4	Φ

and the frequent sequences (L_i's) discovered by GSP for each iteration (i) are listed in Table 2.2.

GSP is an efficient algorithm. However, the number of database scans it requires is determined by the length of the longest frequent sequences. Consequently, if there are very long frequent sequences and if the database is huge, the I/O cost of GSP could be substantial.

PrefixSpan

Subsequently, the works in Zaki (1998), Pei, Han, and Mortazavi-Asl (2001), and Ayres, Gehrke, and Yiu (2002) investigate depth-first memory-based methods to mine sequence patterns. The depth-first approaches generally perform better than the breadth-first approaches if the data resides in memory. This is because GSP bears three inherent non-trivial costs: (1) potentially huge set of candidate sequences, (2) multiple scans of databases, and (3) difficulties at mining long sequential patterns.

Adapting the idea of FP-tree, Han, Pei, and Mortazavi-Asl (2000) develop a sequential mining method called FreeSpan. The general idea is to use frequent items to recursively project sequence databases into a set of smaller projected databases and grow sub-sequences fragments in each projected database. In order to further improve the performance of FreeSpan, Pei, Han, and Mortazavi-Asl (2001) introduce PrefixSpan, that is, Prefix-projected Sequential PAtterN mining. The basic idea is to use a set of locally frequent items to grow patterns.

PrefixSpan (Pei, Han, & Mortazavi-Asl, 2001) mines frequent sequences by intermediate database generation instead of the tradition approach of candidate sequence generation. It is an efficient algorithm when sufficient amount of memory is available. The algorithm assumes without loss of generality that all items within an itemset are listed in alphabetical order.

Given two sequences $s_1 = <t_1, t_2, ..., t_n>$, $s_2 = <t_1', t_2', ..., t_{1m}'> (m \leq n)$, s_2 is called a prefix of s_1 if (1) $t_i = t_i'$ for $i \leq m-1$; (2) $t_m' \subseteq t_m$; and (3) all items in $t_m - t_m'$ are alphabetically ordered after those in t_m'. For example, if $s_1 = <\{a\}, \{b,c,d\}, \{e\}>$, $s_2 = <\{a\}, \{b\}$, $s_3 = <\{a\}, \{d\}>$, then s_2 is a prefix of s_1, but s_3 is not.

Given a sequence s_1 and one of its sub-sequences s_2 (i.e., $s_2 \subseteq s_1$), a sequence p is called the projection of s_1 w.r.t. prefix s_2, if (1) $p \subseteq s_1$; (2) s_2 is a prefix of p; (3) p is the "maximal" sequence that satisfies conditions (1) and (2), that is, there does not exist p', s.t. $(p \subseteq p' \subseteq s_1)$ and $(p \neq p')$ and $(s_2$ is a prefix of p'). For example, if $s_1 = <\{a\}, \{b, c, d\}, \{e\}, \{f\}>$, $s_2 = <\{a\}, \{c, d\}>$, then p $= <\{a\}, \{c, d\}, \{e\}, \{f\}>$ is the projection of s_1 w.r.t. prefix s_2.

If p is the projection of s_1 w.r.t. prefix s_2, then s_3 obtained by removing the prefix s_2 from p is called the postfix of s_1 with respect to prefix s_2. For example, if $s_1 = <\{a\}, \{b, c, d\}, \{e\}, \{f\}>$, $s_2 = <\{a\}, \{c, d\}>$, then p $= <\{a\}, \{c, d\}, \{e\}, \{f\}>$ is the projection of s_1 w.r.t. prefix s_2, and the postfix of s_1 with respect to prefix s_2 is $<\{e\}, \{f\}>$. If s_2 is not a sub-sequence of s_1, then both the projection and the postfix of s_1 w.r.t. s_2 are empty.

There are three major steps in the PrefixSpan algorithm.

1. Find frequent length-1 sequences.

    In this step, PrefixSpan scans the database D once to find all frequent items. The set of frequent length-1 sequences is $L_1 = \{ <\{i\}> \mid i$ is a frequent item$\}$. For example, given the database shown in Table 2.2, and a support count threshold of 3, the set of frequent items is $\{A, B, E\}$.

2. Divide search space into smaller sub-spaces.

    The set of all frequent sequences can be divided into several groups, such that the sequences within a group share the same prefix item. For example, if $\{A, B, E\}$ is the set of frequent items discovered in the first step, then all the frequent sequences can be divided into three groups, corresponding to the three prefixes $<\{A\}>$, $<\{B\}>$, and $<\{E\}>$.

3. Discover frequent sequences in each sub-space.

    In this step, PrefixSpan finds frequent sequences in each sub-space.

We use an example to illustrate the procedure. Let us use the running example to find the frequent sequences with prefix $<\{A\}>$. PrefixSpan first projects the database D to get an intermediate database $D_{<\{A\}>}$. For every sequence s in D, $D_{<\{A\}>}$ contains the postfix of s with respect to $<\{A\}>$. The projected database $D_{<\{A\}>}$ is shown in Table 2.3. In the table, an underscore '_' preceding an item x indicates that x is contained in the same itemset of the last item in the prefix. For example, w.r.t. the prefix $<\{A\}>$, the postfix sequence $<\{\_B,\_C\}, \{E,G\}, \{C,D\}>$ indicates that the items B and C are contained in the same itemset of A in an original database sequence. After obtaining

Table 2.3. Projected database

Customer ID	Postfix sequence
1	<{_B,_C}, {E,G}, {C,D} >
2	<{_B}, {A,D,E} >
3	<{_F}, {B,E}>
4	<{_B,_F}, {C,E}>

$D_{<\{A\}>}$, PrefixSpan scans $D_{<\{A\}>}$ once to get all frequent items in $D_{<\{A\}>}$. In our example, the frequent items are {_B, E}. Hence, there are in total two length-2 frequent sequences with prefix <{A}>, namely, <{A,B}> and <{A}, {E}>. Then recursively, the database $D_{<\{A\}>}$ is projected w.r.t. the prefixes <{_B}> and <{E}> to obtain $D_{<\{A, B\}>}$ and $D_{<\{A\}, \{E\}>}$. Each one is recursively mined to obtain frequent sequences with the corresponding prefix.

PrefixSpan differs from GSP in that it discovers frequent sequences by projecting databases and counting items' supports. This implies that only the supports of sequences that actually occur in the database are counted. In contrast, a candidate sequence generated by GSP may not appear in the database at all. The time for generating such a candidate sequence and checking whether such a candidate is a sub-sequence of database sequences is wasted. This factor contributes to the efficiency of PrefixSpan over GSP.

The major cost of PrefixSpan is that of generating projected databases. It can be shown that for every frequent sequence discovered, a projected database has to be computed for it. Hence, the number of intermediate databases is very large if there are many frequent sequences. If the database D is large, then PrefixSpan requires substantial amount of memory.

SPADE

GSP and PrefixSpan assume a *horizontal database representation*. In this representation, each row in the database table represents a transaction. Each transaction is associated with a customer ID, a transaction time stamp, and an itemset. Table 2.4 shows an example database in the horizontal representation.

Zaki (2001) observes that a *vertical* representation of the database may be better suited for sequence mining. In the vertical representation, every item in the database is associated with an ID-list. For an item *a*, its ID-list is a list of (customer ID, transaction time stamp) pairs. Each such pair identifies a unique transaction that contains a. A vertical database is composed of the ID-lists of all items. Table 2.5 shows the vertical representation of the database shown in Table 2.4.

Zaki (2001) proposes an algorithm called SPADE that uses a vertical database to mine frequent sequences and shows that it outperforms GSP for small databases. SPADE utilizes two terms: generating sub-sequences and sequence ID-list. For a sequence s such that |s| ≥ 2, the two generating sub-sequences of s are obtained by removing the first or the second item of s. Similar to the ID-list of an item, we can also associate an ID-list to a sequence. The ID-list of a sequence *s* is a list of (customer ID, transaction time stamp) pairs. If the pair (C, t) is in the ID-list of a sequence s, then s is contained in the sequence of Customer C, and that the first item of s occurs in the transaction of Customer C at time stamp t. Table 2.6 shows the ID-list of <{A}, {C}>.

We note that if ID-lists are available, counting the supports of sequences is trivial. In particular, the support count of a length-1 sequence can be ob-

Table 2.4. Horizontal database

Customer ID	Transaction time stamp	Itemset
1	110	A
1	120	B C
2	210	A
2	220	C D

Table 2.5. Vertical database

Item	Customer ID	Transaction time stamp
A	1	110
	2	210
B	1	120
C	1	120
	2	220
D	2	220

Table 2.6. ID-list of <{A}, {C}>

Customer ID	Transaction time stamp
1	110
2	210

tained by inspecting the vertical database. In general, the support count of a sequence s is given by the number of distinct customer ID's in s's ID-list. The problem of support counting is thus reduced to the problem of sequence ID-list computation.

With the vertical database, only the ID-lists of length-1 sequences can be readily obtained. The ID-lists of longer sequences have to be computed. The ID-list of a sequence s can be computed easily by *intersecting* the ID-lists of the two generating sub-sequences of s.

The key steps of SPADE can be summarized as follows.

1. Find frequent length-1 sequences.

    As we have explained, the support count of a length-1 sequence can be obtained by simply scanning the ID-list of the lone item in the sequence. The first step of SPADE is to discover all frequent length-1 sequences by scanning the vertical database once.

2. Find frequent length-2 sequences.

    Suppose there are M frequent items, then the number of candidate frequent length-2 sequences is $O(M^2)$. If the support counts of these length-2 sequences are obtained by first computing their ID-lists using the intersection procedure, we have to access ID-lists from the vertical database $O(M^2)$ times. This could be very expensive. Instead, SPADE solves the problem by building a horizontal database on the fly that involves only frequent items. In the horizontal database, every customer is associated with a list of (item, transaction time stamp) pairs. For each frequent item found in Step 1, SPADE reads its iD-list from disk and the horizontal database is updated accordingly.

For example, if the frequent items of our example database (Table 2.5) are {A, C}, then the constructed horizontal database is shown in Table 2.7. Af-

Table 2.7. Horizontal database generated for computing L2

Customer ID	(item, transaction time stamp) pairs
1	(A 110) (C 120)
2	(A 210) (C 220)

ter obtaining the horizontal database, the supports of all candidate length-2 sequences are computed from it.

Note that maintaining the horizontal database might require a lot of memory. This is especially true if the number of frequent items and the vertical database are large.

3.   Find long frequent sequences.

In Step 3, SPADE generates the ID-lists of long candidate sequences (those of length ≥3) by the intersection procedure. SPADE carefully controls the order in which candidate sequences (and their id-lists) are generated to keep the memory requirement at a minimum.

Although SPADE has been shown to be an efficient algorithm, it has the following drawbacks. First, SPADE requires a vertical representation of the database. In many applications, a horizontal database is more natural. Hence, in order to apply SPADE, the database has to be converted to the vertical representation first, which could be computationally expensive. Second, SPADE generates ID-lists and a horizontal database, which require a large amount of memory. The memory requirement of SPADE grows with the database. For example, we implemented GSP and SPADE, and executed them on a synthetic database of 1 million sequences. GSP required 38MB of memory, while SPADE needed 354MB. With a larger database of 1.5 million sequences, GSP required about the same amount of memory, while SPADE took 575MB. Hence, unless memory is abundant, SPADE is efficient only when applied to small databases.

Incremental Sequence Mining

Parthasarathy, Zaki, and Ogihara (1999) design an incremental sequence mining algorithm based on SPADE. The algorithm ISM is able to handle database updates where new transactions are appended to existing sequences, or whole new sequences are added to the database. Similar to SPADE, ISM requires the availability of a vertical database. Besides that, it requires the following information with respect to the old database D:

1.   All frequent sequences (and their support counts);

2.   All sequences (and their support counts) in the negative border (NB).

Under ISM, a sequence s is in the negative border (NB) if s is not frequent and either $|s| = 1$ or both of s's generating sub-sequences are frequent. This information is used to construct an *increment sequence lattice*, or ISL. A sequence that is frequent in D or is in the NB of D is represented by a node in the ISL. The node also contains the support count of the sequence w.r.t.D. Edges in the ISL connect a sequence with its generating sub-sequences.

ISM assumes that the ISL of the old database is available before the incremental update. This ISL is obtained, for example, by a priori execution of SPADE or ISM. We summarize the three key steps of ISM.

1.   Update ISL if the support count requirement is changed.

    After obtaining ISL, ISM checks whether there are new sequences added to the old database D in the update. If there are, ISM computes the new support count threshold and adjusts ISL accordingly. In the adjustment, frequent sequences may remain frequent, be moved to the negative border, or be deleted from ISL. Also, sequences in the negative border may stay in the negative border or be removed.

2.   Update support counts.

    The next step of ISM is to update the support counts of the sequences that are present in ISL. Since the support of s w.r.t. the old database is known, the updated support count can be efficiently found. In this step, some sequences in the negative border may be moved to the frequent sequence set.

3.   Capture sequences that were not originally in ISL.

    The third step of ISM is to check whether there are new sequences that should be added to ISL due to the update. Here, ISM executes a SPADE-like procedure for generating candidate sequences and counting their supports by ID-list intersection.

In general, ISM is efficient under two conditions: (1) the ISL structure derived from the database is small, and (2) the amount of update to the database (and hence the amount of adjustment made to ISL) is small. The former happens, for example, when there are relatively few items in the database. Otherwise, SPADE could be more efficient than ISM even for the incremental update problem. Being derived from SPADE, ISM has a similar memory requirement as that of SPADE. Finally, ISM does not handle database updates where transactions or sequences are deleted from the database.

Closed Sequence Mining

To address the problem of mining frequent sequences in the presence of noise, Yang, Wang, and Yu (2002a) make use of a compatibility matrix, which provides a probabilistic connection from the observation to the underlying true value. However, the limitation is that the performances degrade dramatically when the length of the sequences is long and the minimum support threshold is low. This is not surprising since a long sequence contains a combinatorial number of frequent sub-sequences. Such mining generates an explosive number of sub-sequences for long sequences.

Currently, an interesting solution, called mining closed sequence patterns, is proposed to overcome this difficulty. The problem of mining closed sequences is to find the set of sequences such that there is no sequence which has a super-sequence with the same support. Yan, Han, and Afshar (2003) is the first to present an algorithm CloSpan to mine closed sequence patterns. It introduces the concept of equivalence of projected databases, which unifies two pruning optimizations: backward sub-pattern and backward super-pattern in a single step. However, CloSpan still follows the candidate-maintenance-and-test paradigm and has to maintain the set of already mined closed sequence candidates. To overcome this problem, Wang and Han (2004) introduces the BI-directional extension checking scheme, a new closure checking and ScanSkip optimization technique. Based on the technique, the authors present a solution BIDE, which can find the set of closed sequences without keeping track of any single historical frequent closed sequences for a new pattern's closure checking.

Constrained Sequence Mining

At the same time, many researchers (Garofalakis, Rastogi, & Shim, 1999; Mannila, Toivonen, & Verkamo, 1995; Pei, Han, & Wang, 2002) have shifted their attention towards mining sequences by incorporating constraints to reduce search space. Mannila, Toivonen, and Verkamo (1995) study the problem of finding a frequent episode in a sequence of events by posing constraints on the event in the form of acyclic graphs. Garofalakis, Rastogi, and Shim (1999) propose regular expressions as constraints for sequence pattern mining and develops a family of SPIRIT algorithms while members in the family achieve various degrees of constraint enforcement. Following that, Pei, Han, and Wang (2002) conduct a systematic study on constraint sequence pattern mining and classifies various kinds of constraints into two categories according to their application semantics and roles in sequence pattern mining.

Summary

In this chapter, we have examined three issues in time series mining, namely, similarity measures, data reduction, and data discretization. We have also reviewed existing works in periodic pattern mining and sequence mining. We observed that current research in periodic pattern mining is focused on discovering partial periodic patterns, asynchronous periodic patterns, patterns with unknown periods, and gap requirement. In Chapter III, we will describe an efficient method called DPMiner to discover short periodic patterns, also known as dense periodic patterns, in small segments of the time series data.

For sequence mining, we have seen that the state-of-the art techniques include PrefixSpan, GSP, and SPADE. In Chapter IV, we will analyze the I/O cost of GSP and present a more efficient algorithm called MFS as well as the incremental versions of GSP and MFS for mining sequence patterns in evolving databases. We will also introduce a new kind of pattern called progressive confident rules in Chapter V. This class of pattern captures sequences of states with an increasing confidence that lead to a particular end state. We design new pruning strategies and employ the concise set analysis of rules in the mining of progressive confident rules to achieve efficiency and scalability.

References

Agrawal, R., & Srikant, R. (1995). Mining sequential patterns. In *Proceedings of the IEEE International Conference on Database Engineering,* Taipei, Taiwan, March 6-10 (pp. 3-14). Los Alamitos, CA: IEEE Computer Society Press.

Agrawal, R., & Srikant, R. (1996). Mining sequential patterns: Generalizations and performance improvements. In *Proceedings of the International Conference on Extending Database Technology,* Avignion, France, March 25-29 (pp. 3-17). Berlin/Heidelberg: Springer.

Agrawal, R., Giuseppe, P., & Edward, W. L. (1995). Querying shapes of histories. In *Proceedings of the International Conference on Very Large Databases,* Zurich, Switzerland, September 11-15 (pp. 502-514). San Francisco, CA: Morgan Kaufmann.

Aref, W. A., Elfeky, M. G., & Elmagarmid, A. K. (2004). Incremental, online, and merge mining of partial periodic patterns in time series databases. *IEEE Transactions on Knowledge and Data Engineering, 16*(3), 332-342.

Ayres, J., Gehrke, J., & Yiu, T. (2002). Sequential pattern mining using a bitmap representation. In *Proceedings of the ACM SIGKDD International Conference on Knowledge Discovery and Data Mining,* Edmonton, Alberta, Canada, July 23-26 (pp. 429-435). New York: ACM Press.

Berberidis, C., Aref, W. G., & Atallah, M. J. (2002). Multiple and partial periodicity mining in time series databases. In *Proceedings of the European Conference on Artificial Intelligence,* Lyon, France, July 21-26 (pp. 370-374). Amsterdam, The Netherlands: IOS Press.

Berndt, D., & Clifford, J. (1994). Using dynamic time warping to find patterns in time series. In *Proceedings of the American Association for Artificial Intelligence (AAAI) Workshop on Knowledge Discovery in Database,* Seattle, Washington, USA, July 31-August 4 (pp. 359-370). Menlo Park, CA: AAAI Press.

Chan, F., & Fu, A. (1999). Efficient time series matching by wavelets. In *Proceedings of the 15th IEEE International Conference on Data Engineering,* Sydney, Australia, March 23-26 (pp. 126-133). Los Alamitos, CA: IEEE Computer Society Press.

Chan, K. P., Fu, A., & Yu, C. (2003). Haar wavelets for efficient similarity search of time series: With and without time warping. *IEEE Transactions on Knowledge and Data Engineering, 15*(3), 686-705.

Elfeky, M. G., Aref, W. G., & Elmagarmid, A. K. (2004). Using convolution to mine obscure periodic patterns in one pass. In *Proceedings of International Conference on Extending Database Technology,* Heraklion, Crete, Greece, March 14-18 (pp. 605-620). Berlin/Heidelberg: Springer.

Elfeky, M. G., Aref, W. A., & Elmagarmid, A. K. (2005). Periodicity detection in time series databases. *IEEE Transactions on Knowledge and Data Engineering, 17*(7), 875-887.

Faloutsos, C., Ranganathan, M., & Manolopoulos, Y. (1994). Fast subsequence matching in time-series databases. In *Proceedings of the ACM SIGMOD International Conference on Management of Data,* Minneapolis, Minnesota, USA, May 24-27 (pp. 419-429). New York: ACM Press.

Fu, T.-C., Chung, F.-L., & Ng, V. (2001). Pattern discovery from stock time series using self-organizing maps. In *ACM SIGKDD Workshop on Temporal Data Mining,* San Francisco, California, USA, August 26. New York: ACM Press.

Fu, W.-C., Keogh, E., & Lau, Y. H. (2005). Scaling and time warping in time series querying. In *Proceedings of the International Conference on Very Large Databases,* Trondheim, Norway, August 30-September 2 (pp. 649-660). New York: ACM Press.

Garofalakis, M., Rastogi, R., & Shim, K. (1999). SPIRIT: Sequential pattern mining with regular expression constraints. In *Proceedings of the International Conference on Very Large Data Bases,* Edinburgh, Scotland, UK, September 7-10 (pp. 223-234). San Francisco, CA: Morgan Kaufmann.

Gilbert, A. C., Kotidis, Y., & Muthukrishnan, S. (2001). Surfing wavelets on streams: One-pass summaries for approximate aggregate queries. In *Proceedings of the International Conference on Very Large Databases,* Roma, Italy, September 11-14 (pp. 79-88). San Francisco, CA: Morgan Kaufmann.

Han, J., Dong, G., & Yin, Y. (1999). Efficient mining of partial periodic patterns in time series databases. In *Proceedings of the IEEE International Conference on Data Engineering,* Sydney, Australia, March 23-26 (pp. 106-115). Los Alamitos, CA: IEEE Computer Society Press.

Han, J., Gong, W., & Yin, Y. (1998). Mining segment-wise periodic patterns in time-related databases. In *Proceedings of the ACM SIGKDD International Conference on Knowledge Discovery and Data Mining,* New York City, New York, USA, August 27-31 (pp. 214-218). Menlo Park, CA: AAAI Press.

Han, J., Pei, J., & Mortazavi-Asl, B. (2000) FreeSpan: Frequent pattern-projected sequential pattern mining. In *Proceedings of the 6th Int. Conf. on Knowledge Discovery and Data Mining,* Boston, Massachusetts, USA, August 20-23 (pp. 20-23). New York: ACM Press.

Huang, K.-Y., & Chang, C.-H. (2005). SMCA: A general model for mining asynchronous periodic patterns in temporal databases. *IEEE Transactions on Knowledge and Data Engineering, 17*(6), 774-785.

Itakura, F. (1975). Minimum prediction residual principle applied to speech recognition. *IEEE Transactions on Acoustics, Speech and Signal Processing, 23,* 52-72.

Keogh, E. (2002). Exact indexing of dynamic time warping. In *Proceedings of 28th International Conference on Very Large Data Bases,* Hong Kong, China, August 20-23 (pp. 406-417). San Francisco, CA: Morgan Kaufmann.

Keogh, E., Palpanas, T., & Zordan, V. B. (2004). Indexing large human-motion databases. In *Proceedings of the 30th International Conference on Very Large Data Bases,* Toronto, Canada, August 31-September 3 (pp. 780-791). San Francisco, CA: Morgan Kaufmann.

Keogh, E. J., Chakrabarti, K., & Pazzani, M. J. (2001a). Locally adaptive dimensionality reduction for indexing large time series databases. In *Proceedings of the ACM SIGMOD International Conference on Management of Data,* Santa Barbara, California, USA, May 21-24 (pp. 151-162). New York: ACM Press.

Keogh, E. J., Chakrabarti, K., & Pazzani, M. J. (2001b). Dimensionality reduction for fast similarity search in large time series databases. *Knowledge and Information Systems, 3*(3), 263-286.

Keogh, E. J., & Pazzani, M. J. (2000). Scaling up dynamic time warping for data mining applications. In *Proceedings of the ACM SIGKDD International Conference on Knowledge Discovery and Data Mining,* Boston, Massachusetts, USA, August 20-23 (pp. 285-289). New York: ACM Press.

Kim, S., Park, S., & Chu, W. (2001). An index-based approach for similarity search supporting time warping in large sequence databases. In *Proceedings of the 17th IEEE International Conference on Data Engineering,* Heidelberg, Germany, April 2-6 (pp. 607-614). Los Alamitos, CA: IEEE Computer Society Press.

Korn, F., Jagadish, H., & Faloutsos, C. (1997). Efficiently supporting ad hoc queries in large datasets of time sequences. In *Proceedings of the ACM SIGMOD International Conference on Management of Data,* Tucson, Arizona, USA, May 13-15 (pp. 289-300). New York: ACM Press.

Kruskall, J. B., & Liberman, M. (1983). The symmetric time warping algorithm: From continuous to discrete. In D. Sankoff, & J. B. Kruskall (Eds.), *Time warps, string edits and macromolecules: The theory and practice of sequence comparison.* Boston, MA: Addison-Wesley.

Lin, J., Keogh, E., & Lonardi, S. (2003). A symbolic representation of time series, with implications for streaming algorithms. In *Proceedings of the 8th ACM SIGMOD Workshop on Data Mining and Knowledge Discovery,* San Diego, California, USA, June 13 (pp. 2-11). New York: ACM Press.

Ma, S., & Hellerstein, J. L. (2001). Mining partially periodic event patterns with unknown periods. In *Proceedings of the 17th IEEE International Conference on Data Engineering,* Heidelberg, Germany, April 2-6 (pp. 205-214). Los Alamitos, CA: IEEE Computer Society Press.

Mannila, H., Toivonen, H., & Verkamo, A.I. (1995). Discovering frequent episodes in sequences. In *Proceedings of the International Conference on Knowledge Discovery and Data Mining,* Montreal, Canada, August 20-21 (pp. 210-215). Menlo Park, CA: AAAI Press.

Morchen, F., & Ultsch, A. (2005). Optimizing time series discretization for knowledge discovery. In *Proceedings of the ACM SIGKDD International Conference on Knowledge Discovery and Data Mining,* Chicago, Illinois, USA, August 21-24 (pp. 660-665). New York: ACM Press.

Parthasarathy, S., Zaki, M. J., & Ogihara, M. (1999). Incremental and interactive sequence mining. In *Proceedings of the 8th ACM International Conference on Information and Knowledge Management,* Kansas City, Missouri, USA, November 2-6 (pp. 251-258). New York: ACM Press.

Pei, J., Han, J., & Mortazavi-Asl, B. (2001). PrefixSpan: Mining sequential patterns efficiently by prefix-projected pattern growth. In *Proceedings of the IEEE International Conference on Data Engineering,* Heidelberg,

Germany, April 2-6 (pp. 215-224). Los Alamitos, CA: IEEE Computer Society Press.

Pei, J., Han, J., & Wang, W. (2002). Mining sequential patterns with constraints in large databases. In *Proceedings of the ACM CIKM International Conference on Information and Knowledge Management,* McLean, Virginia, USA, November 4-9 (pp. 18-25). New York: ACM Press.

Rabiner, L., & Juang, B. (1993). *Fundamentals of speech recognition.* Englewood Cliffs, NJ: Prentice Hall.

Ratanamahatana, C. A., & Keogh, E. (2004). Everything you know about dynamic time warping is wrong. In *ACM SIGKDD Workshop on Mining Temporal and Sequential Data,* Seattle, Washington, USA, August 22. New York: ACM Press.

Sakoe, H., & Chiba, S. (1978). Dynamic programming algorithm optimization for spoken word recognition. *IEEE Transactions on Acoustics, Speech and Signal Processing, 26,* 43-49.

Wang, J., & Han, J. (2004). BIDE: Efficient mining of frequent closed sequences. In *Proceedings of the International Conference on Data Engineering,* Boston, Massachusetts, USA, March 30-April 2 (pp. 79-90). Los Alamitos, CA: IEEE Computer Society Press.

Wang, W., Yang, J., & Yu, P. S. (2001) Meta-patterns: Revealing hidden periodic patterns. In *Proceedings of the IEEE International Conference on Data Mining,* San Jose, California, USA, November 29-December 2 (pp. 550-557). Los Alamitos, CA: IEEE Computer Society Press.

Yan, X., Han, J., & Afshar, R. (2003). CloSpan: Mining closed sequential patterns in large datasets. In *Proceedings of the SIAM International Conference on Data Mining,* San Francisco, California, USA, May 1-3. Philadelphia, PA: SIAM.

Yang, J., Wang, W., & Yu, P. (2000). Mining asynchronous periodic patterns in time series data. In *Proceedings of the ACM SIGKDD International Conference on Knowledge Discovery and Data Mining,* Boston, Massachusetts, USA, August 20-23 (pp. 275-279). New York: ACM Press.

Yang, J., Wang, W., & Yu, P. (2001). InfoMiner: Mining surprising periodic patterns. In *Proceedings of the ACM SIGKDD International Conference on Knowledge Discovery and Data Mining,* San Francisco, California, USA, August 26-29 (pp. 395-400). New York: ACM Press.

Yang, J., Wang, W., & Yu, P. S. (2002a). Mining long sequential patterns in a noisy environment. In *Proceedings of the ACM SIGMOD International Conference on Management of Data,* Madison, Wisconsin, USA, June 3-6 (pp. 406-417). New York: ACM Press.

Yang, W., & Lee, G. (2004). Efficient partial multiple periodic patterns mining without redundant rules. In *28th Annual International Computer Software and Applications Conference,* Hong Kong, September 28-30 (pp. 430-435). Los Alamitos, CA: IEEE Computer Society Press.

Yi, B. K., & Faloutsos, C. (2000). Fast time sequence indexing for arbitrary Lp norms. In *Proceedings of the 26th International Conference on Very Large Data Bases,* Cairo, Egypt, September 10-14 (pp. 385-394). San Francisco, CA: Morgan Kaufmann.

Yi, B. K., Jagadish, H., & Faloutsos, C. (1998). Efficient retrieval of similar time sequences under time warping. In *Proceedings of the IEEE International Conference on Data Engineering,* Orlando, Florida, USA, February 23-27 (pp. 201-208). Los Alamitos, CA: IEEE Computer Society Press.

Zaki, M. (1998). Efficient enumeration of frequent sequences. In *Proceedings of the International Conference on Information and Knowledge Management,* Bethesda, Maryland, USA, November 3-7 (pp. 68-75). New York: ACM Press.

Zaki, M. J. (2001). SPADE: An efficient algorithm for mining frequent sequences. *Machine Learning Journal, Special Issue on Unsupervised Learning, 42*(1), 31-60.

Zhang, M., Kao, B., & Cheung, D. W. (2005). Mining periodic patterns with gap requirement from sequences. In *Proceedings of the ACM SIGMOD International Conference on Management of Data,* Baltimore, Maryland, USA, June 14-16 (pp. 623-633). New York: ACM Press.

Zhao, Y., & Zhang, S. (2006). Generalized dimension-reduction framework for recent-biased time series analysis. *IEEE Transactions on Knowledge and Data Engineering, 18*(2), 231-244.

Zhu, Y., & Shasha, D. (2003). Warping indexes with envelope transform for query by humming. In *Proceedings of the ACM SIGMOD International Conference on Management of Data,* San Diego, California, USA, June 9-12 (pp. 181-192). New York: ACM Press.

Chapter III

Mining Dense Periodic Patterns in Time Series Databases

co-authored with

Chang Sheng, National University of Singapore, Singapore

Discovering periodic patterns from an entire time series has proven to be inadequate in applications where the periodic patterns occur only within small segments of the time series. Consider the following scenario: Tom is an employee who drives his car to work every day. However, his route may change from month to month. In the first month, he follows the route of "home → BLOCK A → BLOCK D → company"; In the second month, he follows the route of "home → BLOCK B → BLOCK K → company"; and in the third month, he changes to the route "home → BLOCK C → BLOCK F → company". Existing periodicity detection algorithms treat all potential periods as equal and will not be able to discover Tom's travelling habits since they are present in only a third of the entire three months period. We observe that, in general, users are only concerned with patterns of short periods because short period patterns are likely to be accurate and useful. For example, we prefer to report patterns of period 5, instead of the patterns of multiples of period 5, say 10 and 15.

In this chapter, we describe a new periodicity detection algorithm to efficiently discover short period patterns that may exist in only a limited range of the time series. We refer to these patterns as the dense periodic patterns, where the periodicity is focused on part of the time series. We present a dense periodic pattern mining algorithm called DPMiner to find dense periodic patterns, and design a pruning strategy to limit the search space to the feasible periods. Experimental results on both real-life and synthetic datasets indicate that DPMiner is both scalable and efficient.

The rest of this chapter is organized as follows. We will first give the formal notations and definitions. Then we will describe the basic idea behind the proposed method for mining dense periodic patterns before giving the details of the algorithm DPMiner. We present the results of the experiments to study the performance of DPMiner. Finally, we conclude with a summary of our findings and contributions.

Notations and Definitions

Given a finite alphabet Σ, we define a *time series* T as a sequence of characters $c_1 \dots c_i \dots c_n$ where $c_i \in \Sigma$.

An *itemset* I is a set of zero or more characters. Examples of itemsets are *{a, b}* and *{a}*. For simplicity, we write *{a}* and *a* interchangeably. An empty itemset, denoted as *, refers to the itemset with no symbol in Σ.

A *pattern* $P = (I_1 I_2 \dots I_p)$, is an ordered sequence of itemsets. The *length* of a pattern $|P|$ is the number of non-*itemsets in P. For example, *(*{b, c} * *)* is a pattern of length 1 and *(a b * *)* is a pattern of length 2.

An *i-pattern* refers to a pattern that contains exactly i characters in Σ. For example, *({b, c} *)* is a 2-pattern and *(a b c *)* is a 3-pattern.

A pattern $(I_1' I_2' \dots I_p')$ is said to be a *sub-pattern* of the pattern $(I_1 I_2 \dots I_p)$ if both patterns have the same length and $I_i' \subseteq I_i$ for all i, $0 \le i \le p$. For example, *(a * b * e)* and *(* * {b, c, d} * e)* are two sub-patterns of the pattern *(a * {b, c, d} * e)*.

A time series $T = c_1 \dots c_n$ of n characters can be partitioned into a set of *segments* S_i of length k, where $0 \le i < \lceil n/k \rfloor$ and $S_i = c_{i|k|+1} \dots c_{i|k|+k}$. Given a pattern $P = (I_1 I_2 \dots I_k)$ of period k and a segment $S_i = c_{i1}, \dots, c_{ik}$, we say that P matches S_i (or S_i supports P) if and only if, for each position $j (1 \le j \le k)$, either $I_j = *$ or $c_{ij} \in I_j$.

A segment is called a frequent segment of a pattern P if the segment supports P, otherwise, it is an infrequent segment. The *frequency_count* of a pattern P is the total number of frequent segments in the time series. The *confidence* of a pattern P is defined as the ratio of frequency count over the total segment count, that is,

confidence (P)= frequency_count(P) / m,

where m = $\lceil n/k \rfloor$.

Given the minimum confidence min conf, we say that a pattern P is *frequent* in the time series if its confidence is greater than or equal to the minimal confidence, *confidence (P) ≥ min conf.*

Dense Periodicity

Density is a familiar concept in the area of data mining and has been widely used in many density-based clustering methods (Ester, Kriegel, & Sander, 1996; Sander, Ester, & Kriegel, 1998). The traditional definition of density relates to the spatial distance. To adapt to the requirement of time series, we define the concept of density of a symbol in the alphabet Σ.

Density in Time Series

The distance between any two characters, say c_i and c_j, in the time series T = $c_1 \ldots c_n$, is defined to be $|i - j|$.

For example, in Figure 3.1, the distance between x and y is $|9 - 6| = 3$, and the distance between y and z is $|10 - 9| = 1$.

Figure 3.1. Example of a time series T

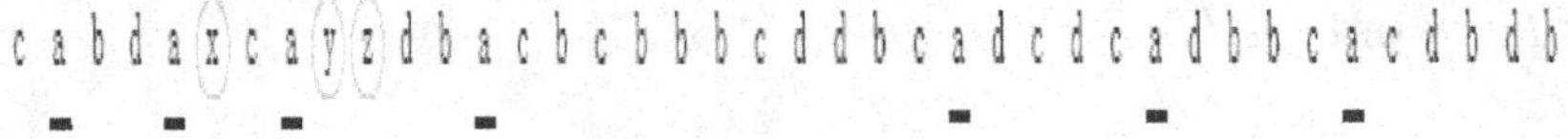

Definition 1: Given a time series $T = c_1 c_2 \ldots c_n$, and a maximum distance, dmax, two characters c_i and c_j are said to be **directly density-reachable** if c_i and c_j are of the same symbol in Σ and there is no other character in the segment $c_{i+1} \ldots c_{j-1}$ that is of the same symbol. Furthermore, the distance between c_i and c_j is less than or equal to d_{max}.

Consider again Figure 3.1. Suppose $d_{max} = 10$. Then the two characters of the symbol 'a' in positions 2 and 5 are directly density-reachable because their distance is 3, which is less than d_{max}. On the other hand, the two characters of the symbol 'a' in position 13 and 25 are not directly density-reachable because their distance is 12, which exceeds d_{max}.

Definition 2: For a symbol $s \in \Sigma$, we extract an ordered sequence of characters of the symbol s from time series T. If any two neighboring characters in this sequence are directly density-reachable, and there is no other character of the same symbol s in T that can be directly density-reachable to any character in this ordered sequence, we say that this ordered sequence is a **closure set** for s, denoted as Cl_s.

In Figure 3.1, the sequence of characters of the symbol a is $(a_2, a_5, a_8, a_{13}, a_{25}, a_{30}, a_{35})$. We observe that the distance between a_{13} and a_{25} is greater than $d_{max} = 10$ whereas the distance between all other neighboring pairs are less than d_{max}. In other words, we can form two closure sets for the symbol a: $\{a_2, a_5, a_8, a_{13}\}$ and $\{a_{25}, a_{30}, a_{35}\}$.

Definition 3: Let bpos and epos be the beginning and ending positions of the first and last characters in the closure set of symbol s. A **dense fragment** of s in the time series T is the continuous sequence of characters in T from position bpos to position epos, denoted as $F_{s,(bpos,epos)}$.

Definition 4: The **dense fragment set** of s in the time series T is the set of all the dense fragments of s, denoted as FS_s.

We calculate the length of a dense fragment $F_{s,(bpos,epos)}$ to be $epos - bpos$, denoted as $|F_{s,(bpos,epos)}|$. Similarly, the $|FS_s|$ is the sum of the length of all the dense fragments. For example, in Figure 3.1, the dense fragment set FS_a for symbol a includes two dense fragments, $F_{a,(2,13)}$ and $F_{a,(25,35)}$. $|F_{a,(2,13)}| = 11$, $|F_{a,(25,35)}| = 10$, and $|FS_a| = 11+10 = 21$. It is obvious that the length of a dense fragment set of any symbol is less than $|T|$.

Lower Bound Period in Fragments

In this section, we derive a lower bound on the period as implied by the symbol's density.

Traditionally, for a time series data with unknown periods, the mining algorithm needs to iteratively inspect all the possible periods from 2 to half of the length of the time series data. This is very expensive.

Here, we show that for a given d_{max} (the maximum allowable distance between two directly density-reachable characters) and *min_conf* (the minimum confidence), we can deduce a lower bound period for all the possible 1-patterns containing the symbol $s \in \Sigma$.

Theorem 1 (Lower Bound Period): For a given symbol s $\in \Sigma$, we can obtain the closure set of s, denoted as Cls, and a dense fragment of s, denoted as Fs,(bpos, epos). The lower bound period of all possible 1-patterns containing symbol s in Fs,(bpos,epos) is equal to

$$\left| \frac{|F_{s,(bpos,epos)}| \times min\_conf \times d_{max}}{|Cl_s| \times d_{max} - |F_{s,(bpos,epos)}| \times (1 - min\_conf)} \right|$$

Proof: From the definition of closure set, we know that Cls contains |Cls| occurrences for symbol s in the fragment $F_{s,(bpos,epos)}$. In order to determine the minimum period, we require that the patterns within this period be frequent. With this in mind, we partition Cl_s into two sets. The first set, called *Type-I* characters, contain characters that occur in the frequent segments (whose count determine whether a pattern is a frequent pattern). The second set, called *Type-II* characters, contains the remaining characters that occur in the infrequent segments. Clearly, we have

$$|Cl_s| = Count_{Type-I} + Count_{Type-II}$$

Since the period of a frequent pattern is determined by the characters in the set Type-I, by assigning as many characters as possible to Type-I, we hope to increase the density of this symbol within the frequent segments, thus leading to the minimum period. More specifically, we have the count in Type-I:

$$Count_{Type-I} = \left\lfloor \frac{|F_{s,(bpos,epos)}|}{period_{min}} \right\rfloor \times min\_conf$$

where period$_{min}$ is the minimal period that we want to compute.

Once we have obtained the count of characters in *Type-I*, the count of the characters in the set *Type-II* is computed by spreading the remaining characters as widely as possible, i.e. d_{max}.

$$Count_{Type-II} = \frac{|F_{s,(bpos,epos)}| - Count_{Type-I} \times period_{min}}{d_{max}}$$

Integrating the formula of *Count$_{Type-I}$*, we have

$$Count_{Type-II} \approx \frac{|F_{s,(bpos,epos)}| - |F_{s,(bpos,epos)}| \times min\_conf}{d_{max}}$$

Finally, by combining the formulae of *Count$_{Type-I}$* and *Count$_{Type-II}$*, the minimal period can be computed as follows:

$$period_{min} = \frac{|F_{s,(bpos,epos)}| \times min\_conf \times d_{max}}{|Cl_s| \times d_{max} - |F_{s,(bpos,epos)}| \times (1 - min\_conf)}$$

For example, in Figure 3.1, suppose we let *min_conf*=0.8 and d_{max}=10, we can easily compute the minimum period of fragment $F_{a,(2,13)}$ as follows: period$_{min}$ = (12×0.8×10) / (4×10−12×0.2) ≈2.55.

The minimum period obtained indicates that it is not possible to find frequent patterns containing the symbol a within a period of 2. A closer look reveals that with a specified period of 2, $F_{a,(2,13)}$ contains 6 segments, in which it requires at least $\lceil 6 \times 0.8 \rfloor = 5$ *a* in the frequent segments. However, we only have $|Cl_a| = 4$ a. In other words, the 1-patterns of period 2 containing 'a' (i.e., (a *) and (* a)) are impossible to be frequent in $F_{a,(2,13)}$.

This theorem allows us to prune the search space of all the periods that are less than the lower bound computed.

Density-Based Pruning

Having found the lower bound periods of the 1-patterns that allow us to prune the search space of all those periods that are less than the lower bound computed, we now need to extend the pruning to the k-patterns, $k > 1$. For simplicity, we assume that the entire time series is divided into segments of period p. Our goal is to identify all the promising high density regions and perform mining only in these regions.

Consider the time series in Figure 3.2 with $min\_conf = 0.7$ and $d_{max} = 5$. There are two overlapping fragments: $F_{a,(13,32)}$ is a dense fragment for symbol a of lower bound period 2, and $F_{b,(25,39)}$ is a dense fragment for symbol b of lower bound period 3. The overlapped portion, from 13 to 39, can be divided into three parts: (13, 24) which only belongs to $F_{a,(13,32)}$, (25, 32) belongs to both $F_{a,(13,32)}$ and $F_{b,(25,39)}$, and (33, 39) which only belongs to $F_{b,(25,39)}$.

Let us first consider the case of period 2. Here, the 2-patterns (i.e., (a b) or (b a)) are not likely to exist in $F_{b,(25,39)}$, because the lower bound period for $F_{b,(25,39)}$ is 3. As for (13,24), we need to inspect whether there are other b's fragments with lower bound of 2 that overlap with it. In other words, we can eliminate (25, 39) from the mining of 2-patterns with period 2. For period 3 or more, we have the following four cases.

Figure 3.2. Fragments for symbols "a" and "b"

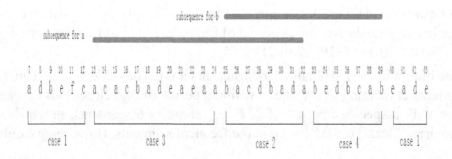

Case 1. The partial time series does not belong to the fragments of symbol *a* nor the fragments of symbol *b*. In other words, the distance between any two arbitrary *a* or *b* is more than d_{max}. This implies that both *a* and *b* occur sparsely, and can be pruned.

Case 2. This is the overlapping region. Here, it is certainly possible to find the frequent segments that support patterns consisting of *a* and *b*.

Case 3. In this case, the time series belong to *a*'s fragments but do not belong to any of the *b*'s fragments. Due to the low density of *b*, it is unlikely to include the frequent segments which support the patterns containing both symbols except nearer to the overlapped region. By extending the overlapped regions (Case 2) slightly on both ends (see Figure 3.2), we can avoid searching the remaining regions as they are not likely to contain the 2-patterns.

Case 4. In this case, the time series belong to *b*'s fragments but do not belong to any of the *a*'s fragments. The analysis of this case is identical to Case 3.

These four cases can be easily extended to three or more symbols. In other words, to check whether a pattern P is frequent, we only need to check the overlapping dense regions of all the itemsets in P. We will now formally define the pruning strategy.

Definition 5: Given a period p and an itemset $I = \{c_1, c_2, ..., c_m\}$, the dense region of I with period p, DR(I,p), is defined as the union of all the dense fragments of c_i, $1 \leq i \leq m$, where the lower bound period of each dense fragment is less than or equal to p.

The dense region of the empty itemset * is defined to be the entire time series. Note that all the merged dense fragments must have the lower bound less than or equal to p so that we make sure these fragments to satisfy the minimal density requirement.

Definition 6: For a pattern P with period p, $(I_1, ..., I_p)$, the dense interval of P, DI(P, p), is defined to be the intersection of all the dense regions of its itemset members, namely DI(P, p)= $DR(I_1, p) \cap ... \cap DR(I_p, p)$.

Given a period p, alphabet Σ, and the dense fragments of all symbols in Σ, we detect the frequent 1-patterns from these dense fragments. To mine the k-patterns, $k > 1$, we only need to check the intersection regions, namely the dense intervals of the k-pattern.

DPMiner

In this section, we show how the proposed density-based pruning strategy can be incorporated into our mining algorithm DPMiner (Dense Periodic pattern Miner). The algorithm mines dense periodic patterns in two phases.

The first phase (Steps 1 to 5 in Algorithm DPMiner) scans the time series once to obtain the dense fragments for each symbol s in Σ. To avoid having too many short and trivial fragments, a parameter $\mu \in (0, 1]$ is used so that only the fragments whose lengths exceed $\mu \times$ length of time series are accepted as dense fragments.

The second phase (Steps 6 to 12 in Algorithm DPMiner) utilizes a top-down method that is similar to the one proposed by Han, Dong, and Yin (1999). The work in Han et al. (1999) defines the *max-pattern*, P_{max}, to be the maximal pattern which can be obtained by merging all frequent 1-patterns F1. For example, if the $F_1 = \{a * * *, c * * *, * b * *, * * * d\}$, the max-pattern will be $\{a, c\}\ b * d$.

Algorithm DPMiner
Input: A time series $T = c_1 c_2 \dots c_n$
    Alphabet Σ
    Maximal distance of two characters in fragments d_{max}
    Fragment length coefficient μ
    Periodicity threshold min_{conf}
Output: Periodic patterns for T
// The periods of the output patterns are in the range of $[2, d_{max}]$

1. *Scan T once to find fragment set S_s for each symbol $s \in \Sigma$;*
2. *FOR each symbol $s \in \Sigma$ DO*
3.   *Delete the fragments of length less than $\mu \times |T|$ from S_s;*
4.   *Compute the lower bound period of every fragment in S_s;*
5. *ENDFOR*

6. *FOR period p = 2 to d$_{max}$*
7.   *For symbol s, discover the frequent 1-patterns, |F1$_s$|, from S$_s$;*
8.   *Merge all |F1$_s$|, s ∈ Σ, to obtain max-pattern P$_{max}$;*
9.   *Let P$_{max}$ with period p be root node of max-subpattern tree R,*
10.   *Compute the dense support DS(R,p);*
11.   *Scan DS(P,p) to construct R;*
12.   *Traverse R to output the frequent patterns.*
13. *ENDFOR*
End Algorithm DPMiner

Given the max-pattern P_{max}, a sub-pattern of P_{max} is *hit* by a segment S_i if it is the maximal sub-pattern of P_{max} in S_i. For example, if $P_{max} = \{a, c\}\, b * d$, the sub-pattern $c\, b * d$ is hit by segment $S_i = c\, b\, d\, d$.

A data structure called *max-subpattern tree* is designed to facilitate the registration of the hit sub-patterns and their counts. The root node of the max-subpattern tree is the max-pattern P_{max}. Each sub-pattern of P_{max} with one non-* letter missing is a direct child node of the root. The tree is constructed by the recursive insertion of the max-subpatterns. If the node of the corresponding max-subpatterns already exists, the hit count of that node is increased by 1; otherwise, a new node is created.

The top-down algorithm can be summarized in three steps. The first step finds the set of frequent 1-patterns F_1 by scanning the time series once, and thereby forming the max-pattern, Pmax. The second step constructs the max-subpattern tree by scanning the time series once again. The last step is the mining procedure from which the frequent patterns are derived according to the constructed max-subpattern tree.

Note that instead of scanning the entire time series as is done in the algorithm in Han et al. (1999), the proposed Algorithm DPMiner only scans the union of the dense regions of the corresponding root nodes' itemsets.

Definition 7: For a max-subpattern tree R taking the max-pattern P$_{max}$ with period p, (I$_1$,...,I$_p$), as its root node, the **dense support** of tree R, DS(R, p), is defined to be the union of all the dense regions of its root node's itemsets, namely DS(R, p)= DR(I$_1$,p) ∪ ... ∪ DR(I$_p$,p).

The dense support of tree R thoroughly covers all segments supporting the max-pattern or its sub-patterns. In other words, only those segments in DS(R) are useful for the construction of max-subpattern tree. This allows us to prune away many unnecessary segments.

We also make modifications to the structure of the max-subpattern tree as follows. Besides the hit count in each node, we also calculate and store the patterns' dense fragments. An example of the modified tree is shown in Figure 3.3.

Let us now discuss how to build the max-subpattern tree and how we can mine patterns from the tree. We first compute the dense support of a max-subpattern tree R according to its max-pattern and Definition 7. Note that we only scan the the dense support of tree R to build its max-subpattern tree, instead of the time series (this is also a reason why DPMiner gives better performance). For every segment in dense support of R, we check whether it supports the max-pattern P_{max} or any sub-pattern of max-pattern it. If yes, this maximal sub-pattern P' will be found by starting from the root node Pmax and along the branches. If the node of P' is found, its count is increased by 1. Otherwise, a new node of P' is created (together with any non-existent ancestors) and the dense interval for P' is computed accordingly.

Consider the example in Figure 3.3. Let a segment cbd be in dense support of R. Then it supports the sub-pattern $(cb*)$ since $cbd \wedge P_{max} = c\ b\ d \wedge (\{a\ c\}\ b\ b) = (\ c\ b\ *)$. This sub-pattern will be found along the route $(\{a\ c\}\ b\ b) \rightarrow (c\ b\ b)(c\ b\ *)$ or $(\{a\ c\}\ b\ b) \rightarrow (\{a\ c\}\ b\ *) \rightarrow (c\ b\ *)$.

Figure 3.3. Example of a max-subpattern tree

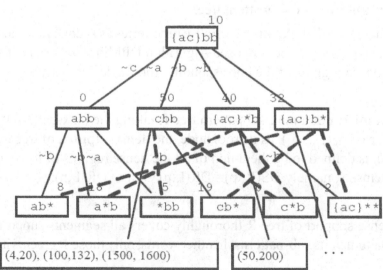

Analysis

Phase 1 in Algorithm 1 scans the time series once. Step 7 in phase 2 scans $min\{|T|, |S_{c1}| + ... + |S_{ci}| + ... + |S_{ck}|\}$ characters, where T is the time series and $c_i \in \Sigma$. Step 10 scans $|DS(R, p)|$ characters, which is also less than $|T|$. The total number of scanned characters for an iteration in phase 2 is $\alpha \times |T|$, where $\alpha \leq 2$ and α is bounded by the time series. For a range of $k(= d_{max})$ period values, we scan $k \times \alpha \times |T|$ characters. Thus, the total number of characters scanned in DPMiner is $(1 + k \times \alpha) \times |T|$, for mining periodic patterns of k periods.

Experiment Evaluation

In this section, we present the results of the experiments that have been carried out to evaluate the performance of Algorithm DPMiner. We implement the DPMiner algorithm in Java. The experiments are performed on a Pentium 4 3Ghz PC with 1GB of memory, running Windows XP. Both synthetic datasets and real-life datasets are used.

Synthetic Datasets

We use the Elfeky's program (available at http://www.cs.purdue.edu/~mgelfeky/Source) to generate the synthetic time series data. By adjusting different parameters such as data distribution (uniform and normal), length of time series, period, and alphabet size, we obtain two synthetic datasets.

1. DATA-6-10000 is a time series satisfying normal distribution with 6 symbols and 10000 characters;
2. DATA-21-75000 is a time series satisfying normal distribution with 21 symbols, and it consists of 75000 characters.

Real-Life Dataset

The PACKET time series dataset (available at http://www.cs.ucr.edu/eamonn/TSDMA/packet.data) serves as the real-life dataset in our experiment studies.

This dataset records the packet Round Trip Time (RTT) delay. We discretize the values into 360K-length characters of alphabet 26.

Sensitivity Experiments

The dense fragments are significant to the final mining result. If the fragment set for a symbol cover too many segments, it is not easy to satisfy the minimal confidence requirement. The extreme case is the entire time series, in which the mining performance and discovered patterns are the same to the previous max-subpattern tree hit set (MTHS) method. Otherwise, the dense fragments should not be extremely short to avoid the patterns within them to be trivial. We will observe the effect of two parameters, namely the maximum distance dmax and the minimal length of dense fragment μ, on the running time of DPMiner, and select the best μ value to ensure adequate dense fragments.

We first vary the value of d_{max} from 10 to 120, and fix the value of μ at 0.01. Figure 3.4 shows the time taken by DPMiner on the PACKET dataset. We observe that d_{max} has a direct effect on the runtime, which can explain that d_{max} affect the length of dense fragments as follows. According to Definitions 1 and 2, the lower the d_{max} value, the more characters are included in

Figure 3.4. Experiment to find optimal value for dmax

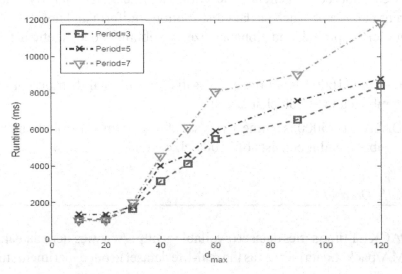

Figure 3.5. Experiment to find optimal value for μ

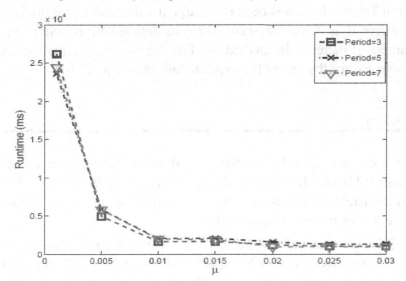

the closure set. This leads to longer dense fragments, and the dense support of max-subpattern tree covers more segments. Hence, we will need more time to search for patterns.

Next, we set the value of dmax to 30, and vary the value of μ from 0.001 to 0.03. μ is the parameter to control the minimal length of dense fragment, and only the dense fragments whose lengths exceed $\mu \times |T|$ are accepted as dense fragments, where T is the time series. Figure 3.5 shows the runtime of DPMiner on the PACKET dataset. We observe that the smaller the value of μ, a lot of dense fragments will be generated, and more time is needed to search for patterns.

Table 3.1. Number of patterns found for varying values of μ

μ	Period=3	Period=5	Period=7
0.001	0	0	0
0.005	1	3	2
0.01	1	4	4
0.015	0	1	1
0.02	0	0	0
0.025	0	0	0
0.03	0	0	0

On the other hand, a large μ value will lead to limited frequent patterns, as shown in Table 3.1. This is because a large μ value will cause no fragment to be accepted as dense fragment. By considering both running time and the number of patterns discovered, we find the $\mu = 0.01$ yields the optimal performance. For the rest of the experiments, we set $\mu = 0.01$.

Efficiency

Next, we run our algorithm on the three datasets and compare its running time with MTHS method. We set dmax = 30 and μ =0.01. Figure 3.6 shows the experimental results. Note that the period '0' on the axis y denotes the time needed for the initialization phase.

Figure 3.6(a) shows that DPMiner has nearly the same performance as MTHS method for the DATA-6-10000 dataset. Figures 3.6(b) and 3.6(c) show that DPMiner outperforms MTHS method for the datasets DATA-21-75000 and PACKET.

This is because the dense support of the max-subpattern tree is greatly affected by the alphabet size of the dataset. For time series data with small alphabet size, the dense support of the tree is equivalent to the entire dataset. In this case, DPMiner will hardly prune any data. On the contrary, for time series data composed of a large alphabet, DPMiner can successfully omit a lot of meaningless data since only a few of characters of alphabet are the itemsets of max-pattern. In other words, only their dense fragments are useful for building the max-subpattern tree. For the reason, DPMiner exhibited better performance on DATA-21-75000 (alphabet size is 21) and PACKET (alphabet size is 26).

Effectiveness

We also compare the patterns discovered by DPMiner and MTHS method. Besides d_{max} = 30 and μ =0.01, we set *min_conf* =0.3. Table 3.2 shows the patterns found by DPMiner with the period range from 2 to 5 on the synthetic dataset DATA-21-75000. Table 3.3 shows the patterns found by DPMiner with the period range from 2 to 6 on real data PACKET. We do not provide the patterns found by MTHS method because it does not discover any frequent patterns on these two datasets.

Figure 3.6. Time comparison of two algorithms

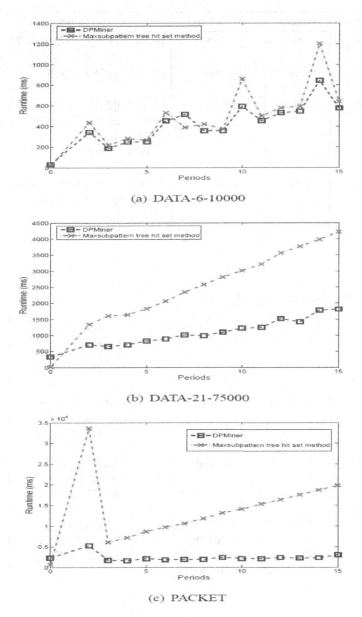

(a) DATA-6-10000

(b) DATA-21-75000

(c) PACKET

We observe that DPMiner can discover the dense periodic patterns as well as their density range. The patterns in DATA-21-75000 are expected since we generate this dataset only in these ranges. The patterns mined from the PACKET dataset are meaningful to keep track of the network traffic.

Table 3.2. Patterns in DATA-21-75000

Period	Pattern	Confidence	Dense Interval
2	be	0.4094	[9002, 12998][21002, 25997]
3	eea	0.3804	[8, 2993][9460, 10436]
4	**be	0.3182	[2, 2174][2216, 2998] [9002, 12998][21002, 25997] [59193, 60040] [60075, 60997]
5	d*ebc	0.3813	[21004,25995][54004,55010] [56939,58454][59193,60040] [60075, 60994]

Table 3.3. Patterns in PACKET

Period	Pattern	Confidence	Dense Interval
2	aa	0.30474216	[148187,155084] [181413,186097] [300522, 304372]
3	*aa	0.3124757	[148187,155084] [181413,186097] [300522, 304372]
4	aa**	0.3103627	[148187,155084] [181413,186097] [300522, 304372]
5	aa*** *aa** ***aa *a*a*	0.3001943 0.30829015 0.32901555 0.31606218	[148187,155084] [181413,186097] [300522, 304372]
6	a**a** ***aa* ****aa	0.30120483 0.31053245 0.34317917	[148187,155084] [181413,186097] [300522, 304372]

Figure 3.7. Runtime on varying dataset size

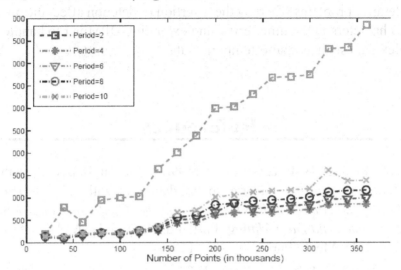

Scalability

Finally, we study the scalability of DPMiner by varying the length of the time series data from 20K to 360K. We also set d_{max} = 30 and μ =0.01. Figure 3.7 shows that the execution time of DPMiner is linearly proportional to the size of the time series.

Summary

In this chapter, we have introduced the notion of dense periodic patterns where the periodicity is focused on part of time series and defined the problem of mining dense periodic patterns. We discussed the concepts of density and fragment, and designed a pruning strategy to limit the search space to just the feasible periods. We have developed a mining algorithm called DPMiner to discover the dense periodic patterns. The experiments carried out on both synthetic and real-life datasets prove the effectiveness and efficiency of DPMiner. The results also show that DPMiner outperforms the existing max-subpattern tree hit set (MTHS) method, especially on the large alphabet datasets. Future research direction include investigating error tolerance problems whereby the insertion or deletion affect the positions of the characters in the time series, and extending DPMiner to handle more complex data such as spatio-temporal data.

References

Ester, M., Kriegel, H.-P., & Sander, J. (1996). A density-based algorithm for discovering clusters in large spatial databases with noise. In *Proceedings of the 7th ACM SIGKDD International Conference on Knowledge Discovery and Data Mining,* Portland, Oregon, USA, August 2-4 (pp. 226-231). Menlo Park, CA: AAAI Press.

Han, J., Dong, G., & Yin, Y. (1999). Efficient mining of partial periodic patterns in time series databases. In *Proceedings of the IEEE International Conference on Data Engineering,* Sydney, Australia, March 23-26 (pp. 106-115). Los Alamitos, CA: IEEE Computer Society Press.

Sander, J., Ester, M., & Kriegel, H. P. (1998). Density-based clustering in spatial databases: A new algorithm and its applications. *Data Mining and Knowledge Discovery, 2*(2), 169-194.

Chapter IV

Mining Sequence Patterns in Evolving Databases

Minghua Zhang, National University of Singapore, Singapore

Ben Kao, The University of Hong Kong, Hong Kong

Chi-Lap Yip, The University of Hong Kong, Hong Kong

David W. Cheung, The University of Hong Kong, Hong Kong

In many applications, the content of a database changes over time. For example, new customer sequences are periodically added to a bookstore's database as the store attracts new customers. Similarly, every visit to a Web site will add a new log to the site's log database. There are also situations in which we have to delete sequences from the database. As an example, when mining current access patterns of a Web site, we may need to delete some out-of-date logs such as those that are more than a year old. Since an operational database changes continuously, the set of frequent sequences has to be updated incrementally.

One simple strategy is to apply an existing mining algorithm on the updated database. However, this strategy fails to take advantage of the valuable information obtained from a previous mining exercise. We note that this information is particularly useful if the updated database and the old one share a significant portion of common sequences. An incremental update algorithm that makes use of a previous mining result should therefore be much more efficient than a mining-from-scratch approach.

In this chapter, we analyze and improve the I/O performance of the GSP algorithm (Agrawal & Srikant, 1996). We also study the problem of incremental maintenance of frequent sequences.

The rest of this chapter is organized as follows. We first give a formal definition of the problem of mining frequent sequences and that of incremental update. Then we present the sequence mining algorithm MFS and its candidate generation function MGen. Next, the pruning technique and two incremental algorithms GSP+ and MFS+ are described. Experiment results comparing the performance of the algorithms given before we conclude the chapter.

Problem Definition

In this section, we formally define the problem of mining frequent sequences and the incremental update problem. We also define some notations to simplify our discussion.

Let $I = \{i_1, i_2, ..., i_m\}$ be a set of literals called items. An itemset X is a set of items (hence, $X \subseteq I$). A sequence $s = <t_1, t_2, ..., t_{-n}>$ is an ordered set of itemsets. The length of a sequence s is defined as the number of items contained in s (denoted by $|s|$). If an item occurs several times in different itemsets of a sequence, the item is counted for each occurrence. For example, if $s = < \{1\}, \{2, 3\}, \{1, 4\} >$, then $|s|=5$.

Consider two sequences $s_1 = <a_1, a_2, ..., a_m>$ and $s_2 = < b_1, b_2, ..., b_n>$. We say that s_1 *contains* s_2, or equivalently, s_2 is a *sub-sequence* of s_1 if there exist integers $j_1, j_2, ..., j_n$, such that $1 \leq j_1 < j_2 < ... < j_n \leq m$ and $b_1 \subseteq a_{j_1}, b_2 \subseteq a_{j_2}, ..., b_n \subseteq a_{j_n}$. We represent this relationship by $s_2 \subseteq s_1$. As an example, the sequence $s_2 = < \{a\}, \{b, c\}, \{d\} >$ is contained in $s_1 = < \{e\}, \{a, d\}, \{g\}, \{b, c, f\}, \{d\} >$ because $\{a\} \subseteq \{a, d\}$, $\{b, c\} \subseteq \{b, c, f\}$, and $\{d\} \subseteq \{d\}$. Hence, $s_2 \subseteq s_1$.

Given a sequence set V and a sequence s, if there exists a sequence $s' \in V$ such that $s \subseteq s'$, we write $s \vdash V$. In words, $s \vdash V$ if s is contained in some sequence of V. Further, a sequence $s \in V$ is *maximal* if s is not contained in any other sequence in V. That is, s is maximal if there does not exist s' such that s' $\in$ V and s' $\neq$ s and s $\subseteq$ s'. We use *Max (V)* to represent the set of all maximal sequences in V.

Given a database D of sequences, the *support count* of a sequence s, denoted by δ_D^s, is defined as the number of sequences in D that contain s. The *fraction* of sequences in D that contain s is called the *support* of s (represented by *sup(s)*). If we use the symbol |D| to denote the number of sequences in D (or the size of D), we have sup(s) = δ_D^s / |D|. If sup(s) is not less than a user specified support threshold ρ_s, s is a *frequent sequence*. We use the symbol L_i to denote the set of all length-i frequent sequences. Further, we use L to denote the set of all frequent sequences. That is $L = \cup_{i=1}^{\infty} L_i$. The problem of mining frequent sequences is to find all *maximal* frequent sequences in a database D (i.e., *Max (L)*).

For the incremental update problem, we assume that a previous mining exercise has been executed on a database D to obtain the supports of the frequent sequences in D. The database D is then updated by deleting a set of sequences Δ^- followed by inserting a set of sequences Δ^+.

Figure 4.1. Definitions of D, D', Δ^-, D^-, and Δ^+

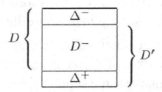

Table 4.1. Notations

Symbol	Description
S	a sequence
δ_X^s	support count of sequence s in database X
ρs	support threshold
|X|	number of sequences in database X
Li	the set of length-i frequent sequences
L	the set of all frequent sequences
D	old database
D'	updated database
Δ-	the set of deleted sequences
Δ+	the set of inserted sequences
D-	the set of sequences shared by D and D'

Let us denote the updated database D'. Note that $D' = (D - \Delta^-) \cup \Delta^+$. Let the set of sequences shared by D and D' be D^-, hence, $D^- = D - \Delta^- = D' - \Delta^+$. Since the relative order of the sequences within a database does not affect the mining results, we may assume (without loss of generality) that all deleted sequences are located at the beginning of the database and all new sequences are appended at the end, as illustrated in Figure 4.1.

The incremental update problem is to find all maximal frequent sequences in the database D' given Δ^-, D^-, and Δ^+, and the result of mining D. Table 4.1 summarizes the notations we use in this chapter.

Algorithm MFS

In this section, we describe the algorithm MFS which aims to reduce the I/O cost of algorithm GSP (Agrawal & Srikant, 1996) when mining huge databases.

The general strategy of MFS is two-fold. First, it efficiently finds an estimate of the set of frequent sequences. Second, it refines the estimate successively until no more refinement can be achieved. If the initial estimate is sufficiently close to the final result, then only a few iterations (database scans) of the refinement step are needed, resulting in an I/O-efficient algorithm.

An initial estimate, S_{est}, can be obtained in several ways. One possibility is to mine a small sample, say 10%, of the database using GSP. In this case, the sample could be mined using the same support threshold as used to mine the whole dataset. As another possibility, if the database is updated and mined regularly, the result obtained from a previous mining exercise can be used as S_{est}. In the latter case, no effort is spent in obtaining the estimated set. This makes MFS suitable for the incremental update problem.

The MFS algorithm has four inputs: the database D, the support threshold ρ_s, the set of all items I, and an estimated set of frequent sequences S_{est}. Algorithm MFS maintains a set MFSS, which is composed of all and only those *maximal* frequent sequences known so far. Since all the sub-sequences of a frequent sequence are frequent, MFSS is sufficient to represent the set of all frequent sequences known.

No frequent sequences are known when the algorithm starts. Hence, MFSS is initialized to the empty set. MFS then scans the database once to count the supports of all length-1 sequences and all the sequences contained in S_{est}. The maximal frequent sequences found in this step are put in the set MFSS. After that, MFS iterates the following two steps:

1. Apply a candidate generation function MGen on MFSS to obtain a candidate set.

2. Scan the database to find out which sequences in the candidate set are frequent. Those frequent candidate sequences are then used to update MFSS.

This refinement procedure stops when MFS cannot find any new frequent sequences. The heart of MFS is the MGen function. MGen is a generalization of the GGen function of GSP. It generates a set of candidate sequences of various lengths given a set of frequent sequences (represented by MFSS) of various lengths. MGen takes three parameters, namely, MFSS—the set of all maximal frequent sequences known so far; Iteration—a loop counter that MFS maintains; and AlreadyCounted—a set of sequences whose supports have already been counted.

MGen generates candidate sequences by "joining" MFSS with itself (lines 3-7). For every pair of frequent sequences s_1 and s_2 in MFSS that have a common sub-sequence, x, MGen generates candidates by prepending an item i_1 from s_1 to x and appending an item i_2 from s_2 to x.

Algorithm MFS (D, ρ_s, I, S_{est})
Input: database D,
          support threshold ρ_s,
           set of all items I,
            estimated set of frequent sequences S_{est}.
Output:set of maximal frequent sequences found MFSS

Function MGen (MFSS, Iteration, AlreadyCounted)
1   CandidateSet = Φ
2   for each pair of s_1, s_2 in MFSS such that $|s_1|$>Iteration-2, $|s_2|$ > Iteration-2 and that s_1, s_2 share at least one common subsequence of length ≥ Iteration-2
3   for each common subsequence s of s_1, s_2 such that $|s|$ ≥ Iteration-2

4          $NewCandidate = \{<i_1 s, i_2>^3 | <i_1, s> \subseteq s_1, <s, i_2> \subseteq s_2\}$
5          $CandidateSet = CandidateSet \cup NewCandidate$
6          $NewCandidate = \{<i_2, s, i_1> | <i_2, s> \subseteq s_2, <s, i_1> \subseteq s_1\}$
7          $CandidateSet = CandidateSet \cup NewCandidate$
8   *for each sequence s ∈ CandidateSet*
9   *if (s |– MFSS) delete s from CandidateSet*
10   *if (s ∈ AlreadyCounted) delete s from CandidateSet*
11   *for any subsequence s' of s with length |s|-1*
12   *if not(s' |– MFSS) delete s from CandidateSet*
13   *AlreadyCounted = AlreadyCounted ∪ CandidateSet*
14   *for each sequence s ∈ AlreadyCounted*
15   *if (|s| = Iteration) delete s from AlreadyCounted*
16   *Return CandidateSet*
End Function MGen

Begin Algorithm MFS
17   $MFSS = \Phi$
18   $CandidateSet = \{<\{i\}> | i \in I\} \cup \{s | s |– S_{est}, |s| >1\}$
19   *Scan D to get* δ_D^s *for every sequence s in CandidateSet*
20   $NewFrequentSequences = \{s | s \in CandidateSet, \delta_D^s \geq \rho_s |D|\}$
21   $AlreadyCounted := \{s | s |– S_{est}, |s| >1\}$
22   *Iteration = 2*
23   *while (NewFrequentSequences ≠ Φ)*
24       $MFSS = Max(MFSS \cup NewFrequentSequences)$
25       $CandidateSet = MGen (MFSS, Iteration, AlreadyCounted)$
26   *Scan D to get* δ_D^s *for every sequence s in CandidateSet*
27       $NewFrequentSequences := \{s | s \in CandidateSet, \delta_D^s \geq \rho_s |D|\}$
28   *Iteration := Iteration+1*
29   *Return MFSS*
End Algorithm MFS

For example, if $s_1 = <\{A,B\}, \{C\}, \{D,E,F\} >$ and $s_2 = <\{B\}, \{C,G\}, \{H\}>$, then a common subsequence would be $<\{B\}, \{C\} >$.

By this generation rule, MGen would generate the candidates $<\{A,B\}, \{C,G\} >$ and $<\{A,B\}, \{C\}, \{H\}>$.

Note that, unlike GGen, the generating sequences s_1 and s_2 have different lengths. After a candidate sequence s is generated, it is removed (from the candidate set) if any one of the following conditions is true (lines 8-12):

1. $s \vdash$ MFSS. This implies that s is already known to be frequent.

2. $s \in$ AlreadyCounted. This implies that the support of s has been counted already.

3. Some sub-sequences of s with length $|s|$ -1 are not known to be frequent. This implies that s cannot be frequent.

We can prove that MFS is correct, and that MGen does not generate any unnecessary candidates. When there is no initial estimate S_{est}, MFS and GSP are equivalent in the sense that they consider the same set of candidate sequences. For details of proofs, we refer readers to Kao, Zhang, and Yip (2005).

Incremental Update Algorithms

In this section, we describe a pruning technique that, when applied to GSP and MFS, leads to two efficient incremental update algorithms GSP+ and MFS+. In our model, the database is updated continuously and incrementally. In the following discussion, D is an old database version, Δ^- and Δ^+ are the sets of sequences removed from and added to D, respectively. The update results in a new database version D'. The algorithms can be similarly applied when the database is subsequently changed again with D' taking the role of D, and so forth.

The general idea of the incremental update algorithms is that, given a sequence s, we use the support count of s in D (if available) to deduce whether s could have enough support in the updated database D'. In the deduction process, the portion of the database that has been changed, namely, Δ^- and Δ^+, might have to be scanned. If we deduce that s cannot be frequent in D', s's support in D^- (the portion of the database that has not been changed) is not counted. If D^- is large compared with Δ^- and Δ^+, the pruning technique saves much CPU cost.

Before we present the algorithms, let us consider a few mathematical equations that allow us to perform the pruning deductions. Readers are referred to Table 4.1 for the symbol definitions. First of all, since $D' = D - \Delta^- \cup \Delta^+ = D^- \cup \Delta^+$, we have, for any sequence s,

$$\delta_D^{\ s} = \delta_{D^-}^{\ s} + \delta_{\Delta^-}^{\ s} \qquad (1)$$

$$\delta_{D'}{}^{s} = \delta_{D\text{-}}{}^{s} + \delta_{\Delta+}{}^{s} \tag{2}$$

$$\delta_{D'}{}^{s} = \delta_{D}{}^{s} + \delta_{\Delta+}{}^{s} - \delta_{\Delta\text{-}}{}^{s} \tag{3}$$

Let us define $b_{X}{}^{s} = \min_{s'} \delta_{X}{}^{s'}$ for any sequence s and database X, where $(s' \subseteq s) \cup (|s'|=|s|\text{-}1)$. That is to say, if s is a length-k sequence, $b_{X}{}^{s}$ is the smallest support count of the length-(k-1) sub-sequences of s in the database X. Since the support count of a sequence s must not be larger than the support count of any subsequence of s, $b_{X}{}^{s}$ is an *upper bound* of $\delta_{X}{}^{s}$.

The reason for considering $b_{X}{}^{s}$ is to allow us to estimate $\delta_{X}{}^{s}$ without counting it. As we will see later, under both GSP+ and MFS+, a candidate sequence s is considered (and may have its support counted) only if all of s's sub-sequences are frequent. Since frequent sequences would already have their supports counted (in order to conclude that they are frequent), we would have the necessary information to deduce $b_{X}{}^{s}$ when we consider s.

To illustrate how the bound is used in the deduction, let us consider the following lemmas:

Lemma 1. If a sequence s is frequent in D', then $\delta_{D}{}^{s} + b_{\Delta+}{}^{s} \geq \delta_{D}{}^{s} + b_{\Delta+}{}^{s} - \delta_{\Delta\text{-}}{}^{s}$ $\geq |D'|\, \rho_{s}$.

Given a sequence s, if s is frequent in D, we know $\delta_{D}{}^{s}$. If $b_{\Delta+}{}^{s}$ is available, we can compute $\delta_{D}{}^{s} + b_{\Delta+}{}^{s}$ and conclude that s is not frequent in D' if the quantity is less than $|D'|\times\rho_{s}$. Otherwise, we scan $\Delta^{\text{-}}$ to find $\delta_{\Delta\text{-}}{}^{s}$. We conclude that s is not frequent in D' if $\delta_{D}{}^{s} + b_{\Delta+}{}^{s} - \delta_{\Delta\text{-}}{}^{s}$ is less than the required support count ($|D'|\times\rho_{s}$). Note that in these cases, the deduction is made without processing $D^{\text{-}}$ or Δ^{+}.

If a sequence s is not frequent in D, $\delta_{D}{}^{s}$ is unavailable. The pruning tricks derived from Lemma 1 are thus not applicable. However, being not frequent in D means that the support of s (in D) is *small*. The following Lemma allows us to prune those sequences.

Lemma 2. If a sequence s is frequent in D' but not in D, then $b_{\Delta+}{}^{s} \geq b_{\Delta+}{}^{s} - \delta_{\Delta\text{-}}{}^{s}$ $\geq \delta_{\Delta+}{}^{s} - \delta_{\Delta\text{-}}{}^{s} > (|\Delta^{+}| - |\Delta^{\text{-}}|)\, \rho_{s}$.

Given a candidate sequence s that is not frequent in the old database D, we first compare $b_{\Delta^+}^s$ against $(|\Delta^+| - |\Delta^-|) \rho_s$. If $b_{\Delta^+}^s$ is not large enough, s cannot be frequent in D', and hence s can be pruned. Otherwise, we scan Δ^- to find $b_{\Delta^+}^s - \delta_{\Delta^-}^s$ and see if s can be pruned. If not, we scan Δ^+ and consider $\delta_{\Delta^+}^s - \delta_{\Delta^-}^s$.

Similar to Lemma 1, Lemma 2 allows us to prune some candidate sequences without completely counting their supports in the updated database.

Interested readers may refer to Zhang, Kao, and Cheung (2002) and Kao, Zhang, and Yip (2005) for proofs of the two Lemmas.

Algorithm GSP+

Based on Lemma 1 and 2, we modify algorithm GSP (Agrawal & Srikant, 1996) to incorporate the pruning techniques mentioned to obtain a new algorithm, GSP+.

GSP+ shares the same structure with GSP. GSP+ is an iterative algorithm. During each iteration i, a set of candidate sequences C_i is generated based on L_{i-1} (the set of frequent sequences of length i-1). Before the database is scanned to count the supports of the candidate sequences, the pruning tests derived from Lemmas 1 and 2 are applied. Depending on the test results, the datasets Δ^- and/or Δ^+ may have to be processed to count the support of a candidate sequence.

GSP+ carefully controls when such countings are necessary. If all pruning tests fail on a candidate sequence s, GSP+ checks whether s is frequent in D. If so, δ_D^s is available. Hence, $\delta_{D'}^s$ can be computed by $\delta_D^s + \delta_{\Delta^+}^s - \delta_{\Delta^-}^s$. Finally, if s is not frequent in D, the unchanged part of the database, D^-, is scanned to find out the actual support of s. Since D^- is typically much larger than Δ^+ and Δ^-, saving is achieved by avoiding processing D^- for certain candidate sequences.

As we will see later in the experiment section, the pruning tests can prune up to 60% of the candidate sequences. This demonstrates that the tests are quite effective.

In terms of I/O performance, GSP+ generally has a slightly higher I/O cost compared to applying GSP directly on the updated database D'. This is because GSP+ scans and processes Δ^-, the deleted portion of the database, which is not needed by GSP. However, in some cases, the pruning tests (in GSP+) remove all candidate sequences during an iteration of the algorithm.

Under such cases, GSP+ saves some database passes, and is slightly more I/O efficient than GSP.

Algorithm MFS+

The pruning tests can also be applied to MFS. We call the resulting algorithm MFS+. The interesting thing about MFS+ is that it uses the set of frequent sequences (L_{old}) of the old database D as an initial estimate of the set of frequent sequences of the new database D'.

These sequences together with all possible length-1 sequences are put into a candidate set *CandidateSet*. It then scans Δ^+, Δ^-, and D^- to obtain $\delta_{\Delta^+}{}^s$, $\delta_{\Delta^-}{}^s$ and $\delta_{D^-}{}^s$ for each sequence s in *CandidateSet*. From these counts, we can deduce which sequences in *CandidateSet* are frequent in D'. The *maximals* of such frequent sequences are put into the set MFSS. MFS+ then executes a loop, trying to refine MFSS.

During each iteration, MFS+ generates a set of candidate sequences *CandidateSet* from MFSS. MFS+ then deduces which candidate sequences must not be frequent by applying the pruning tests. In the process, the datasets Δ^- and Δ^+ may have to be scanned. For those sequences that are not pruned by the tests, D^- is scanned to obtain their exact support counts. Since sequences that are originally frequent in the old database D have already had their supports (with respect to D') counted in the initial part of MFS+, all candidate sequences considered by MFS+ in the loop section are not frequent in D.

Hence, only those pruning tests resulting from Lemma 2 are used. MFS+ terminates when no refinement is made to MFSS during an iteration.

Performance Study

We carried out a number of experiments to compare the various algorithms for the sequence mining problem and the incremental update problem. We study the amount of I/O savings MFS could achieve, and how effective sampling is in discovering an initial estimate of the set of frequent sequences S_{est}. We also study the effectiveness of the pruning technique when applied to GSP and MFS in solving the incremental update problem. The experiment was done on a Sun Enterprise 4000 machine with 12 UltraSparc II 250MHz

CPUs and 3G main memory running Solaris 7. In this section, we present some representative experiment results.

Experimental Dataset

We used synthetic data as the test databases. The data is generated using the generator of the IBM Quest data mining project. The values of the parameters used in the data generation are listed in Table 4.2.

Coverages and I/O Savings

Recall that MFS requires an estimated frequent sequence set, S_{est}. Obviously the number of frequent sequences contained in S_{est} will affect how much I/O gain MFS can achieve. In one extreme case, if S_{est} contains no frequent sequences, MFS reduces to GSP, and it needs the same number of I/O passes as GSP. In the other extreme case, if S_{est} contains all frequent sequences, MFS can finish the whole mining process in only two database scans. One pass to get all frequent sequences; the other pass to verify no other frequent sequences can be found.

Here, we study how the "coverage" of S_{est} affects the performance of MFS. By coverage, we refer to the fraction of all the frequent sequences that are contained in S_{est}. We formally define coverage by:

Table 4.2. Parameters and values for data generation

Parameter	Description	Value
|C|	Average no. of transactions(itemsets) per sequence	10
|T|	Average no. of items per transaction(itemset)	2.5
|S|	Average no. of itemsets in maximal potentially frequent sequences	4
|I|	Average size of itemsets in maximal potentially frequent sequences	1.25
NS	Number of maximal potentially frequent sequences	5,000
NI	Number of maximal potentially frequent itemsets	25,000
N	Number of items	10,000

$$\text{Coverage} = | \{s| s |\text{-} S_{est}\} \cap (\cup_{i=2}^{\infty} L_i) | / | \cup_{i=2}^{\infty} L_i |$$

where L_i represents the set of all frequent sequences of length i.

Notice that we only consider those frequent sequences of length-2 or longer. This is because all length-1 sequences *will* be checked by MFS during its first scan of the database (see Figure 2.2, line 20). Therefore, whether S_{est} contains frequent length-1 sequences or not is immaterial to the number of I/O passes required by MFS.

In our first experiment, we generate a database of about 131,000 sequences using the parameter values listed in Table 4.2. We then apply GSP on the database to obtain all frequent sequences. After that, we randomly select some frequent sequences to form an estimated set S_{est}. MFS is then applied on the database with the S_{est} obtained. The number of I/O passes taken by MFS is noted. We perform the experiment using different support thresholds ρ_s. The results for $\rho_s = 0.3\%$, 0.4%, and 0.5% are shown in Figure 4.2.

In Figure 4.2, the x axis is the coverage of S_{est}, and the y axis is the number of I/O passes taken by MFS. We use three kinds of points (`◊`, `+`, `□`) to represent three support thresholds 0.3%, 0.4%, 0.5%, respectively.

For example, point A is represented by □ and its coordinates are (0.718, 4). This means that when the support threshold was 0.5% and the coverage of S_{est} was 0.718, MFS took 4 I/O passes. Note that the lines connecting points of the same kind are there for legibility reason only and should not be interpreted as interpolation.

We observe that when coverage increases, the number of I/O passes required by MFS decreases. In general, the curves show the following trend:

1.   When coverage = 0 (e.g., when S_{est} is empty), MFS degenerates to GSP. Therefore, the number of I/O passes taken by MFS is the same as that of GSP. Hence, the y-intersects of the curves show the I/O costs of GSP under their respective support thresholds.

2.   When coverage is small, S_{est} would contain very few long frequent sequences. This is because if S_{est} covers a long frequent sequence s, it also covers every sub-sequence of s. These sub-sequences are frequent and if s is long they are numerous. The coverage of S_{est} would thus be high. Since few long frequent sequences are covered by S_{est}, quite a number of I/O passes are required to discover them. Hence, with a small coverage, MFS does not reduce the I/O cost at all.

Figure 4.2. No. of I/O passes needed by MFS versus coverage under differ-ent ρ_s

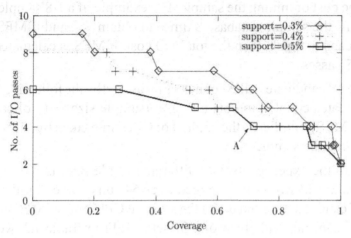

3. When coverage is moderate, MFS becomes more effective. The amount of I/O savings increases with the coverage.

4. When coverage is 100%, that is, S_{est} covers all frequent sequences in the database, MFS requires only two passes over the database: one pass to verify that the sequences in S_{est} are all frequent, another pass to verify that no more frequent sequences can be found.

Sampling

As we have mentioned, one way to obtain S_{est} is to mine a sample of the whole database. We perform a set of experiments to study the effectiveness of the sampling approach.

In this set of experiments, we use a database of about 131,000 sequences and we fixed the support threshold at $\rho_s =0.4\%$. The experiments are carried out as follows. We first apply GSP on our synthetic dataset to obtain the number of I/O passes it required.

Then a random sample of the database is drawn. After that, we run GSP on the sample to obtain S_{est} for MFS. When mining the sample, GSP use a sample support threshold $\rho_{s\_sample} = \rho_s = 0.4\%$. We then execute MFS with the S_{est} found. This exercise is repeated 64 times, each with a different random sample. Finally, the experiment is repeated using various sample sizes.

We compare the performance of GSP and MFS in three aspects—I/O cost, the number of candidates they counted, and CPU cost. The I/O cost of MFS includes the cost of mining the sample. For example, if a 1/8 sample is used, if GSP scans the sample database 8 times to obtain S_{est}, and if MFS takes 4 database scans to finish, then the total I/O cost of MFS is calculated as: 1/8 $\times$ 8 + 4 = 5 passes.

The number of candidates MFS counted is measured by the following formula: (# of candidates counted to obtain S_{est}) $\times$ (sample size) + (# of candidates counted in MFS). Similarly, the amount of CPU time taken by MFS includes that of mining the sample.

The result of the experiments with different sample sizes is shown in Table 4.3. The values of MFS are averaged over 64 runs. Note that the average number of candidates counted and the average CPU cost of MFS are shown in relative quantities with those of GSP set to 1. From Table 4.3, we see that MFS required fewer I/O passes than GSP (8 passes). As the sample size increases, the coverage of S_{est} becomes higher, and fewer I/O passes are required for MFS to discover all the frequent sequences given S_{est}. This accounts for the drop of I/O cost from 6.777 passes to 5.807 passes as the sample size increases from 1/128 to 1/8. As the sample size increases further, however, the I/O cost of mining the sample becomes substantial. The benefit obtained by having a better-coverage S_{est} is out weighted by the penalty of mining the sample. Hence, the overall I/O cost increases as the sample size increases from 1/8 to 1/2. Similar trends are observed for the number of candidates being counted and the CPU cost.

Table 4.3. Performance of MFS vs. sample size (ρ_s =0.4%, ρ_{s_sample} = 0.4%)

Sample size	1/128	1/64	1/32	1/16	1/8	1/4	1/2	0
Avg. coverage	0.718	0.758	0.788	0.793	0.861	0.900	0.924	n/a
Avg. I/O cost	6.777	6.533	6.090	6.059	5.807	6.262	7.945	8
Avg. # of cand.	1.685	1.279	1.149	1.106	1.146	1.265	1.503	1
Avg. CPU cost	3.693	1.699	1.320	1.198	1.174	1.249	1.441	1

The experiment results show that sampling is a good way to determine S_{est}. For example, even if the sample size is as small as 1/128, the coverage of S_{est} is over 70%. The results also show that MFS can achieve good I/O efficiency by sampling. Given a 1/8 sample, for example, MFS reduces about (8-5.807)/8 = 27% of the I/O cost at the expense of a 17% increment in CPU cost. In all our experiments, we find that a sample size of 1/8 or 1/16 generally gives a large reduction in I/O cost with a small expense in CPU cost.

In these experiments, the support threshold used in mining the sample (ρ_{s_sample}) is the same as the support threshold used for mining the whole database (ρ_s). What if we use a different ρ_{s_sample} compared with ρ_s? Intuitively, if $\rho_{s\_sample} <$ ρ_{s_sample}, more sequences in the sample will satisfy the support requirement. Therefore, more sequences will be included in S_{est}. This will potentially improve the coverage of S_{est}, and hence a larger reduction in I/O cost is achieved. The disadvantage is a larger CPU cost, since more support counting would have to be done in the sample-mining process as well as in verifying which sequences in S_{est} are frequent.

To study the effect of using a smaller ρ_{s_sample}, we conduct an experiment varying the ratio ρ_{s_sample} / ρ_s from 1.0 to 0.7. In the experiment, we fix the sample size at 1/8 and ρ_s at 0.4%. Figure 4.4 shows the performance of MFS. The average I/O cost and the average CPU cost of MFS use the left scale and the

Figure 4.3. Performance of MFS vs. ρ_{s_sample} / ρ_s

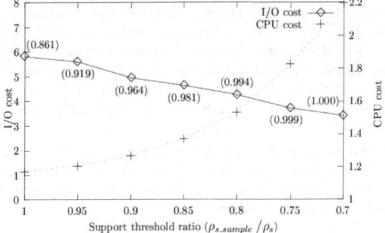

right scale, respectively. The number associated with each point shows the average coverage of S_{est} given the corresponding ρ_{s_sample} / ρ_s value.

From Figure 4.3, we observe that a smaller ρ_{s_sample} gives a smaller I/O cost and a larger CPU cost. For example, when ρ_{s_sample} equals $0.9 \times \rho_s$, MFS took about 5 passes over the data (GSP took 8) at a CPU penalty of 27%. Figure 4.4 shows that MFS is a flexible algorithm: one can adjust ρ_{s_sample} to achieve efficiency based on the system's characteristics. For example, if the machine on which mining is performed has a fast CPU but a slow storage device, a small ρ_{s_sample} should be used.

CPU Cost

Our previous experiments show that in order to achieve I/O efficiency, MFS has to pay a non-trivial CPU penalty. In this section, we discuss the CPU requirement of MFS. We will show that the relative CPU cost of MFS (compared with GSP) decreases when the database size increases. For large databases, the CPU penalty is negligible.

Compared with GSP, there are two reasons why MFS might require a higher CPU cost. First, there is the cost of mining a sample. Second, the candidate generation function MGen is more complicated than GGen. There are usually more sub-sequence testing in the generation process, and more pruning tests to check. However, we note that the generation function is executed once per iteration of the algorithm, and it is *independent* of the database size.

On the other hand, there is a factor that causes MFS to be more CPU efficient than GSP. Recall that under MFS or GSP, during each iteration, each sequence s in the database is matched against a set of candidate sequences to see which candidates are contained in s, and to increase their support counts. Since MFS performs fewer database scans compared with GSP, the database sequences are matched against candidate sequences fewer times. This makes MFS more CPU efficient. We note that the larger the database, the more prominent is the saving achieved. Let us call this factor the *support counting benefit*.

We perform an experiment varying the database size from the original setting of 131,000 sequences to 2.5 million sequences. Again, a 1/8 sample is used and ρ_s is set to 0.4%. Figure 4.5 shows the relative CPU cost of MFS (over GSP) as the database size changes.

Figure 4.4. Relative CPU cost of MFS versus database size

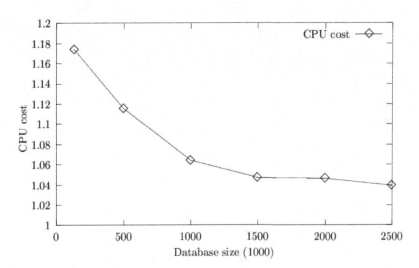

Figure 4.4 shows that as the database size increases, the relative CPU cost of MFS decreases. This is because the penalty of a more expensive candidate generation process suffered by MFS does not grow with the database size. Hence, when the database is very large, the candidate generation penalty is negligible compared with the other two factors that affect MFS's CPU performance, namely, the sampling penalty and the support counting benefit. Since these two factors are affected by the database size in a similar way, the relative CPU cost of MFS approaches a constant factor as the database becomes very large.

From Figure 4.4, we observe that under our experiment setting, the CPU penalty of MFS is only about 4% for large databases. We note that the relative I/O saving achieved by MFS is unaffected by the database size.

MFS vs. SPADE

In this section, we compare the performance of MFS and SPADE in a limited-memory environment. To study the effect of memory availability on SPADE's performance, we compare the performance of SPADE and MFS running on a PC with 512M memory. As we have discussed in Chapter II, SPADE is a very efficient algorithm for small databases. Its performance,

Figure 4.5. Execution time of MFS and SPADE under different database sizes

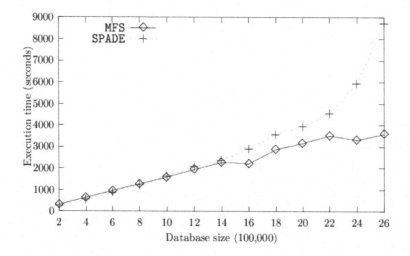

however, is less impressive if the database size is relatively large compared with the amount of memory available.

Figure 4.5 shows that when the database size is large (e.g., when there are more than 1.4 million sequences), the performance of SPADE degrades greatly due to memory paging.

Incremental Update

In this section we study the performance of the algorithms GSP, MFS, GSP+, and MFS+ when they are applied to the incremental update problem. For GSP, the algorithm is simply applied to the updated database D'. For MFS, it is applied to D' using the set of frequent sequences of the old database D as S_{est}. Both GSP+ and MFS+ use the mining result of D and the pruning technique to discover the frequent sequences in D'.

We conduct a series of experiments using a database D of 1.5 million sequences. We first execute a sequence mining program on D to obtain all frequent sequences and their support counts. Then, 10% (150,000) of the sequences in D are deleted. These sequences form the dataset Δ^-. Another 10% (150,000) sequences which form the set Δ^+, are added into D to form the updated database D'. After that, the four algorithms are executed to mine D'. We vary the support threshold ρ_s from 0.35% to 0.65%.

We compare the CPU costs and I/O costs of the four algorithms. I/O cost is measured in terms of database scans normalized by the size of D'. For example, if GSP scans D' 8 times, then the I/O cost of GSP is 8. For an incremental algorithm, if it reads Δ^- n_1 times, D^- n_2 times, and Δ^+ n_3 times, then its I/O cost is

$$(n_1 \, |\Delta^-| + n_2 \, |D^-| + n_3 \, |\Delta^+|) \, / \, |D'|.$$

We note that while the I/O costs of GSP and MFS are integral numbers (because D' is the only dataset they read), those of GSP+ and MFS+ could be fractional. Figure 4.7 shows the experiment results.

Figure 4.6(a) shows that as ρ_s increases, the CPU costs of all four algorithms decrease. This is because a larger ρ_s means fewer frequent sequences, and thus there are fewer candidate sequences whose supports need to be counted. Among the four algorithms, GSP has the highest CPU cost. Since MFS uses the mining result of D as the estimate, S_{est}, no time is spent on mining a sample. Because of the support counting benefit, MFS is more CPU efficient than GSP for incremental update.

We also observe that GSP+ and MFS+ are more CPU efficient than their respective counterparts. The saving is obtained by the pruning effect of the incremental algorithms: some candidate sequences are pruned by processing only Δ^- and/or Δ^+; the set D^- is avoided. In our experiment setting, the size of D^- is 9 times that of Δ^- and Δ^+. Avoid counting the supports of the pruned candidate sequences in D^- results in a significant CPU cost reduction.

Table 4.4 Effectiveness of pruning tests

ρs	0.35%	0.40%	0.45%	0.5%	0.55%	0.6%	0.65%
Total # of candidates	34,065	18,356	10,024	5,812	3,365	2,053	1,160
# of candidates requiring δD-s	13,042	7,161	3,966	2,313	1,353	867	509
Percentage	38%	39%	40%	40%	40%	42%	44%

Table 4.4 shows the effectiveness of the pruning tests used in GSP+. The total number of candidate sequences processed by the pruning tests is shown in the second row, and the number of them that require the scanning of D⁻ is shown in the third row. We observe that only about 40% of the candidate sequences require the processing of D⁻ to obtain their support counts. In other words,

Figure 4.6. Comparison of four algorithms under different support thresholds

C10T2.5S4I1.25 D1500-150+150(thousand)

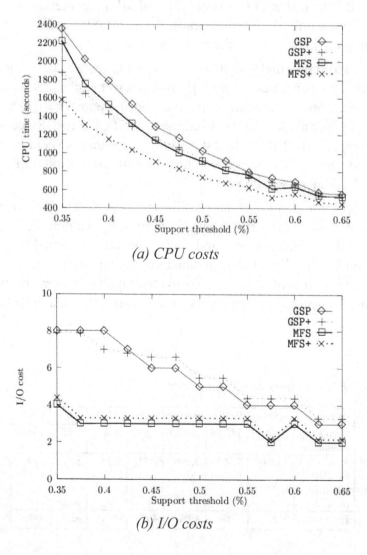

(a) CPU costs

(b) I/O costs

about 60% of the candidate sequences are pruned. This accounts for the saving in CPU cost achieved by GSP+ over GSP. Similarly, MFS+ outperforms MFS, mainly due to candidate pruning.

Finally, when ρ_s becomes large, the CPU times of the algorithms are roughly the same. This is because a large support threshold implies short and few frequent sequences. In such a case, GSP and MFS take similar number of iterations, and hence the CPU saving of MFS over GSP is diminished. Moreover, there are much fewer candidate sequences when ρ_s is large, and there are much fewer opportunities for the incremental algorithms to prune candidate sequences.

Figure 4.6(b) shows the I/O costs of the four algorithms. We see that as ρ_s increases, the I/O costs of the algorithms decrease. This is due to the fact that a larger ρ_s leads to shorter frequent sequences. Hence, the number of iterations (and database scans) the algorithms take is small. Comparing GSP and MFS, we see that MFS is a very I/O-efficient algorithm. Since MFS uses the frequent sequences in D as an estimate of those in D', this gives MFS a head start and allows MFS to discover all maximal frequent sequences in much fewer database scans.

The incremental algorithms generally require a slightly higher I/O cost than their non-incremental counterparts. The reason is that the incremental algorithms scan and process Δ^- to make pruning deductions, which is not needed by GSP or MFS. However, in some cases, the pruning tests remove all candidate sequences during an iteration of the algorithm. In such cases, incremental algorithms save some database passes. For example, when ρ_s <0.45%, GSP+ has a smaller I/O cost than GSP (see Figure 4.6(b)).

We can conclude that GSP has a high CPU cost and a high I/O cost. GSP+ reduces the CPU requirement but does not help in terms of I/O. MFS is very I/O-efficient and it also performs better than GSP in terms of CPU cost. MFS+ is the overall winner. It requires the least amount of CPU time and its I/O cost is comparable to that of MFS.

Varying $|\Delta^+|$ and $|\Delta^-|$

As we have discussed, GSP+ and MFS+ achieve efficiency by processing Δ^+ and Δ^- to prune candidate sequences. The performance of GSP+ and MFS+ is thus dependent on how large Δ^+ and Δ^- are. Intuitively, a large delta requires more effort. We run an experiment to investigate how $|\Delta^+|$ and $|\Delta^-|$ affect the performance of GSP+ and MFS+. In the experiment, we set $|D| = |D'| = 1.5$ million sequences, $\rho_s = 0.5\%$, and we vary $|\Delta^+|$ and $|\Delta^-|$ from 15,000 to 600,000 (1% – 40% of $|D|$). Figure 4.7 shows the experiment results.

Figure 4.7. Comparison of four algorithms under different insertion and deletion sizes

C10T2.5S4I1.25 D1500-x+x (thousand)

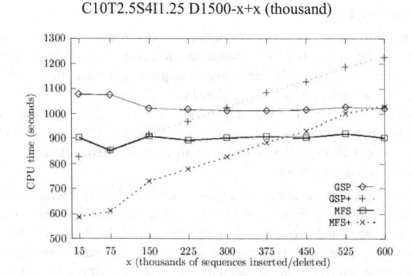

(a) CPU costs

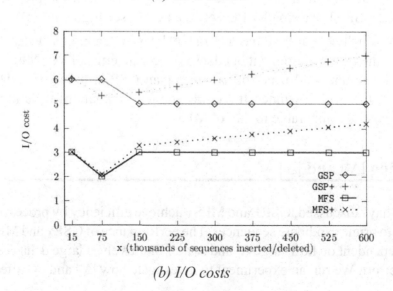

(b) I/O costs

Figure 4.7(a) shows that the CPU costs of GSP and MFS stay relatively steady. This is expected since |D'| does not change. The CPU costs of GSP+ and MFS+, on the other hand, increase linearly with the size of Δ^+ and Δ^-. This increase is due to a longer processing time taken by GSP+ and MFS+ to deal with Δ^+ and Δ^-. MFS+ outperforms the other methods even when the database is changed substantially. In particular, if $|\Delta^+|$ and $|\Delta^-|$ are less than 375,000 sequences (or 25% of |D|), MFS+ is most CPU-efficient. For cases in which only a small fraction of the database is changed, the incremental algorithms can achieve significant performance gains.

Finally, GSP+ and MFS+ usually have slightly higher I/O costs than their non-incremental counterparts, since they have to read Δ^-. Therefore, the I/O performance difference between GSP and GSP+ (and also that between MFS and MFS+) widens as $|\Delta^-|$ increases. This is shown in Figure 4.7(b).

We also perform experiments with settings of varying $|\Delta^+|$ and fixed $|\Delta^-|$, varying $|\Delta^-|$ and fixed $|\Delta^+|$, varying $|\Delta^+|$ and $|\Delta^-|=0$, and varying $|\Delta^-|$ and $|\Delta^+|=0$. The results of these experiments are same as the ones we described here.

Summary

In this chapter, we have described the details of an I/O-efficient algorithm MFS for mining frequent sequences. Its candidate generation function MGen can generate candidate sequences of various lengths given a set of frequent sequences of various lengths. Because long sequences are generated and processed early, MFS can effectively reduce the I/O cost. Experiment results show that MFS saves I/O passes significantly compared with GSP, especially when an estimate (S_{est}) of the set of frequent sequences with a good coverage is available.

We have shown how mining a small sample of the database led to a good S_{est}. By using a smaller support threshold (ρ_{s_sample}) in mining the sample, we showed that MFS outperformed GSP in I/O cost by a wide margin. The I/O saving is obtained, however, at a mild CPU cost. Further, the CPU penalty was insignificant for large databases. We have also presented a candidate pruning technique for incremental update of frequent sequences. By applying the pruning technique on GSP and MFS, we designed two efficient incremental algorithms GSP+ and MFS+. Extensive experiments comparing the performance of the incremental algorithms and their non-incremental counterparts showed that the pruning technique is very effective. In particular, MFS+ is shown to be both I/O and CPU efficient.

References

Agrawal, R., & Srikant, R. (1996). Mining sequential patterns: Generalizations and performance improvements. In *Proceedings of the International Conference on Extending Database Technology,* Avignion, France, March 25-29 (pp. 3-17). Berlin/Heidelberg: Springer.

Kao, B., Zhang, M., & Yip, C.-L. (2005). Efficient algorithms for mining and incremental update of maximal frequent sequences. *Data Mining and Knowledge Discovery, 10*, 87-116.

Zhang, M., Kao, B., & Cheung, D. (2002). Efficient algorithms for incremental update of frequent sequences. In *Proceedings of the 6th Pacific-Asia Conference on Knowledge Discovery and Data Mining*, Taipel, Taiwan, May 6-8 (pp. 186-197). Berlin/Heidelberg: Springer.

Chapter V

Mining Progressive Confident Rules in Sequence Databases

co-authored with

Minghua Zhang, National University of Singapore, Singapore

Real-life objects can be described by its attribute values. For example, a person has attributes such as gender, date of birth, education level, and job, and so forth. While the gender and date of birth of a person do not change, the education level and job may change with time. If we denote the set of attribute values of an object as its state, then the state of an object changes as the attribute values change with time. The states of an object at different time stamps form a state sequence.

In many applications, an object's state sequence over time is usually more interesting than its current state because the state sequence depicts the object's behavior characteristics. For example, if we only look at the current stock price, we cannot tell its behavior in the next week. However, if we look at its price history over several months, we could have a better idea about its trend in the future.

The state sequence of an object also captures more information than the current state for classification. For example, it is hard to determine whether a patient has chronic lymphocytic leukemia if we only know that he currently has anemia. However, if we track the patient's medical history over a period of time, then the doctor will be able to make a better judgement.

Table 5.1 shows a sample database that records the symptom sequences of patients and whether they have Chronic Lymphocytic Leukemia (CLL). The first column is the patient's ID. The second column is the patient's symptom sequence over time. For example, for patient ID "1", he/she first has night sweat and hypodynamia, followed by fever, then achroacytosis, and finally anemia. We regard the set of symptoms at a time point as the state of a patient at that time. Thus, the first state of patient 1 is {night sweat, hypodynamia}, and his last state is anemia. The last column in Table 5.1 is the doctor's diagnosis on Chronic Lymphocytic Leukemia(CLL). The first four patients have CLL, while the last four do not.

If we examine the last state of each patient, or their last symptom, we find that three patients with anemia have CLL (IDs 1-3), while the other three patients with anemia do not (IDs 6-8). Thus it is not clear whether a patient with anemia will have CLL. However, if we study the patients' state sequences, or their sequence of symptoms, we see that most CLL patients (IDs 1-3) have the following symptom sequence which does not occur in non-CLL patients: nightsweat → fever → achroacytosis → anemia.

We observe that patient 5 in Table 5.1 does not have CLL although his symptom sequence is the same as the 3 leading symptoms of CLL patients (nightsweat → fever → achroacytosis). It is possible that he may have CLL later, and a doctor could advise on preventive measures in advance.

Table 5.1. Example diagnosis on chronic lymphocytic leukemia

Patient	Sequence of Symptoms	CLL
1	{Nightsweat, hypodynamia } → Fever → Achroacytosis → Anemia	Y
2	Nightsweat → Fever → Achroacytosis → Anemia	Y
3	Nightsweat → Fever → Achroacytosis → Anemia	Y
4	Nightsweat → Fever → Achroacytosis → Splenomegalia	Y
5	Nightsweat → Fever → Achroacytosis	N
6	Nightsweat → Fever → Anemia	N
7	Nightsweat → Splenomegalia → Anemia	N
8	Nightsweat → Sleepy → Anemia	N

Let us call the symptom sequence nightsweat $\rightarrow$ fever $\rightarrow$ achroacytosis $\rightarrow$ anemia as p, and show how p could play a role in predicting patients getting CLL. Based on Table 5.1, four patients (IDs 1-4) with symptom night sweat have CLL. The total number of patients with night sweat is eight. We use conf(nightsweat, CLL) to denote the probability of symptom night sweat leading to CLL, that is, conf(nightsweat, CLL) = 4/8 = 0.5. Similarly, we have

conf(nightsweat $\rightarrow$ fever, CLL) = 4/6 = 0.67

conf(nightsweat $\rightarrow$ fever $\rightarrow$ achroacytosis, CLL)=0.8

conf(p, CLL)=1

From the four confident values, we see that the probability of a patient getting CLL becomes higher and higher as his symptoms change according to the symptom sequence p.

Suppose a new patient comes in with symptom nightsweat. From conf(nightsweat, CLL), the doctor knows the current probability of the patient catching CLL is not high (0.5), but could monitor whether the next symptoms in p appear later. If fever $\rightarrow$ achroacytosis occurs, as in the case of patient 5 in Table 5.1, the doctor could advise on preventive measures because the chance of having CLL has increased (0.8). However, if the patient becomes sleepy, then according to Table 5.1, we have conf(nightsweat $\rightarrow$ sleepy, CLL) = 0/1 = 0 < conf(nightsweat, CLL), and the chance of having CLL is very small.

In this chapter, we discuss a new kind of pattern that describes the changing states of objects with increasing probabilities that lead to some end state C, for example, CLL in Table 5.1. We call the pattern progressive confident rules. The general form of a progressive confident rule is $X_1 \rightarrow X_2 \rightarrow \ldots \rightarrow X_n$ where X_i is a state, and a state in the left hand side of "$\rightarrow$" occurs earlier in time than a state in the right hand side of "$\rightarrow$". By progressive confident, we mean the probability of an object achieving state C in the future becomes higher and higher as state X_i, $1 \le i \le n$, appears one after another. We call this the progressive confident condition.

For the rules to be more meaningful, we have three additional requirements. First, there is a minimum support of the rule to ensure that the rule is general. Second, the probability of the first state X_1 leading to the ending state C should be no less than some threshold min_conf$_1$. This removes rules that begin with unrelated states. For example, if we know that cataract has nothing to do with CLL, we will not be interested in a rule like cataract → nights-sweat → fever → achroacytosis → anemia for CLL. Third, the probability of the entire rule leading to C should be no less than a threshold min_conf$_2$. This ensures that the rule is interesting. For example, people do not regard night sweat → fever as a rule for CLL, because many diseases also have this symptom sequence.

We note that the set of all progressive confident rules usually contains redundant information. For example, it is possible that both nightsweat → fever → achroacytosis → anemia and nightsweat → fever → achroacytosis are progressive confident rules. In fact, the former rule subsumes the latter one. We will examine how to discover the concise set of progressive confident rules that does not contain redundant information.

As in most mining problems, the search space for finding progressive confident rules is enormous. Many algorithms use the Apriori property (Agrawal, Imielinski, & Swami, 1993) to prune the search space. The Apriori property states that if a pattern satisfies the mining requirement, so do all its sub-patterns. However, this property does not hold for progressive confident rules because we consider the confidence of the rules. Although the support of a pattern is no larger than the support of its sub-patterns, this is not true for confidence.

Another property for pruning the search space is the prefix anti-monotonic property (Pei, Han, & Wang, 2002). This property states that if a pattern P is in the mining result, so is any pattern Q obtained by removing some ending items from P. However, this property does not hold for the progressive confident condition either. By removing some ending items, an itemset may change to its subset, and the confidence of a subset is not necessarily no less than its super-set. Hence, previous pruning methods are not applicable and new pruning strategies are needed. We will describe a depth-first mining algorithm which utilizes the concise set analysis in the mining process to further reduce the huge search space.

Finally, we demonstrate how progressive confident rules can be utilized to predict an object's future state. This is a classification problem in essence. We incorporate the rules into three representative classifiers C4.5 (Quinlan, 1993), SVM (Cortes & Vapnik, 1995), and Bayes Classifier (Friedman & Goldszmidt, 1996) to improve their classification accuracy. Experiments on both synthetic and real data show that the rules greatly improve the classification accuracy.

The rest of the chapter is organized as follows. We first give a formal definition of progressive confident rules and their concise set. Then we describe our algorithm for mining progressive confident rules and present the results of experiments to evaluate the performance of the algorithm. Finally, we compare the classification accuracy of existing classifiers with and without the utilization of progressive confident rules before we conclude the chapter.

Problem Definition

In this section, we give a formal definition of progressive confident rules and the notion of a concise set of rules.

Let $I = \{i_1, i_2, \ldots, i_m\}$ be a set of literals called items. A state or an itemset $X \subseteq I$ is a set of items. The semantic meaning of item and itemset is as follows. Every item is related with a characteristic. If a state (an itemset) contains an item, it means the item's corresponding characteristic appears in the state. For example, if item a represents the symptom "sick", item b represents the symptom "fever", and item c represents the symptom "headache", then state $\{a, b\}$ means the patient feels sick and has a fever but does not have a headache, while state $\{b, c\}$ means the patient has a fever and headache but does not feel sick.

A pattern $P = X_1 \rightarrow X_2 \rightarrow \ldots \rightarrow X_n$ is an ordered set of states. The length of P is defined as the number of states in P. We use $|P|$ to represent the length of P. For example, if $P = \{a\} \rightarrow \{b, c\} \rightarrow \{d\}$, then $\{P\} = 3$.

An observation o is an itemset T with a time stamp (tid), that is, $o = <tid, T>$. If a state $X \subseteq T$, we say X is contained in the observation o. Sometimes we omit the time stamp tid and represent an observation by its itemset T only,

A sequence s is composed of a sequence id (sid) and an ordered list of observations, that is, $s = <sid, o_1, o_1, \ldots, o_n>$. Given a sequence $s = <sid, o_1, o_1, \ldots, o_n>$ and a pattern $P = X_1 \rightarrow X_2 \rightarrow \ldots \rightarrow X_m$, we say that s matches P, or equivalently, P is contained in s, if there exist integers $j_1, j_1, \ldots, j_m$ such that $1 \leq j_1 < j_2 < \ldots < j_m \leq n$, and X_1 is contained in o_{j1}, X_1 is contained in o_{j1}, ..., X_2 is contained in o_{j2}, ..., X_m is contained in o_{jm}. We represent this relationship by $P \angle s$. As an example, pattern $P = \{a\} \rightarrow \{b,c\} \rightarrow \{d\}$ is contained in sequence $s_1 = <sid1, \{e\}, \{a, d\}, \{g\}, \{b,c,f\}, \{d\}>$ because $\{a\} \subseteq \{a, d\}$, $\{b,c\} \subseteq \{b,c,f\}$, and $\{d\} \subseteq \{d\}$. Hence, $P \angle s_1$. On the other hand, P is not contained in $s_2 = $ <sid2, {a, d}, {d}, {b,c,f}> because {b, c} occurs before {d} in P, which is not the case in s_2.

A database D is composed of a number of sequences whose end states are known. We use D_C to represent the set of sequences in D that end with state C, and $D_{C'}$ represent the set of sequences in D that does not end with state C. Thus, $D = D_C \cup D_{C'}$. The sequences in D_C do not necessarily have the same end states, that is, there can be more than two end states in the database. We say that sequences with end state C are in class C.

The support of a pattern P in class C (represented by sup(P, C)) is defined as the number of sequences in D_C that match P. If sup(P, C) is no less than a user specified threshold ρ_s, we say P is a frequent pattern in class C. We use sup(P, C') to represent the number of sequences in $D_{C'}$ that match P. The confidence of a pattern P resulting in class C is defined as

$$conf(P, C) = sup(P, C) / (sup(P, C) + sup(P, C')$$

Given a pattern $P = X_1 \rightarrow X_2 \rightarrow ... \rightarrow X_n$, if $conf(X_1, C) \leq conf(X_1 \rightarrow X_2, C) \leq ... \leq conf(P, C)$, we say P satisfies the progressive confident condition. Finally, if a pattern P satisfies the following four conditions:

$$sup(P, C) \geq \rho_s \tag{1}$$

$$conf(X_1, C) \geq min\_conf_1 \tag{2}$$

$$conf(X_1, C) \leq conf(X_1 \rightarrow X_2, C) \leq ... \leq$$
$$conf(X_1 \rightarrow X_2 \rightarrow ... \rightarrow X_n, C) \tag{3}$$

$$conf(X_1 \rightarrow X_2 \rightarrow ... \rightarrow X_n, C) \geq min\_conf_2 \tag{4}$$

where min_conf_1, min_conf_2 and ρ_s are three user specified parameters, we say P together with its confidence values is a progressive confident rule.

We observe that the set of all progressive confident rules contains redundant information. We will now discuss how a concise set of progressive confident rules can be obtained.

Suppose $P = \{a\} \rightarrow \{b, c\}$ and $Q = \{a\} \rightarrow \{b, c\} \rightarrow \{d\}$ are two progressive confident rules. If conf(P, C) = 1, then by definition of confidence, conf(Q, C) must also be 1, and the information captured in Q is redundant. But suppose conf(P, C) < 1, then all the information in P is already contained in Q.

Given a pattern Q, we use Q[i] to represent the i-th state (itemset) in Q, and Q[i, j] (j > i) to represent the pattern Q[i] $\rightarrow$ Q[i + 1] $\rightarrow$ ... $\rightarrow$ Q[j]. For example, if Q = $\{a\} \rightarrow \{b, c\} \rightarrow \{d\}$, then Q[1] = $\{a\}$, Q[2] = $\{b, c\}$, Q[3] = $\{d\}$, and Q[1, 2] = $\{a\} \rightarrow \{b, c\}$.

A base-pattern of a pattern Q is a pattern obtained by removing the last several states (itemsets) from Q. For example, if Q = $\{a\} \rightarrow \{b, c\} \rightarrow \{d\}$, then $\{a\} \rightarrow \{b, c\}$ is Q's base-pattern, and $\{a\} \rightarrow \{b\}$ is not. If P is a base-pattern of Q, we also say Q is an extender of P. Give a pattern Q, if conf(Q, C) = 1 and none of its base-pattern P satisfies the condition conf(P, C) = 1, we say Q is a terminator pattern. Given a set of patterns V and a pattern P $\in$ V, if *P* is not a base-pattern of any other pattern *P'* in *V*, we say *P* is a *maximal pattern* in *V*.

Based on this discussion, we can obtain a concise set of rules from a set of progressive confident rules R in two steps: (1) delete all extenders of terminator patterns in R; and (2) remove non-maximal patterns.

We define the problem of mining progressive confident rules as finding the concise set of all progressive confident rules in a given database D and a class C.

Mining Concise Set of PCR

One common issue for data mining problems is that the search space is huge. As a result, many mining algorithms make use of the *Apriori* property to reduce the search space to a manageable one. Unfortunately, this property does not hold in the progressive confident condition. We illustrate this fact with an example.

Consider the database in Table 5.2. Let the three user input parameters be set as $\rho_s = 2$, min_conf$_1$=0.5 and min_conf$_2$ = 0.9. The pattern $P = \{a\} \rightarrow \{b, c\} \rightarrow \{d\}$ is a progressive confident rule because sup(P, C) = 2 $\geq \rho_s$; conf($\{a\}$, C)= 3/(3+3) = 0.5 $\geq$ min_conf$_1$; conf($\{a\} \rightarrow \{b, c\}$, C) = 2/(2+1) = 0.67 $\geq$ conf($\{a\}$, C); conf($\{a\} \rightarrow \{b, c\} \rightarrow \{d\}$, C) = 2/(2+0) = 1 $\geq$ conf($\{a\} \rightarrow \{b,$

Table 5.2. Sample database

Class C

Sequence Id	Observations	
	Tid	Itemset
1	1	{a, e}
	2	{b, c}
	3	{d}
2	4	{a}
	5	{b, c}
	6	{d, f}
3	7	{a}
	8	{g}
	9	{e}

Classes not of C

Sequence Id	Observations	
	Tid	Itemset
4	11	{a}
	12	{b, c, d}
	13	{e}
5	14	{a}
	15	{b, d}
	16	{f}
6	17	{a}
	18	{d}
	19	{b}

c}, C); conf({a} → {b, c} → {d}, C) = 1 ≥ min_conf$_2$. However, P's sub-pattern Q = {a} → {b} does not satisfy the progressive confident condition, because conf({a} → {b}, c+ = 2/(2+3) = 0.4 < conf({a}, C) = 0.5. Therefore, the Apriori property does not hold.

Another property that can be used to prune the search space is the prefix anti-monotonic property (Pei, Han, & Wang, 2002). This property states that if a pattern P_1 meets the mining requirement and another pattern P_2 is obtained by removing some ending items from P_1, then P_2 also satisfies the mining requirement. In our example, Q is obtained by removing ending items c and d from P. Although P is a progressive confident rule, Q does not satisfy the progressive confident condition. Hence, the prefix anti-monotonic property is also not applicable for our problem here.

We put forward two theorems can help to reduce the huge search space.

Theorem 1: Suppose a pattern P satisfies the following three conditions:

$sup(P, C) \geq \rho_s$;

$conf(P[1], C) \geq min\_conf_1$;

$conf(P[1], C) \leq conf(P[1,2], C) \leq \ldots \leq conf(P, C)$.

If Q is a base-pattern of P, then Q also satisfies the three conditions:

$\sup(Q, C) \geq \rho_s;$

$\text{conf}(Q[1], C) \geq \text{min\_conf}_1;$

$\text{conf}(Q[1], C) \leq \text{conf}(Q[1,2], C) \leq \ldots \leq \text{conf}(Q, C).$

Proof: Let the base-pattern Q be $Q = P[1, i]$ $(1 \leq i < |P|)$. Since Q is a base-pattern of P, we have $\sup(Q, C) \geq \sup(P, C) \geq \rho_s$. Q meets the first condition. From $Q = P[1, i]$, we get $\text{conf}(Q[1], C) = \text{conf}(P[1], C) \geq \text{min\_conf}_1$, Q also satisfies the second requirement. Since $Q = P[1, i]$, we have $\text{conf}(Q[1], C) = \text{conf}(P[1], C) \leq \text{conf}(P[1,2], C) = \text{conf}(Q[1,2], C) \leq \ldots \leq \text{conf}(P[1,i], C) = \text{conf}(Q, C)$. Therefore, Q also obeys the progressive confident condition.

Theorem 1 states that if a pattern Q does not satisfy either one of the support requirement, min_conf_1 requirement or progressive confident condition, then none of Q's extenders will meet the requirements or condition. Thus, if we find such a pattern Q in the mining process, we do not need to consider Q's extenders as potential progressive confident rules. This will prune off a huge amount of search space.

We denote the property described in Theorem 1 as the base anti-monotonic property. All the mining problems that satisfy the Apriori property also satisfy the prefix anti-monotonic property. All mining problems that obey the prefix anti-monotonic property also obey the base anti-monotonic property. Therefore, an algorithm that solves a problem with the Apriori property is not necessarily applicable to the problems with the prefix anti-monotonic property or the base anti-monotonic property. Similarly, an algorithm that solves a problem with the prefix anti-monotonic property may not be suitable for problems with the base anti-monotonic property.

The work in Pei, Han, and Wang (2002) proposes a projection framework for mining sequential patterns with constraints that satisfy the prefix anti-monotonic property. The efficiency of the framework lies in the prefix anti-monotonic property. When this property holds, by continuous database projections on individual items, no subset testing and candidate generation are required. Further, the number of projections in each level is bounded by the number of frequent items in the database, that is, O(N). The problem of mining progressive confident rules does not follow the prefix anti-monotonic property. However, with Theorem 1, we can modify the framework in Pei,

Han, and Wang (2002) by projecting on itemsets, and not on items. Unfortunately, this approach is inefficient because subset testing will be unavoidable when making projections on itemsets. Candidate generation is necessary, otherwise one needs to enumerate all the itemsets in a database sequence. Further, the number of projections for each level is bounded by the number of frequent itemsets in the database, which is $O(2^n)$, much larger than $O(n)$ when projecting on items.

If a pattern P satisfies the progressive confident condition and the support requirement, we need to consider P's extender $P \rightarrow X$. At this point, conf(P, C) is already known. In order to check whether conf($P \rightarrow X$, C) $\geq$ conf(P,C), we should know conf($P \rightarrow X$, C). According to the definition of conf($P \rightarrow$ X, C), one needs to calculate both sup($P \rightarrow X$, C) and sup($P \rightarrow X$, C'). The following theorem helps us to avoid computing sup($P \rightarrow X$, C) when $P \rightarrow$ X does not satisfy the progressive confident condition.

Theorem 2: Given a pattern P and a state X, if conf(P, C) < 1 and conf($P \rightarrow$ X, C) $\geq$ conf(P, C), we have

sup(P, C) $\geq$ sup($P \rightarrow X$, C') * (conf(P, C)/(1 − conf(P, C))) and

sup(X, C) $\geq$ sup($P \rightarrow X$, C') * (conf(P, C)/(1 − conf(P, C)))

Proof: From conf($P \rightarrow X$, C) $\geq$ conf(P, C), we get

1 − conf($P \rightarrow X$, C) $\leq$ 1− conf(P, C).

Therefore,

conf($P \rightarrow X$,C)/(1−conf($P \rightarrow X$,C)) $\geq$ conf(P,C)/(1− conf(P, C)).

By definition,

conf($P \rightarrow X$,C)/(1−conf($P \rightarrow X$,C)) = sup($P \rightarrow X$,C)/sup($P \rightarrow X$, C').

Hence,

sup($P \rightarrow X$, C)/sup($P \rightarrow X$, C') $\geq$ conf(P, C)/(1 − conf(P, C)) or

sup($P \rightarrow X$, C) $\geq$ sup($P \rightarrow X$, C') * (conf(P, C)/(1 − conf(P, C)))

We have

$$sup(P, C) \geq sup(P{\rightarrow}X, C) \geq$$
$$sup(P{\rightarrow}X, C') * conf(P, C)/(1 - conf(P, C)) \text{ and}$$
$$sup(X, C) \geq sup(P{\rightarrow}X, C) \geq$$
$$sup(P{\rightarrow}X, C') * conf(P, C)/(1 - conf(P, C))$$

Theorem 2 provides a pruning test on whether to extend a pattern P to P→ X. If sup(P, C) or sup(X, C) is not large enough (compared with sup(P→ X, C')*conf(P, C)/(1 − conf(P, C)), we have conf(P→X, C) < conf(P, C). This is a contradiction to the progressive confident condition, and we do not need to extend P to P→X, which saves the time for counting sup(P→X, C). Note that Theorem 2 does not handle the case when conf(P, C) = 1. This is inconsequential since conf(P, C) = 1 implies that P is a terminator pattern. No extenders of P will be in the concise set, and we do not need to consider P→X in the algorithm.

Algorithm FMP

Based on Theorem 1 and Theorem 2, we design an efficient depth-first algorithm for mining the concise set of all progressive confident rules. We call it FMP (Fast Mining of Progressive confident rules). Algorithm FMP first finds all frequent itemsets in class C. Then for each frequent itemset that satisfies min_conf$_1$ requirement, FMP processes its extenders in a depth-first order to search for other potential progressive confident rules.

The core of FMP lies in extend function (lines 6-26). Given a pattern P, the function finds out all extenders of P that are in the concise set of progressive confident rules. FMP checks whether conf(P, C) is equals to 1. If yes, then P is a terminator pattern and we can ignore all P's extenders because they are not in the concise set. P will be output. If conf(P, C) is not equals to 1, we check whether we need to append a state X to the end of P with the help of Theorem 2. If X passes the test, we check whether P → X meets the support requirement and progressive confident condition. If yes, we call the extend function with a new parameter value P → X. Finally, if P could not be extended anymore, that is, P is a maximal pattern and conf(P, C) ≥ min_conf$_2$, we output P and the function terminates. The support of P → X is counted from the ID lists of P and X, not by scanning the database. The ID list of a pattern records the sequences and the time stamps in which a pattern appears.

The depth-first order and the careful control of the extend function guarantees that the rules in the output belongs to the concise set. The efficiency of the FMP algorithm mainly comes from two aspects. One is the utilization of the two theorems to effectively reduce the search space. The other is by incorporating the concise set analysis in the mining process to avoid checking the extenders of terminator patterns, which further reduces the search space.

Algorithm FMP
Input: Database D;
        Thresholds ρ_s, min_conf$_1$, min_conf$_2$;
Output: Set of progressive confident rules

1. *find frequent itemsets in class C: $L_X =\{X \mid sup(X, C) \geq \rho_s\}$;*
2. *$\forall X \in L_X$*
3.   *calculate conf(X, C);*
4.   *if conf(X, C) $\geq$ min_conf$_1$*
5.   *extend (X);*

Function extend (pattern P)
6. *if conf(P, C) = 1*
7.   *output P;*
8.   *return;*
9. *ext = false;*
10. *$\forall X \in L_X$*
11.   *count sup(P $\rightarrow$ X, C');*
12.   *stand = sup(P $\rightarrow$ X, C') * (conf(P, C)/1 $-$ conf(P,C));*
13.   *if sup(P, C) < stand*
14.   *continue with next itemset in L_X;*
15.   *if sup(X, C) < stand*
16.   *continue with next itemset in L_X;*
17.   *count sup(P $\rightarrow$ X, C);*
18.   *if sup(P $\rightarrow$ X, C) < ρ_s*
19.   *continue with next itemset in L_X;*
20.   *count conf(P $\rightarrow$ X, C);*
21.   *if sup(X, C) < conf(P, C)*
22.   *continue with next itemset in L_X;*
23.   *ext = true;*
24.   *extend (P $\rightarrow$ X);*
25. *if (ext = false AND conf(P) $\geq$ min_conf$_2$)*
26.   *output P;*
End Algorithm FMP

Experiments

We have carried out experiments to study the performance of Algorithm FMP and evaluate the effectiveness of progressive confident rules in classification. We compare Algorithm FMP with a naive algorithm DMP (Direct Mining of Progressive confident rules). Algorithm DMP first makes use of the SPADE algorithm to find out all frequent patterns. It then removes those frequent patterns that do not satisfy the other requirements of progressive confident rules. Finally, DMP computes the concise set of rules and output it. Note that both FMP and DMP utilize the ID lists to count the support of a pattern, which makes their performance comparison reasonable. We implemented both algorithms in C++. The experiments were executed on a Sunfire 4800 midframe sever with 750MHz Ultra Sparc III CPU and 1GB RAM, running SunOS 5.8.

Synthetic Data Generation

We generate the test dataset in three steps as follows. In the first step, we generate a table of potentially frequent itemsets. The size of each itemset is computed as a Poisson distributed random number with mean equal to I. Except for the first itemset, every other itemset shares some common items with its immediate preceding one. The number of items to be shared is controlled by an exponentially distributed random number. We generate N_I itemsets from N different items.

Each generated itemset is assigned a confidence value c. This confidence value determines the probability an itemset will appear in class C. The confidence value c is r if $0 \leq r \leq 1$; c is 0 if $r < 0$ and c is 1 if $r > 1$, where r is a normal-distributed random number with mean equal to 0.5.

In the second step, we generate two pattern tables for dataset D_C (corresponding to class C) and $D_{C'}$ (corresponding to class C'), respectively. We call the two pattern tables T_C and $T_{C'}$. The length of a pattern p is determined by a Poisson distributed random number with mean equal to S. The content of p is a series of itemsets generated in the first step. The itemsets are selected randomly from the itemset table. If the confidence of a selected itemset is c, we append it to a pattern belonging to T_C with a probability of c, and append it to a pattern in $T_{C'}$ with the probability of 1- c. When a pattern reaches its length, we insert it into the corresponding pattern table, and continue to generate the next pattern for the same pattern table. We generate a total of N_s patterns for both T_C and $T_{C'}$.

For each generated pattern p, we assign a weight and a corruption level to it. The weight represents the probability of p being picked for generating a sequence in the third step, and the corruption level controls how many items will be randomly dropped from p before it is inserted into a sequence.

In the third step, we generate sequences in our test database. Sequences in D_C is computed from pattern table T_C, and sequences in $D_{C'}$ is generated from $T_{C'}$. When generating a sequence, we first calculate its length, which is determined by a Poisson distributed variable whose mean is O, and the average number of items in its itemsets, which is a Poisson distributed variable with mean equal to T. We then randomly choose a pattern from the corresponding pattern table to fill in it. If the pattern is too large for the sequence, we discard it in half the cases, and push it into the sequence in the rest of the cases. In this step, we generate a total $|D_C|$ and $|D_{C'}|$ sequences from the tables T_C and $T_{C'}$ respectively.

Table 5.3 summarizes the parameters of the generator and their default values used in the experiments.

Table 5.3. Parameters and values for data generation

Parameter	Description	Value
|D|	Number of sequences in database D	100,000
|DC|	Number of sequences in class C	50,000
|DC'|	Number of sequences in class C'	50,000
O	Average number of observations per sequence	8
T	Average number of items per observations	2.5
S	Average number of itemsets in maximal potentially frequent patterns	6
I	Average size of itemsets in maximal potentially frequent patterns	1.25
NS	Number of maximal potentially frequent patterns	500
NI	Number of maximal potentially frequent itemsets	2,500
N	Number of items	1,000

Figure 5.1. Performance of DMP and FMP vs. support threshold

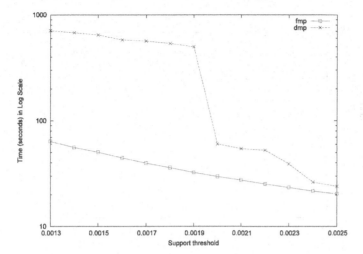

Effect of Varying Support Threshold

In the first experiment, we evaluate the performance of algorithms FMP and DMP under varying support thresholds. The result is presented in Figure 5.1.

The x-axis in Figure 5.1 is the support threshold, and the y-axis is the runtime in log scale. We see that FMP runs much faster than DMP. When support threshold is low ($\rho_s \leq 0.0019$), FMP is one order faster than DMP. This is because with a low ρ_s, there are many frequent patterns, and DMP has to discover all of them. In contrast, FMP only needs to deal with a subset of the patterns that satisfy not only support requirement but also the confidence requirements.

When the support threshold increases, there are fewer frequent patterns, and DMP requires less effort to mine them, thus narrowing the gap between the two algorithms. However, FMP is still about two times faster than FMP.

Effect of Varying Confidence Thresholds

Next, we examine the influence of the parameters min_conf$_1$ and min_conf$_2$ on the two algorithms. Figure 5.2 shows the running time of DMP and FMP

Figure 5.2. Performance of DMP and FMP vs. min_conf₁

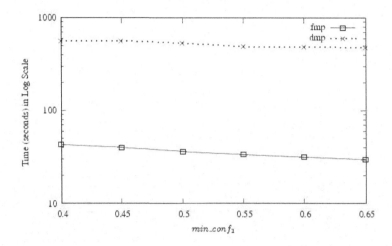

in log scale when min_conf₁ changes from 0.4 to 0.65. We observe that when min_conf₁ increases, the running times of both algorithms decrease. For DMP, a higher min_conf₁ implies that more patterns could be pruned before carrying out the progressive confident condition test and concise set computation. Thus, the running time decreases. When min_conf₁ increases from 0.4 to 0.65, DMP saves about 15% of the execution time.

Algorithm FMP incorporates the test of min_conf₁ into the mining process, that is, it does not extend an itemset if its confidence is less than min_conf₁. Hence, the influence of min_conf₁ on FMP is higher than that on DMP. When min_conf₁ changes from 0.4 to 0.65, the running time of FMP is reduced by about 31% .

Figure 5.3 shows the execution time of DMP and FMP when min_conf₂ changes from 0.75 to 1. The performance of both two algorithms stays relatively steady. Since FMP does not use min_conf₂ for pruning, min_conf₂ has nearly no effect on its performance. For DMP, the savings on progressive confident condition check and concise set calculation by deleting patterns which do not meet the min_conf₂ requirement is also negligible.

Figure 5.3. Performance of DMP and FMP vs. min_conf$_2$

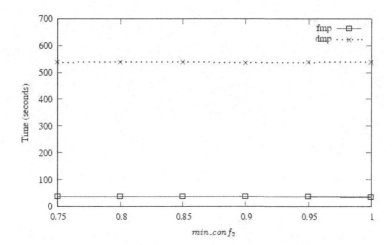

Effect of Parameters O, T, S, and I

We also study the influence of generator parameters O, T, S, and I on the performance of the algorithms. We first fix the values of T, S, I, and change O (the average number of observations per sequences) from 6 to 12. The execution times of DMP and FMP are shown in Figure 5.4. We observe that as O increases, the running time of both algorithms increases as well. Recall that O represents the average length of sequences. A larger O implies more frequent patterns and more progressive confident rules, and hence additional execution time. The increase in running time of FMP is much smaller than that of DMP. The reason is that FMP could efficiently avoid processing many new frequent patterns that are not new progressive confident rules in the concise set; while DMP has to work on all the new frequent patterns.

Next, we fix the values of O, S, I, and change T (the average number of items in the itemset). Figure 5.5 shows the performance of DMP and FMP when T changes from 2 to 5. We see that the running time of DMP varies greatly under different T values. Recall that when generating a sequence in the synthetic database, we repeatedly append a random pattern to the end of the sequence until the sequence exceeds its size limit. At this point, the current pattern will be inserted into the sequence or be discarded randomly. Since T is used to control the size limit of a sequence, different T values result in different

Figure 5.4. Performance of DMP and FMP vs. O

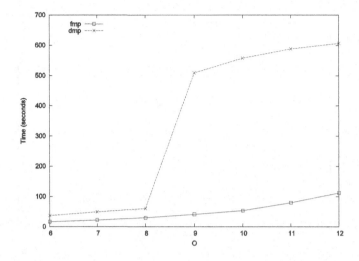

Figure 5.5. Performance of DMP and FMP vs. T

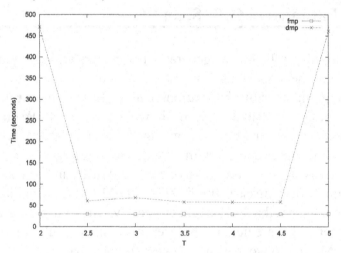

databases and different set of frequent sequences. Hence, the performance of DMP, which mines all frequent sequences, varies as T changes. On the other hand, T does not influence the pattern table, which contains potential progressive confident rules. By mining progressive confident rules directly, the performance of FMP is not influenced as much as DMP is.

In the next experiment, we fix O, T, I, and change S (average length of potentially maximal frequent patterns) from 3 to 8. The experiment result is shown in Figure 5.6. Since a larger S implies more frequent patterns and more progressive confident rules, both algorithms need more processing time. As S increases, the running time of FMP increases slowly, while that of DMP increases dramatically.

Figure 5.6. Performance of DMP and FMP vs. S

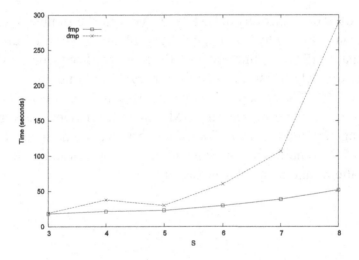

Figure 5.7. Performance of DMP and FMP vs. I

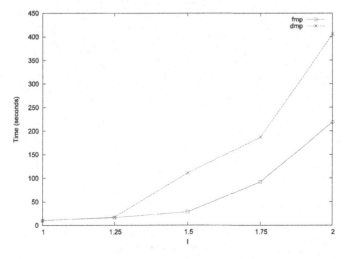

We also examine the performance of DMP and FMP when the average number of items in an itemset (I) changes. Figure 5.7 shows the results. With a larger I, the frequencies of items increase in the database, which results in more frequent patterns and more progressive confident rules. Hence, the execution times of both DMP and FMP increase as I increases. Again, the rate of increase rate for FMP is slower than that for DMP, because FMP incorporates other condition checks in the mining process to prune the search space.

Scalability

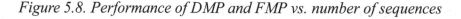

Finally, we test the scalability of DMP and FMP with the number of sequences ranging from 100,000 to 1,000,000. The result is shown in Figure 5.8. We observe that FMP scales linearly with the number of sequences. Algorithm DMP scales linearly at first, and runs of memory when the number of sequences reaches 400,000. The reason is that the increase in the number of sequences leads to longer ID lists of patterns. DMP mines all frequent patterns before the filtering part and requires a lot of memory to store the long ID lists. In contrast, FMP combines the mining and filtering phases and is able to prune a lot of patterns and their ID lists directly.

Figure 5.8. Performance of DMP and FMP vs. number of sequences

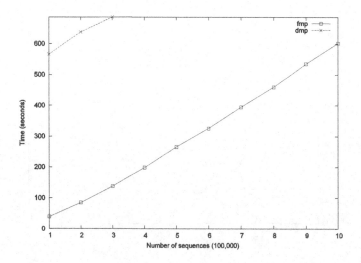

Application of PCR in Classification

One application of the progressive confident rule is to predict a future state of an object based on its past state sequence. In this section, we will describe how progressive confident rules can be utilized in three representative classifiers C4.5, Support Vector Machine (SVM), and Bayes Classifier (BC). All the three classifiers—C4.5, SVM, and BC—require input objects to be described by {feature, value} pairs. For objects with state sequences, the classifiers can run directly on their last states. However, in order to utilize the state sequences in the classifiers, some mappings have to be carried out first.

We map each progressive confident rule r in the concise set to a new feature f_r. If the state sequence of an object matches r, then the value of f_r is set to 1. Otherwise, it is set to 0. Given n progressive confident rules, the state sequence of an object is transformed to n {feature, value} pairs. The three classifiers are run on the converted new feature set.

Given a training dataset and a test dataset of state sequences, we first mine the concise set of progressive confident rules in the training data for every class (end state). Then we utilize the discovered rules to convert the original training data and test data to {feature, value} pair databases. Finally, we run the classifiers on the transformed datasets.

We carry out experiments on both synthetic and real data to evaluate the performance of classifiers incorporated with progressive confident rules (PCRs). We use C4.5_PCR (C4.5 with Progressive Confident Rules), SVM_PCR and BC_PCR to represent the three classifiers incorporated with PCRs, respectively. C4.5, SVM, and BC is used to represent the three classifiers running on the last states of objects, that is, not incorporating PCRs.

The first set of experiment is carried out on the synthetic dataset described in the previous section. There are two classes C and C' in this dataset. Each class has 50,000 cases. We select 50% of the cases from each class for training, and use the remaining cases for testing. The mining algorithm generated 1,154 progressive confident rules from the two classes.

Table 5.4 shows the classification accuracy of C4.5, SVM, BC, C4.5_PCR, SVM_PCR, and BC_PCR for the two classes as well as the entire test dataset. We observe that classifiers incorporated with PCRs outperform their counterparts. On average, there is an increase of 12% in the accuracy.

We also carried out experiments on a real-life dataset which captures the retinal examination data of 10,845 diabetic patients. Each patient has around

Table 5.4. Classification result on synthetic dataset

Data	Class C	Class C'	Total
Training cases	25,000	25,000	50,000
Test cases	25,000	25,000	50,000
Classifier Accuracy	Class C	Class C'	Average
C4.5	74.08%	79.44%	76.76%
C4.5_PCR	77.70%	99.62%	88.66%
SVM	75.99%	77.49%	76.74%
SVM_PCR	99.63%	77.69%	88.66%
BC	88.06%	62.23%	75.15%
BC_PCR	99.12%	74.60%	86.86%

2 to 6 examination records at different times. All the records for a patient form his state sequence. Items of this dataset are related to symptoms such as drusen, cataract, and hypertension. We are interested in discovering whether a patient has developed maculopathy in his last exam record (state). There are two classes in this dataset. In one class, the patients' last examination records show maculopathy. We call it class FMAC-Y. There are 111 patients in this class. In the other class, maculopathy does not appear in the last exams. We call it FMAC-N. This class has 10,734 patients. Suppose a patient has five exam records. We predict whether maculopathy appears in the fifth record from the first four records. We say a prediction is correct if it is the same as what is shown in the last exam record. Otherwise, the prediction is wrong.

Note that this real-life dataset is very biased. The size of class FMAC-N is about 100 times that of class FMAC-Y. If a classifier assigns all the test cases to FMAC-N, the average accuracy is high. However, no cases in FMAC-Y could be recognized. For such biased data, we use the geometric mean (g_mean) to measure the total classification accuracy for all classes. We have g_mean = sqrt (TP * TN) where TP is the recall or true positive rate, and TN is the true negative rate. When a classifier gives all the test cases the same label, either TP or TN is 0, and g_mean is 0.

We set the training size of two classes to be 90% that of class FMAC-Y, that is, 100. There are 1,268 progressive confident rules in the training data. Table 5.5 shows the classification accuracy of the classifiers in two classes and the g_mean values. From g_mean value, we see that C4.5 and BC perform poorly, while C4.5_PCR and BC_PCR could improve the classification accuracy of their counterparts greatly. SVM_PCR also outperforms SVM by a wide margin.

Table 5.5. Classification result on diabetic retina dataset

Data	FMAC-N	FMAC-Y	Total
Training cases	100	100	200
Test cases	10634	11	10645
Classifier Accuracy	Class C	Class C'	Average
C4.5	57.22%	9.09%	22.81%
C4.5_PCR	76.47%	27.27%	45.67%
SVM	67.84%	63.64%	65.70%
SVM_PCR	64.25%	90.91%	76.42%
BC	89.21%	18.18%	40.27%
BC_PCR	60.06%	90.91%	73.89%

Finally, we also run an experiment on the diabetic retinal dataset using only part of the rules. We select the rules with top K support values in each class. Hence, the total number of rules used is 2*K. Figure 5.9 shows the g_mean values of C4.5_PCR, SVM_PCR and BC_PCR under different K values. When K = 650, all the rules are utilized. We see that the accuracy of SVM_PCR and BC_PCR remains relatively unchanged. But the performance of C4.5_PCR changes as K varies. The g_mean values of C4.5, SVM and BC are not related to K. We see that under all K values, C4.5_PCR, SVM_PCR and BC_PCR have a better accuracy than their counterparts C4.5, SVM and BC respectively.

Figure 5.9. Classification result on diabetic retina dataset using selected progressive confident rules

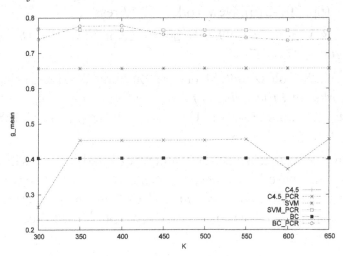

Summary

In this chapter, we have described a new kind of pattern called progressive confident rules. The rules capture the state change of objects that leads to a certain end state with increasing confidence. We have given a formal definition of progressive confident rules and their concise set. We also presented new pruning strategies to reduce the huge search space. A novel depth-first mining algorithm FMP is designed based on the new pruning strategies. FMP incorporates the concise set analysis in the mining process to further prune the search space. Experiment results indicate that FMP is one order faster than a straight forward method DMP.

We have also illustrated an application of progressive confident rules in predicting a future state of an object given its past state sequence. We describe how to utilize the progressive confident rules in three representative classifiers C4.5, SVM, and BC. Experiment results on both synthetic and real data demonstrate that all three classifiers incorporated with progressive confident rules could improve the classification accuracy greatly.

References

Agrawal, R., Imielinski, T., & Swami, A. (1993). Mining association rules between sets of items in large databases. In *ACM SIGMOD International Conference on Management of Data,* Washington, D.C., USA, May 25-28 (pp. 207-216). New York: ACM Press.

Cortes, C., & Vapnik, V. (1995). Support-vector networks. *Machine Learning, 20*(3), 273-297.

Friedman, N., & Goldszmidt, M. (1996). Building classifiers using Bayesian networks. In *Proceedings of American Association of Artificial Intelligence,* Portland, Oregon, USA, August 4-8 (pp. 1277-1284). Menlo Park, CA: AAAI Press.

Pei, J., Han, J., & Wang, W. (2002). Mining sequential patterns with constraints in large databases. In *Proceedings of the ACM CIKM International Conference on Information and Knowledge Management,* McLean, Virginia, USA, November 4-9 (pp. 18-25). New York: ACM Press.

Quinlan, J. R. (1993). *C4.5: Programs for machine learning.* San Francisco, CA: Morgan Kaufmann Publishers.

Chapter VI

Early Works in Spatio-Temporal Mining

Spatio-temporal data mining is an emerging area with increasing importance in a variety of applications, such as homeland security, mobile services, surveillance systems, and health monitoring applications. However, mining in spatio-temporal databases is still in its infancy. Existing work on spatio-temporal data mining has mainly focused on three types of patterns: evolution patterns of natural phenomena, frequent movements of objects over time, and space-time clusters. While there has been much research on association rule mining on transactional, spatial, and temporal data, there is little literature on finding interesting associations in spatio-temporal data. In this chapter, we introduce the early attempts at spatio-temporal data mining and review the techniques to discover various interesting spatio-temporal patterns. This is followed by a review of the traditional association rules mining algorithms and their variants on transactional data, temporal data, and spatial data.

Spatio-Temporal Patterns

Evolution Patterns

A system called CONQUEST (Mesrobian, Muntz, & Shek, 1995; Stolorz, Nakamura, & Mesrobian, 1995) has been developed to find the evolution patterns of natural phenomena. This system allows some means of accessing and interpreting spatio-temporal data. It provides an environment that enables geophysical scientists to easily formulate queries of spatio-temporal patterns on massive data, such as cyclones, hurricanes, and fronts.

Following that, many researchers (Steinbach, Tan & Kumar, 2001; Tan, Steinbach, & Kumar, 2001) have attempted to mine interesting spatio-temporal patterns in earth science data. They apply existing data mining techniques to find clusters, predictive models, and trends, and they state that existing data mining algorithms cannot discover all the interesting patterns in spatio-temporal data (Tan, Steinbach, & Kumar, 2001).

Recently, Tsoukatos and Gunopulos (2001) presented an algorithm to discover frequent sequences in a depth-first manner over all locations in spatio-temporal databases. This is essentially a sequence mining algorithm whereby each location is treated as a transaction. The algorithm is able to find the common temporal relationships of events in some locations, but not the relationships of events among these locations.

The work in Basak, Sudarshan, and Trivedi (2004) studies mining patterns from spatial-temporal weather data. It views weather variables as spatio-temporal signals. Under this mapping, a widely-used technique in signal and image processing called independent component analysis (ICA) is applied to mine patterns in weather data. The mining result is validated by matching the independent component activities with the domain knowledge (North Atlantic Oscillation Index; see Bell & Visneck).

Mei, Liu, and Su (2006) study the problem of mining spatio-temporal theme patterns from Web logs. They put forward a novel probabilistic approach to model the sub-topic themes and spatio-temporal theme patterns simultaneously. The proposed model could extract common themes from Web logs; generate theme life cycles for each given location; and compute theme snapshots for each given time period. Spatio-temporal patterns are then discovered from theme life cycles and theme snapshots.

Frequent Movements of Objects

With the development of the global positioning system, moving object databases have received considerable attention. Many research efforts have been focused on finding efficient indexing and querying methods in such databases. However, data mining in moving object databases is still in its infancy.

Peng and Chen (2003) first proposed a method to optimize mobile systems by finding the frequent motion patterns of objects. It first converts the movement log data into multiple sub-sequences, each of which represents a maximal moving sequence. With this, finding frequent moving patterns means finding frequently occurring consecutive sub-sequences among maximal moving sequences. With the mining results of user moving patterns, the authors further develop data allocation schemes that can utilize the knowledge of user moving patterns for proper allocation of both personal and shared data.

Mamoulis, Cao, and Kollios (2004) studied the problem of optimizing spatio-temporal queries through the discovery of spatio-temporal periodic patterns, which are the sequence of object locations that reappear in the movement history periodically. This work uses the concept of dense cluster to identify a valid region instead of a district in the map from the object trajectory. To find spatio-temporal periodic patterns, the study develops a two-phase top-down method. First, it uses a hash-based method to retrieve all frequent 1-patterns (i.e., a set of valid clusters), and replaces the trajectories in the database using cluster-IDs. Next, it uses the same methodology of max-subpattern-tree algorithm to discover all the frequent patterns. After getting all the frequent spatio-temporal periodic patterns, it introduces an index structure, called Period Index, to manage the trajectories of objects by exploiting the discovered periodic patterns.

Laube, Van Kreveld, and Imfeld (2004) studied mining patterns from moving point object data. They are interested in four kinds of patterns, namely flock, leadership, convergence, and encounter. The flock pattern describes objects moving in the same direction and being close to each other. The leadership pattern is similar to the flock pattern, except that one object should be heading in the specified direction for some time. The convergence pattern refers to objects moving to the same location. While the encounter pattern is a special kind of convergence pattern, in which the objects reach the same location at the same time. The authors proposed efficient algorithms for mining these four categories of patterns.

Gudmundsson, Van Kreveld, and Speckmann (2004) also worked on mining flock, leadership, convergence, and encounter patterns. They made use of the approximation technique commonly used in computational geometry. Experiment results show that the proposed approximation algorithms are much faster than their exact counterparts.

Li, Han, and Yang (2004) studied the problem of clustering moving objects. The goal is to capture pattern changes in the motion process and to provide better insight into the essence of the mobile data. The authors employed micro-clustering to catch the spatial-temporal regularities of moving objects and to handle huge datasets. Efficient techniques are proposed to keep the moving micro-clusters geographically small. By dynamically maintaining high-quality moving micro-clusters, the algorithm could obtain competitive clustering results at any given time instance. Experiment results show orders of magnitude improvement on running time over normal K-Means clustering method.

Space-Time Clusters

Another work on spatio-temporal clusters is Neill, Moore, and Sabhnani (2005). They proposed a new cluster detection method to efficiently discover emerging space-time clusters. The work is motivated from prospective disease surveillance, where the ability to automatically detect disease outbreaks is important to reduce the rates of morbidity and mortality. Neill, Moore, and Sabhnani (2005) combined time series analysis with new "emerging cluster" space-time scan statistics. Experiments on two kinds of simulated outbreaks show that their methods could rapidly detect both outbreak types while keeping the number of false positives low. The newly proposed "emerging cluster" scan statistics also consistently outperformed the standard "persistent cluster" scan statistics approach.

Adam, Janeja, and Atluri (2004) studied the problem of detecting anomalies in high dimensional spatio-temporal sensor datasets. They found that in spatial analysis, not only the spatial relationships among objects are important, but also the spatial features in the vicinity and the nearby spatial processes. Both nearby spatial features and spatial processes influence the behavior of objects. An example spatial feature could be a chemical factory or a stream. An example spatial process could be a chemical factory dumping toxic chemicals at the origin of the stream. In Adam et al. (2004), the similarity of objects is measured in terms of the spatial relationships among the objects and the semantic relationships based on spatial processes and spatial features in their vicinity. Spatio-temporal outliers in high dimensions are then detected based on this similarity definition.

These early attempts in spatio-temporal mining clearly show the promises and potentials in this research area. In this book, we focus primarily on a special class of patterns/rules in spatio-temporal databases—the spatio-temporal association rules.

Review of Association Rule Mining

Association rule mining has been applied largely on transactional, spatial, and temporal data. Here we give a brief review before introducing the novel spatio-temporal association mining algorithms in Chapters VII, VIII, and IX.

Mining Association Rules in Transactional Data

Given a set of transactions T (the database), the problem of mining association rules is to discover all association rules that have support and confidence greater than the user-specified minimum support (called *minsup*) and minimum confidence (called *minconf*).

The basic model of association rules is as follows: Let $I = \{i_1, i_2, ..., i_m\}$ be a set of items. Let T be a set of transactions (the database), where each transaction t (a data case) is a set of items such that $t \subseteq I$. An *association rule* is an implication of the form, $X \rightarrow Y$, where $X \subset I$, $Y \subset I$, and $X \cap Y = \varnothing$. The rule $X \rightarrow Y$ holds in the transaction set T with *confidence c* if $c\%$ of transactions in T that support X also support Y. The rule has *support s* in T if $s\%$ of the transactions in T contains $X \cup Y$. The key features of association rule mining are as follows:

- **Completeness:** It finds all possible rules. Other data mining techniques are only able to find a subset of the rules that exist in data.

- **No target item(s) on the right-hand-side:** An item can appear on either side of a rule. This is different from other data mining methods, which typically have some fixed items on the right-hand-side of a rule as targets.

- **Mining with data on hard disk:** It does not need to load the whole data into memory. This makes mining a huge dataset possible. Most of the existing mining techniques require the data to be in memory and thus could not handle large datasets due to the main memory size limit.

An association mining algorithm works in two steps: (1) Generate all *frequent* itemsets that satisfy minsup; (2) Generate all association rules that satisfy minconf using the frequent itemsets. An itemset is simply a set of items. A frequent itemset is an itemset that has transaction support above minsup. For example, suppose we have the following transaction dataset:

Jacket, Boots

Milk, Cheese, Bread, Shoes

Milk, Bread

Milk, Bread, Shoes, GreetingCard, Pork

Cheese, Milk, Shoes, Beef

Jacket, Boots, SkiPants

Let us assume that minimum support = 30%, and minimum confidence = 70%. An example frequent itemset is

{Milk, Bread}   [sup = 3/6]

Two association rules can be generated from the itemset:

Milk → Bread   [sup = 50%, confid = 75%]
Bread → Milk   [sup = 50%, confid = 100%]

We now discuss the mining algorithm. The key behind almost every association rule mining algorithm is the "*Apriori*" or "downward closure" property, which is used to prune those itemsets that are impossible to have sufficient supports.

- **Downward closure property:** If an itemset does not have minimum support then every super-set of this itemset also does not have minimum support.

This property is obvious because as the number of items in an itemset grows, the support cannot increase. We now present the most popular association rule mining algorithm—the Apriori algorithm (Agrawal & Srikant, 1994).

Apriori Algorithm

The Apriori algorithm is one of the most efficient algorithms for association rule mining. Apriori is a breadth-first memory-based algorithm and makes use of the downward closure property by pruning off candidates that have infrequent subset before counting their support. The algorithm makes multiple passes over the data to discover large itemsets. In the first pass, it counts the supports of individual items and determines whether they are frequent. In each subsequent pass, it starts with the seed set of itemsets found to be frequent in the previous pass. It uses this seed set to generate new possibly frequent itemsets, called *candidate itemsets*. The actual supports for these candidate *itemsets* are computed during the pass over the data. At the end of the pass, it determines which of the candidate *itemsets* are actually frequent.

After all the frequent itemsets are discovered, the rules are then generated using the frequent itemsets. This step basically works on each frequent item-set separately, that is, it puts a subset of the items on the right-hand-side and the rest of the items on the right-hand-side to compute the confidence. If the confidence obtained is above minconf, it is an association rule. Otherwise, the rule is discarded. Interested readers can refer to Agrawal and Srikant (1994). Note that the supports for all frequent itemsets are sufficient for rule generation and no access to the original data is needed.

Clearly the search space for all association rules grows exponentially. The mining algorithm exploits the sparseness of data, high minimum support, and minimum confidence values. Whie the algorithm seems to be very expensive, the level-wise search is in fact quite efficient. It makes at most k passes over the data where k is the size of the longest itemset. In practice, k is bounded (≤ 10). Under some conditions, all the rules can be found in linear time and scales up to large datasets since the algorithm does not require the data to reside in main memory.

Since the Apriori algorithm have been proposed, many researchers have worked on different variations that aim to improve the efficiency of the original algorithm. Briefly, the optimizations can be grouped as follows:

- **Reducing the dataset size:** Here the idea is to pick random sample S of the given dataset D and search for frequent itemsets in S instead of D. A lower support threshold is used to find the frequent itemsets local to S to reduce the likelihood of missing the important global frequent itemsets. The sampling approach is good when efficiency is of utmost importance.

- **Reducing number of database scans:** This is based on the technique whereby the database is partitioned into blocks. New candidate itemsets are added for each block with smaller minimum support to obtain the local frequent itemsets. One pass of the database is initiated to associate each itemset with the list of transaction ID (TID) that contains the items in the itemset. This list of TIDs allows the algorithm to find the potentially frequent global itemsets. To confirm that the itemsets are indeed globally frequent, a second pass of the database scan is utilized.

- **Reducing number of candidate itemsets examined:** The idea is to make use of a hash-table to keep track of the number of itemsets. Itemsets whose corresponding bucket count is below the support threshold cannot be frequent and can be removed immediately.

- **Removing the need to generate candidates:** The cost of Apriori algorithm is largely constrained by the number of candidates generated. The idea is to mine the complete set of frequent itemsets without having to generate candidates. The algorithm makes use of the TP-tree to keep a compressed information of the database. To find the long frequent patterns, the algorithm looks for the shorter frequent patterns in the FP-tree recursively and then concatenating the suffix.

Mining Association Rules in Temporal Data

Temporal association rule mining refers to the association rule mining performed on temporal data. Unlike traditional association rule mining, where the problem definition is clear, there is no formal definition on the role that the time plays in temporal association rule mining.

Ozden, Ramaswamy, and Silberschatz (1998) propose the model of cyclic association rules. A cyclic association rule is an association rule that occurs periodically over time, say occurring regularly daily, weekly, and so forth. The rigid requirement of cyclic patterns results in the limited power of describing real-life variations.

Ramaswamy, Mahajan, and Silberschatz (1998) generalize the work in Ozden, Ramaswamy, and Silberschatz (1998) by introducing calendar algebra to describe complicated temporal phenomena. The calendar algebra could deal with multiple granularities of time. However, the requirement of user-defined calendar algebraic expressions implies the user's prior knowledge about the temporal patterns to be discovered.

In order to remove the requirement on user's prior knowledge, Li, Ning, and Wang (2001) propose to use a calendar schema to represent the time intervals during which a temporal association rule holds. An example of a calendar schema is (year, month, day). A calendar pattern is obtained from a calendar schema by assigning concrete values to every element in the schema. For example, a calendar pattern (2006, 5, *) represents all days in May of 2006.

Li, Ning, and Wang (2001) consider two types of temporal association rules: precise-match association rules and fuzzy-match association rules. A precise-match association rule should hold in every interval of a calendar pattern. If the calendar pattern is (2006, 5, *), then the rule must hold on every day in May 2006.

A fuzzy-match association rule should hold in at least m% of the intervals, where m is a user specified threshold. Therefore, if a temporal association rule holds in m% days of May 2006, we say that it is a fuzzy-match rule. Based on the well-known Apriori algorithm, the authors propose two optimization techniques that take advantage of the properties of the calendar-based patterns.

Ale and Rossi (2000) put forward a type of temporal association rules that is based on the lifetime of items. The authors observe that in a supermarket, some products have been sold for a long time, while others may just enter the market several months ago. Hence, judging the popularity of a product by its support in the whole transaction database is not suitable. The support of a new popular product could be much less than the support of an old unpopular product, because the lifetime of the new product is much shorter than that of the old product. Based on this observation, the authors propose to consider a product's support in its lifetime, and not in the whole database time span. With this new measurement, interesting patterns involving new popular products could be discovered. A modified version of the Apriori algorithm is proposed to obtain this type of temporal association rules.

Lee, Lin, and Chen (2001a) study the problem of mining general temporal association rules in a publication database. In the publication database, every item has its exhibition period. A transaction is composed of a set of items. The database contains a set of transactions. The concept of exhibition period is similar to lifetime in Ale and Rossi (2000). Lee, Lin, and Chen (2001a) finds frequent itemsets with respect to their exhibition period. An algorithm called Progressive-Partition-Miner (PPM) is proposed to discover the general temporal association rules. The basic idea of PPM is to first partition the database according to exhibition periods of items. It then progressively accumulates the support count of candidate itemsets to obtain the frequent itemsets.

Chen and Petrounias (2000) propose three types of temporal association rules. The first type is an association rule together with its valid time period during which the association rule holds. For example, the valid time of buying pattern "coffee and egg" is in the morning. The second type is the periodicities that association rules have. The third type is the discovery of association rules with temporal features. The authors implement a prototype system with an integrated query and mining interface (IQMI) and a temporal mining language (TML).

Wang, Yang, and Muntz (2001) examine the problem of mining patterns that are hidden in the evolution of numerical attributes. The authors attempt to find correlations among the change of attribute values over time. For example, ages and salaries of employees are numerical attributes. These values change with time. A resulting pattern may show the relationship between the change of salary and the change of age. Three metrics are proposed to qualify a temporal association rule: support, confidence, and dense. An efficient algorithm utilizing all the three requirements to prune the search space is then proposed. Further, the mining result is presented in a concise form of rule set.

Spatial Association Pattern Mining

Spatial data mining is the process of discovering relationships between spatial data and non-spatial data by using spatial proximity relationships. Spatial data is self-autocorrelated and exhibits a unique property known as Tobler's first law of geography (Tobler, 1979):

"Everything is related to everything else but nearby things are more related than distant things."

Mining patterns from spatial datasets is more difficult than extracting the corresponding patterns from traditional numeric and categorical data due to the complexity of spatial data. Spatial data mining covers a wide spectrum and many approaches for finding patterns in spatial databases. This includes spatial clustering (Guha, Rastogi, & Shim, 1998; Ng & Han, 1994; Sander, Ester, & Kriegel, 1998), spatial characterization and spatial trend analysis (Ester, Frommelt, & Kriegel, 1998), spatial classification (Koperski, Han, & Stefanovic, 1998), spatial association pattern mining (Huang, Xiong, & Shekhar, 2003; Morimoto, 2001; Shekhar & Huang, 2001; Zhang, Mamoulis, & Cheung, 2004), and so forth. A comprehensive survey on techniques to find spatial clustering patterns is given in Han and Kamber (2001).

In the context of spatial data mining, spatial association patterns reflect the relationships of spatial/spatial data or spatial/non-spatial data. To date, two formats of association rules in spatial databases have been introduced: spatial association rules and spatial collocation patterns. Here, we briefly review the techniques to extract these spatial association patterns in spatial databases.

Spatial Association Rules

The problem of mining spatial association rules based on spatial relationships (e.g., adjacency, proximity) of events or objects is first discussed in Koperski and Han (1995) where spatial data are converted to transactions according to a centric reference feature model. Koperski, Adhikary, and Han (1996) introduces the concept of spatial association rules, and design a two-step Apriori method to mine such rules.

Consider a spatial database D, which consists of n number of spatial sub-datasets $D = \{R_1, R_2, ..., R_i\}$, such that each R_i contains all objects that have a particular non-spatial feature f_i. Given a feature f_i, we define a transactional database as follows. For each object o_i in R_i, a spatial query is issued to derive a set of features $I = \{f_j : f_j = f_i \wedge \exists o_j \in R_j, \text{dist}(o_i, o_j) \leq \theta\}$ where θ is the distance threshold.

The collection of all feature sets I for each object in R_i defines a transactional table T_i. T_i is then mined using some item-sets mining method (Agrawal & Srikant, 1994; Han & Pei, 2000). The frequent feature sets I in this table, according to a minimum support value, can be used to define rules of the form:

$$o.\text{label} = f_i \Rightarrow o \text{ close to some } o_j \in R_j, \forall f_j \in I$$

The support of a feature set I defines the confidence of the corresponding rule.

The major limitation of the spatial association rule is that it depends on the concept of explicit transactions in databases. However, due to the continuity of the underlying space, this may not be possible or appropriate in spatial databases. Moreover, many duplicate counts of association rules may result if we define transactions around locations of instances of features.

Further, it is difficult to extend the algorithm for mining spatial association rules to find association rules in spatio-temporal databases. In spatio-temporal databases, association rules should satisfy both spatial proximity relationships and temporal proximity relationships. Since spatio-temporal databases are 3-dimensional, instead of 2-dimensional, the computational cost of processing candidate patterns and computing the interestingness of these patterns is much higher than that of spatial databases. As a result, existing techniques are difficult and not scalable for use to find association rules in spatio-temporal databases.

Spatial Collocation Patterns

Recently, research on spatial association pattern mining has shifted toward mining collocation patterns that are the set of spatial features with instances located in the same neighborhood.

Shekhar and Huang (2001) first define the problem for mining spatial collocation patterns. They use neighborhoods instead of transactions in traditional association rule mining to find event-centric spatial co-location patterns. The work defines a new spatial measure of conditional probability as well as a monotonic measure of prevalence to allow iterative pruning. Based on these concepts, an Apriori-like approach called Co-location Miner is developed to find all the frequent collocation patterns. Co-location Miner initially performs a spatial join to retrieve object pairs which are close to each other, and then it uses the Apriori-based candidate generation algorithm to generate the candidates of length $(k+1)$-pattern from k-patterns and validate the candidates by joining the instances of the k-patterns which share the first $(k-1)$ feature instances. They further study the problem of mining confident co-location rules without a support threshold in their continuous work (Huang, Xiong, & Shekhar, 2003).

Similarly, Morimoto (2001) studies the same problem to find sets of services located close to each other. An algorithm called Apriori_Gen is introduced to find neighboring class sets from spatial databases approximately. Points in the spatial databases are grouped based on the Euclidean distance measure and a Voronoi diagram is used to efficiently determine the nearest point from a set of points. While Apriori_Gen is effective in answering the question of what are the frequent neighboring class sets, the method can only be used to do approximation and the patterns found are typically too general to be useful.

Zhang, Mamoulis, and Cheung (2004) introduces a method to discover collocation patterns by combining the discovery of spatial neighborhoods with the mining process. Specifically, it extends a hash-based spatial join algorithm to operate on multiple feature sets in order to identify such neighborhoods. The algorithm divides the map and partitions the feature sets using a regular grid. While identifying object neighborhoods in each partition, at the same time, the algorithm attempts to discover prevalent and confident patterns by counting their occurrences at production time. However, the approach still follows the candidate-generation-and-test methodology, and has to enumerate all combinations of the spatial features. As a result, performance decreases dramatically as the number of spatial features increases.

From this, we note that all of the methods proposed in Shekhar and Huang (2001), Morimoto (2001), and Zhang, Mamoulis, and Cheung (2004) follow the candidates-maintenance-and-test methodology. Their performances suffer from maintaining many candidates and the need for multiple database scans. Hence, it is difficult to extend them to the discovery of spatio-temporal collocation patterns due to the high computational cost of candidate patterns in higher dimension space.

In Yang, Parthasarathy, and Mehta (2005), a general framework for mining spatial associations and spatio-temporal episodes from scientific datasets is proposed. Unlike previous works, here features are modeled as geometric objects rather than points. When defining distance metrics, objects' shape and extent are taken into account. Therefore, the model is more accurate in capturing the influence of an object on other neighboring objects. In this paper, four different types of spatial object interaction (association) patterns are studied: star, clique, sequence, and minLink. Besides that, the authors also extended their approach to incorporate temporal dimension to mine spatio-temporal episodes. The proposed framework is evaluated on real datasets. Domain knowledge verifies the importance of discovered patterns and episodes. Experiments on enormous datasets also show that the framework is both efficient and scalable.

Summary

From the literature review in this chapter, we observe that there is a limited number of works on spatio-temporal data mining. Most of the research work has been regarded as the generalization of pattern mining in temporal databases. In other words, they map data (i.e., locations of objects or the changes of natural phenomena over time) to sequences of values. Then, the algorithms that discover frequent sequences or find frequent sub-sequences in a long sequence are applied. Although these techniques can discover some interesting patterns in spatio-temporal databases, they cannot be used to discover patterns that reveal the interactions of the events or objects in different locations. In the next few chapters, we propose new algorithms targeted at revealing such interactions.

References

Adam, N. R., Janeja, V. P., & Atluri, V. (2004). Neighborhood based detection of anomalies in high dimensional spatio-temporal sensor datasets. In *Proceedings of the ACM Symposium on Applied Computing,* Nicosia, Cyprus, March 14-17 (pp. 576-583). New York: ACM Press.

Agrawal, R., & Srikant, R. (1994). Fast algorithms for mining association rules in large databases. In *Proceedings of the 20th International Conference on Very Large Data,* Santiago de Chile, Chile, September 12-15 (pp. 487-499). San Francisco, CA: Morgan Kaufmann Publishers.

Ale, J. M., & Rossi, G. H. (2000). An approach to discovering temporal association rules. In *Proceedings of the ACM Symposium on Applied Computing,* Villa Olmo, Como, Italy, March 19-21 (pp. 294-300). New York: ACM Press.

Basak, J., Sudarshan, A., & Trivedi, D. (2004). Weather data mining using independent component analysis. *Journal of Machine Learning Research, 5,* 239-253.

Bell, I., & Visneck, M. North Atlantic Oscillation Index. Retrieved from http://www.ldeo.columbia.edu/NAO

Chen, X., & Petrounias, I. (2000). Discovering temporal association rules: Algorithms, language and system. In *Proceedings of the 16ᵗʰ IEEE International Conference on Data Engineering,* San Diego, California, USA, February 28-March 3 (p. 306). Los Alamitos, CA: IEEE Computer Society Press.

Ester, M., Frommelt, A., & Kriegel, H. P. (1998). Algorithms for characterization and trend detection in spatial databases. In *Proceedings of the 4ᵗʰ International Conference on Knowledge Discovery and Data Mining,* New York City, New York, USA, August 27-31 (pp. 44-50). Menlo Park, CA: AAAI Press.

Gudmundsson, J., Van Kreveld, M., & Speckmann, B. (2004). Efficient detection of motion patterns in spatio-temporal data sets. In *Proceedings of the 12th Annual ACM International Workshop on Geographic information Systems,* Washington, D.C., USA, November 12-13 (pp. 250-257). New York: ACM Press.

Guha, S., Rastogi, R., & Shim, K. (1998). CURE: An efficient clustering algorithm for large databases. In *Proceedings of ACM SIGMOD International Conference on Management of Data,* Seattle, Washington, USA, June 2-4 (pp. 73-84). New York: ACM Press.

Han, J., & Kamber, M. (2001). *Data mining: Concepts and techniques.* San Francisco, CA: Morgan Kaufmann Publishers.

Han, J., & Pei, J. (2000). Mining frequent patterns by pattern-growth: Methodology and implications. *ACM SIGKDD Explorations, Special Issue on Scalable Data Mining Algorithms, 2*(2), 14-20.

Huang, Y., Xiong, H., & Shekhar, S. (2003). Mining confident co-location rules without a support threshold. In *Proceedings of the ACM Sympo-*

sium on Applied Computing, Melbourne, Florida, USA, March 9-12 (pp. 497-501). New York: ACM Press.

Koperski, K., Adhikary, J., & Han, J. (1996). Spatial data mining: Progress and challenges survey paper. In *Proceedings of ACM SIGMOD Workshop on Research Issues on Data Mining and Knowledge Discovery,* Montreal, Quebec, Canada, June 4-6 (pp. 55-70). New York: ACM Press.

Koperski, K., & Han, J. (1995). Discovery of spatial association rules in geographic information databases. In *Proceedings of the International Symposium on Large Spatial Databases,* Portland, Maine, USA, August 6-9 (pp. 47-66). Berlin/Heidelberg: Springer.

Koperski, K., Han, J., & Stefanovic, N. (1998). An efficient two-step method for classification of spatial data. In *Proceedings of the International Symposium on Spatial Data Handling,* Vancouver, Canada, July 12-15 (pp. 45-54). Berlin/Heidelberg: Springer.

Laube, P., Van Kreveld, M., & Imfeld, S. (2004). Finding REMO – Detecting relative motion patterns in geospatial lifelines. In *Proceedings of the 11th International Symposium on Spatial Data Handling,* University of Leicester, UK, August 22-24 (pp. 201-215). Berlin/Heidelberg: Springer.

Lee, C.-H., Lin, C.-R., & Chen, M.-S. (2001a). On mining general temporal association rules in a publication database. In *Proceedings of the IEEE International Conference on Data Mining,* San Jose, California, USA, November 29-December 2 (pp. 337-344). Los Alamitos, CA: IEEE Computer Society Press.

Li, Y., Han, J., & Yang, J. (2004). Clustering moving objects. In *Proceedings of the 10th ACM SIGKDD International Conference on Knowledge Discovery and Data Mining,* Seattle, Washington, USA, August 22-25 (pp. 617-622). New York: ACM Press.

Li, Y., Ning, P., & Wang, S. (2001). Discovering calendar-based temporal association rules. In *Proceedings of the 8th International Symposium on Temporal Representation and Reasoning,* Civdale del Friuli, Italy, June 14-16 (pp. 111-118). Los Alamitos, CA: IEEE Computer Society Press.

Mamoulis, N., Cao, H., & Kollios, G. (2004). Mining, indexing, and querying historical spatiotemporal data. In *Proceedings of the ACM SIGKDD Knowledge Discovery and Data Mining,* Seattle, Washington, USA, August 22-25 (pp. 236-245). New York: ACM Press.

Mei, Q., Liu, C., & Su, H. (2006). A probabilistic approach to spatiotemporal theme pattern mining on Weblogs. In *Proceedings of the 15th international Conference on World Wide Web,* Edinburgh, Scotland, UK, May 23-26 (pp. 533-542). New York: ACM Press.

Mesrobian, E., Muntz, R., & Shek, E. C. (1995). Exploratory data mining and analysis using CONQUEST. In *IEEE Pacific Conference on Communications, Computers, Visualization, and Signal Processing,* Victoria, May 17-19 (pp. 281-286). Los Alamitos, CA: IEEE Computer Society Press.

Morimoto, Y. (2001). Mining frequent neighboring class sets in spatial databases. In *Proceedings of the ACM SIGKDD International Conference on Knowledge Discovery and Data Mining,* San Francisco, California, USA, August 26-29 (pp. 353-358). New York: ACM Press.

Neill, D. B., Moore, A. W., & Sabhnani, M. (2005). Detection of emerging space-time clusters. In *Proceeding of the 11th ACM SIGKDD International Conference on Knowledge Discovery in Data Mining,* Chicago, Illinois, USA, August 21-24 (pp. 218-227). New York: ACM Press.

Ng, R. T., & Han, J. (1994). Efficient and effective clustering methods for spatial data mining. In *Proceedings of the International Conference on Very Large Databases,* Santiago de Chile, Chile, September 12-15 (pp. 144-155). San Francisco, CA: Morgan Kaufmann Publishers.

Ozden, B., Ramaswamy, S., & Silberschatz, A. (1998). Cyclic association rules. In *Proceedings of the International Conference on Data Engineering,* Orlando, Florida, USA, February 23-27 (pp. 412-421). Los Alamitos, CA: IEEE Computer Society Press.

Peng, W. C., & Chen, M. S. (2003). Developing data allocation schemes by incremental mining of user moving patterns in a mobile computing system. *IEEE Transactions on Knowledge and Data Engineering, 15*(1), 70-85.

Ramaswamy, S., Mahajan, S., & Silberschatz, A. (1998). On the discovery of interesting patterns in association rules. In *Proceedings of the International Conference on Very Large Data Bases,* New York City, New York, USA, August 24-27 (pp. 368-379). San Francisco, CA: Morgan Kaufmann Publishers.

Sander, J., Ester, M., & Kriegel, H. P. (1998). Density-based clustering in spatial databases: A new algorithm and its applications. *Data Mining and Knowledge Discovery, 2*(2), 169-194.

Shekhar, S., & Huang, Y. (2001). Discovery of spatial co-location patterns. In *Proceedings of the International Symposium on Advances in Spatial and Temporal Databases,* Redondo Beach, California, USA, July 12-15 (pp. 236-256). Berlin/Heidelberg: Springer.

Steinbach, M., Tan, P. N., & Kumar, V. (2001). Clustering earth science data: Goals, issues and results. In *ACM SIGKDD Workshop on Mining Scientific Dataset,* San Francisco, California, USA, August 26. New York: ACM Press.

Stolorz, P., Nakamura, H., & Mesrobian, E. (1995). Fast spatio-temporal data mining of large geophysical datasets. In *Proceedings of the International Conference on Knowledge Discovery and Data Mining,* Montreal, Canada, August 20-21 (pp. 300-305). Menlo Park, CA: AAAI Press.

Tan, P. N., Steinbach, M., & Kumar, V. (2001). Finding spatio-temporal patterns in earth science data. In *ACM SIGKDD Workshop on Temporal Data Mining,* San Francisco, California, USA, August 26. New York: ACM Press.

Tobler, W. R. (1979). Cellular geography. In S. Gale, & G. Olssen (Eds.), *Philosophy in geography* (pp. 379-386). Dordrecht, Holland: D. Reidel Publishing Company.

Tsoukatos, I., & Gunopulos, D. (2001). Efficient mining of spatiotemporal patterns. In *Proceedings of the International Symposium on Advances in Spatial and Temporal Databases,* Redondo Beach, California, USA, July 12-15 (pp. 425-443). Berlin/Heidelberg: Springer.

Wang, W., Yang, J., & Muntz, R. R. (2001). TAR: Temporal association rules on evolving numerical attributes. In *Proceedings of the 17th IEEE International Conference on Data Engineering,* Heidelberg, Germany, April 2-6 (pp. 283-292). Los Alamitos, CA: IEEE Computer Society Press.

Yang, H., Parthasarathy, S., & Mehta, S. (2005). A generalized framework for mining spatio-temporal patterns in scientific data. In *Proceeding of the 11th ACM SIGKDD international Conference on Knowledge Discovery in Data Mining,* Chicago, Illinois, USA, August 21-24 (pp. 716-721). New York: ACM Press.

Zhang, X., Mamoulis, N., & Cheung, D. W. (2004). Fast mining of spatial collocations. In *Proceedings of ACM SIGKDD International Conference on Knowledge Discovery and Data Mining,* Seattle, Washington, USA, August 22-25 (pp. 384-393). New York: ACM Press.

Chapter VII

Mining Topological Patterns in Spatio-Temporal Databases

Spatial data mining is an interesting area and has received a lot of attention (Guha, Rastogi & Shim, 1998; Koperski, Han & Stefanovic, 1998; Ng & Han, 1994; Sander, Ester & Kriegel, 1998). One special class of spatial patterns is the collocation patterns. Collocation patterns describe a set of features that tend to occur together in close spatial proximity. For example, shopping malls and fast food restaurants tend to be located in the same neighborhood. Recently, some researchers have shifted their attention towards mining of topological patterns. Topological patterns are the set of collocated features that satisfy additional pre-defined spatial relationships. Figure 7.1 shows some examples of topological patterns. Mining topological patterns is an interesting research problem with broad applications, such as mining topological patterns in an e-commerce company, a location-based service, an ecology dataset, and so forth. Thus far, existing works primarily focus on the spatial aspect of the pattern while ignoring the temporal aspect. They discover patterns such as: "There is high probability of the occurrence of earthquakes in a region if there is high atmospheric pressure in the nearby region." However, it is not clear whether this "high atmospheric pressure in the nearby region" is observed a few days prior to the occurrence of the earthquake, or many months before the occurrence of the earthquake. With the prevalence of spatio-temporal databases, mining of topological patterns with temporal information, such as: "There is a higher incidence of earthquakes in a region, where during the same time, there is a high atmospheric pressure occurs in the nearby region." This pattern is more useful and helpful to data analysts and decision makers in understanding the underlying process that controls the changes.

Existing techniques for finding topological patterns (Huang, Xiong, & Shekhar, 2003; Koperski & Han, 1995; Morimoto, 2001; Shekhar & Huang, 2001; Zhang, Mamoulis, & Cheung, 2004) cannot be easily extended to mine patterns in spatio-temporal databases. This is because they follow the candidate-generation-and-test methodology (Agrawal & Srikant, 1994). Such approaches do not scale well when the potential number of candidate patterns is large. In spatio-temporal databases, the candidate space is three dimensional rather than two dimensional. In other words, the number of potential candidate patterns is potentially much more than that in spatial databases. Furthermore, topological patterns must satisfy not only the spatial proximity relationships but also the temporal proximity relationships. This translates to higher computational cost for processing the candidate patterns and computing the interestingness of these patterns. New methods are needed to mine the topological patterns efficiently.

Besides the efficiency of mining topological patterns, we have observed that the spatial features in topological patterns are always prompted by the surrounding geographical objects. To enhance the usefulness of the mined topological patterns, we need to include geographical features in the mining of topological patterns. For example, if we can identify a set of spatial features that always happen together when certain geographical features are present, then decision makers or area developers can have the means to issue a warning ahead of a disaster or consider the available alternatives.

In this chapter, we study the problem of mining topological patterns by imposing temporal constraints into the process of mining collocation patterns. We first introduce a summary structure that summarizes the database with the instances' count information of a feature in a region within a time window. Next, based on the summary structure, we design an algorithm, called TopologyMiner, to find the interesting topological patterns in a depth-first manner. The algorithm follows the pattern growth methodology. We also investigate an efficient way to incorporate geographical features in TopologyMiner.

Our extensive experimental study indicates that our proposed algorithm can discover topological patterns efficiently and is scalable.

Problem Statement

Given a spatio-temporal database D, let $F = \{f_1, ..., f_n\}$ be a set of spatial features and a lexicographic order $\leq_f$ be among the spatial features. Let $I = \{i_1, i_2, ..., i_m\}$ be a set of m instances in the spatio-temporal database D, where each instance is a vector ⟨instance-ID, spatial feature, position, time stamp⟩. The spatial feature f, the position (x, y) and the time stamp t_s of an instance i are denoted as $i.f$, $i.x$, $i.y$ and $i.t_s$ respectively.

Let R be a neighborhood relation over the positions of the instances in the spatio-temporal database D. Here, we define R as a distance threshold. The distance between two instances i_1 and i_2 is computed as $sdist = [(i_1.x - i_2.x)^2 + (i_1.y - i_2.y)^2]^{1/2}$. We say i_1 and i_2 are located close to each other if and only if $sdist \leq R$.

Similarly, let W be a closeness relation over the time stamps of instances in D. We define W as a time window threshold. The distance between the time stamps of two instances is computed as $tdist = |i_1.t_s - i_2.t_s|$. Two instances are said to be near in time if and only if $tdist \leq W$.

To capture the concept of "nearby", a neighbor set N is defined as a set of instances such that not only all pairwise positions of the instances in N are neighbors, but they are also near in time.

Topological Patterns

A *topological pattern* S of length k or k-pattern for short, is a set of spatial features, denoted as $S = \{f_1, f_2, ..., f_k\}$. All the features in S are ordered according to $\leq_f$. A valid instance of S is a set of instances $\{i_1, i_2, ..., i_k\}$ such that the spatial feature of the instance i_j is f_j, i.e., $i_j.f = f_j$. Note that all the features' instances in S must be near in time. A topological pattern P is called a *sub-pattern* of Q if $\forall f_j \in P, f_j \in Q$; and Q is a *super-pattern* of P, denoted as $P \subseteq Q$.

A topological pattern S is a *star-like* pattern if in a valid instance of S, the instance i_j of the feature f_j is located close to other instances while the in-

Figure 7.1. Example of two topological patterns

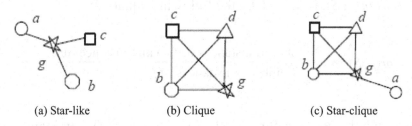

(a) Star-like   (b) Clique   (c) Star-clique

stances of other features are not required to be located close to each other. A star-like pattern is written as $\langle f_j : \{f_1, ..., f_k\}\rangle$. Figure 7.1(a) shows an example of a star-like pattern $\langle g : \{a,b,c\}\rangle$.

A topological pattern S is said to be a *clique* pattern if and only if in a valid instance of S, all pairs of the features' instances are located close to each other. In other words, the closeness relationships of the instances form a clique graph. A clique pattern is denoted as $\langle f_1, f_2, ..., f_k\rangle$. For example, Figure 7.1(b) shows a clique pattern where the instances of the features in the set $\langle b, c, d, g\rangle$ are close to each other.

A topological pattern S is a *star-clique* pattern if S contains a sub-clique pattern S' (i.e. S'$\subset$ S), and there is a feature $f_j \in$ S' such that the instance of fj is close to the instances of the features in S\S' and the instances of the features in S\S' are not required to be close to each other. A star-clique pattern is denoted as $\langle$S'$|f_i :$ S\S'$\rangle$. In essence, star-clique patterns can be generated by combining the star-like patterns with the clique patterns on a common feature. Figure 7.1(c) shows a star-clique pattern $\langle\langle b, c, d, g\rangle \mid g : \{a\}\rangle$.

Two measurements—support (Koperski & Han, 1995) and participation ratio (Shekhar & Huang, 2001)—have been introduced to measure the implication strength of a spatial feature in a topological pattern.

The *support* of a pattern S is defined as the number of instances of S found in the database. The support of a pattern S also defines the *confidence* of the corresponding rule in the form of $f_i \Rightarrow \{f_1, ..., f_s\}$. For example, Figure 7.1(a) defines a rule $g \Rightarrow \{a, b, c\}$, which means that if there is an instance of g, there is high confidence that it is close to the instances of features a, b and c while the instances of features a, b and c do not need to be close to each other.

Different from support, *participation ratio* is used to capture the probability that whenever an instance feature $f_i \in S$ appears on the map, it will participate in an instance of S. The participation ratio of a feature f_i in a pattern S, denoted as $pr(f_i, S)$, is defined by the following equation:

$$pr(f_i, S) = \frac{\text{Number of instances of } f_i \text{ in any instance of } S}{\text{Number of instances of } f_i}$$

Generalizing this to the pattern level, the *prevalence* (Zhang, Mamoulis, & Cheung, 2004) measure is defined. The *prevalence* of a pattern S, denoted as *prevalence(S)*, is the *minimum* participation ratio among all the features of S, that is $prevalence(S) = min\{pr(f_i, S), f_i \in S\}$. Prevalence measure is *monotonic*: if $S \subseteq S'$, then $prevalence(S) \geq prevalence(S')$.

A topology rule has the form $A \Rightarrow B$ where A and B are subsets of spatial features. Further, the prevalence $(A \Rightarrow B)$ is greater or equal to the a pre-defined minimum prevalence threshold. For example, a rule $g \Rightarrow \{b, c, d, g\}$ can be obtained in Figure 7.1(b), which means that if there is an instance of the feature g, there is a high probability that it participates in the instances of the clique pattern $\langle b, c, d, g \rangle$.

Geographical Features

With the concept of topological patterns, we now define the geographical features of topological patterns. Geographical features of topological patterns are entities in the physical world, such as a park, school, zoo, and so forth. These geographical features can be extracted from maps in geographical information systems and are kept in geographical feature databases with the format $\langle$*geographical feature identifier, geographical feature type, minimum bounding rectangles*$\rangle$.

A geographical feature, denoted as g, is indicated by a polygon or a minimum bounding rectangle (MBR) that describes its boundary. A geographical feature is said to be interesting with respect to a topological pattern S if it is always close to the spatial features in an instance of S. We define the distance between an instance i_{jk} of a spatial feature in S and the MBR of g as the minimum Euclidean distance from i_{jk} to g, denoted as $mindist(i_{jk}, g)$. A geographical feature g is frequent if the number of valid instances exceeds a user specified minimum support value.

Let R_g be the distance threshold for measuring the closeness of a geographical feature and the spatial features in a topological pattern. Here, we assume that $R_g \gg R$. This is to ensure that the instances' centroid of a length-k topological pattern S can be used to represent the positions of the spatial features' instances in S such that the interesting geographical features of S are also the interesting geographical features of spatial features in S.

Figure 7.2 shows the distance relation between the centroid and the instances of spatial features in a length-k topological pattern. Let $dist(o, i_{jk})$ be the distance from the centroid o to the instance i_{jk}, $dist(o, i_{jk}) = \mu R$ where $\mu \leq 1$. Let $dist(o, g)$ be the distance from the centroid o to the geographical feature g and $dist(o, g) = R_g = \sigma R, \sigma \gg 1$.

Based on the triangle inequality, we have $(R_g - \mu R) \leq dist(i_{jk}, g) \leq (R_g + \mu R)$. If we regard $dist(o, g)$ as $dist(i_{jk}, g)$, then the error ε obtained is:

$$
\begin{aligned}
\varepsilon &= \frac{|dist(o, g) - dist(i_{jk}, g)|}{dist(i_{jk}, g)} \approx \frac{|dist(o, g) - dist(i_{ik}, g)|}{dist(o, g)} \\[2mm]
&\leq \frac{dist(o, i_{jk})}{dist(o, g)} = \frac{\mu R}{\sigma R} = \frac{\mu}{\sigma} \\[2mm]
&\leq \frac{1}{\sigma}
\end{aligned}
$$

From this equation, we observe that the error is only related to $\sigma = R_g/R$. When σ is big, the distance from the spatial features in an instance of a topological pattern to the geographical feature approximates the distance from the centroid of the instance to the geographical feature, that is $dist(i_{jk}, g) \approx dist(o, g)$.

Note that finding the geographical features of topological patterns involves mining patterns across two types of databases, that is, spatio-temporal databases (e.g., mobile service databases) and geographical feature databases.

With this definition, we can now define the problem to find topological patterns as follows: Given a spatio-temporal database D and a geographical feature database D_g, the distance thresholds R and R_g, a time window threshold W, and the minimum prevalence threshold minprev, we want to find all frequent topological patterns, that is, star-like, clique, and star-clique patterns, and their geographical features.

Figure 7.2. Relationship of distance to geographical feature

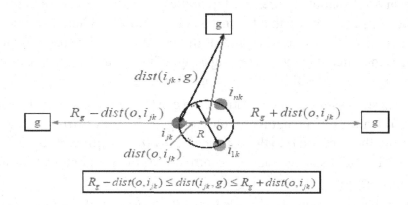

$$R_g - dist(o, i_{jk}) \leq dist(i_{jk}, g) \leq R_g + dist(o, i_{jk})$$

Mining Topological Patterns

Given that there is no explicit transaction concept in a spatio-temporal database, it is difficult to extend existing algorithms such as (Han, Pei, & Yin, 2000) to find topological patterns in spatio-temporal databases. We need to design new algorithms that follow the pattern growth methodology to find topological patterns in spatio-temporal databases.

In this section, we present the algorithm TopologyMiner for finding topological patterns. TopologyMiner finds all frequent patterns in a depth-first manner. It divides search space into a set of partitions. In each partition, it uses a set of locally frequent features to grow the patterns. It consists of two phases.

In the first phase, it divides the space-time dimensions into a set of smaller disjoint cubes. Then, it scans the database once to build a summary structure that records the instances' count information of the features in a cube. It further constructs two indices on the summary structure to facilitate the mining of topological patterns.

The second phase utilizes the count information stored in the summary structure to discover frequent topological patterns in a depth-first manner.

Summary Structure

Let us first introduce the summary structure. Let D be the spatio-temporal database, R be the distance threshold, and W be the time window threshold.

We divide the database D into a set of disjoint cubes $\{\langle c_{x1,y1}, w_1 \rangle, ..., \langle c_{x1,y1}, w_q \rangle, ..., \langle c_{xp,yp}, w_1 \rangle, ..., \langle c_{xp,yp}, w_q \rangle\}$ where $\{c_{x1,y1}, ..., c_{xp,yp}\}$ are two-dimensional cells with width $\frac{R}{\sqrt{2}}$, and $\{w_1, w_2, ..., w_q\}$ are one-dimensional time periods with width $\frac{W}{2}$.

For the instances in a cube $\langle c_{xk,yk}, w_t \rangle$, we can easily determine their neighbors, which should and must be the instances in one of the cubes $\langle c_{xi,yi}, w_s \rangle$ in the set

$$N_{c_{xk,yk},w_t} = \{\langle c_{x_i,y_i}, w_s \rangle \| y_k - y_i | \leq 2 \wedge |t - s| \leq 2 \wedge |x_k - x_i| \leq 2$$

and if $|xk - xi| = 2, |yk - yi| \neq 2\}$.

We call $Nc_{xk,yk}, w_t$ the neighbor-set of the cube $\langle c_{xk,yk}, w_t \rangle$. Note that two instances are near in position if and only if their cubes are neighbors.

Let $L = \{\langle c_{x1,y1}, w_1 \rangle, ..., \langle c_{xi,yi}, w_s \rangle\}$ be a list of cubes. The neighbor-set of L, denoted as N_L, is the join of the neighbor-set of each cube in L, that is, $N_L = Nc_{x1,y1}, w_1 \cap ... \cap Nc_{xi,yi}, w_s$.

Figure 7.4 shows an example of the spatio-temporal database with $R = 45$ and $W = 90$ mins. The space is divided into 48 cells and the time is divided into eight time periods. The neighbor-set of the cell $c_{3,3}$, i.e., $Nc_{3,3}$, is marked in grey. The neighbor-set of the time period w_4 consists of the time periods w_2, w_3, w_4, w_5 and w_6. Hence, the neighbor-set of the cube $\langle c_{3,3}, w_4 \rangle$ is the join of the neighbor-set $Nc_{3,3}$ with $\{w_2, w_3, w_4, w_5, w_6\}$.

After dividing time and space into a set of cubes, we scan the database once, and hash the instances of the features into the corresponding cubes. For each cube $\langle c_{xi,yi}, w_s \rangle$, we keep the instances' count of a feature f_j in the main memory. Note that only those cubes that contain at least one feature instance will be stored in the summary structure. Compared to the original database of N instances, the size of the summary structure is $O(N/k)$, assuming each cube contains k (k $\geq$ 1) instances and N is the number of instances in the database.

To facilitate information retrieval operations in the summary structure, we construct two hash-based indices, called Cube-Feature Index (CFI) and Feature-Cube Index (FCI). Both indices are two-level structures. Specifically, CFI is built with the composite key $(\langle c_{xi,yi}, w_s \rangle, fid)$, and its first level is used to index the cube with the identifier $\langle c_{xi,yi}, w_s \rangle$, and its second level is utilized to index features with the identifier *fid*. With CFI, we can obtain features that occur in a cube $\langle c_{xi,yi}, w_s \rangle$, and retrieve their correspondingly instances' count in the cube in constant time.

FCI is built using the composite key $(fid, \langle c_{xi,yi}, w_s \rangle)$. The first level of FCI is used to index features with the identifier fid, and the second level indexes cubes with the identifier $\langle c_{xi,yi}, w_s \rangle$ respectively. FCI helps to determine corresponding cubes in which a feature fid occurs and obtain its instances' count in constant time.

Figure 7.4 gives an example of the summary structure with the two indices, CFI and FCI, for the database in Figure 7.3.

Figure 7.3. Example of a spatio-temporal database

tid	fid	position	time
1	f_1	(86,185)	15:32:01
2	f_1	(200,180)	9:05:31
3	f_2	(70,202)	15:45:01
4	f_2	(57,59)	19:25:31
5	f_2	(130,120)	13:03:33
6	f_2	(235,200)	9:25:31
7	f_3	(240,180)	11:19:07
8	f_3	(263,15)	12:29:54
9	f_4	(31,62)	19:05:45
10	f_4	(268,28)	11:55:14
11	f_4	(253,12)	11:29:43
12	f_2	(128,125)	10:21:56
13	f_2	(135,115)	14:05:26

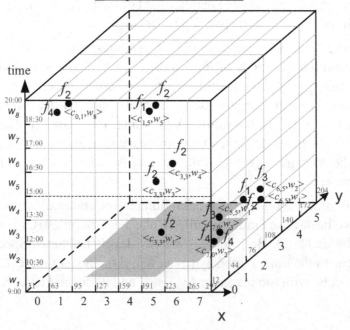

Figure 7.4. Example of summary structure

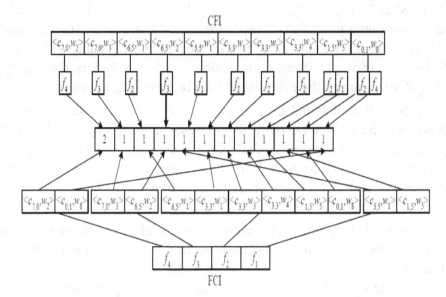

With these two indices, we can approximate the number of instances of a topological pattern. Recall we consider two instances are near in the position if and only if their cubes are neighbors. This means that the instances of a feature f_i in a cube $\langle c_{x1,y1}, w_1 \rangle$ and the instances of a feature f_j in the neighboring cube $\langle c_{x2,y2}, w_2 \rangle$ form the valid instances of a topological pattern $\langle f_i, f_j \rangle$. In other words, the instances' count of a feature in a topological pattern can be obtained from the summary structure directly. With this in mind, we now proceed to explain the process of finding frequent topological patterns.

Projected Database

Now, we discuss the steps to find topological patterns. We first define the projected database of a length-k topological pattern S, and then explain how to construct the projected database of S from the summary structure. Finally, we illustrate the process of mining frequent topological patterns in the projected database of S.

We define the projected database of a topological pattern as a collection of sets of cubes in which instances of the features in a topological pattern occur, and a set of related features.

Let $S = \{f_1, ..., f_k\}$ be a length-k topological pattern. The projected database of S, denoted as P_S, is the collection of entries $\langle L, R_p \rangle$, where L is a list of cubes and R_p is a pointer pointing to a list of features that are related to the pattern S. These features are found either in L or the neighboring cubes of L. Figure 7.5 shows an example of projected database of S. For brevity, we use $P_S.L$ and $P_S.R_p$ to represent the cube-list and the feature-list respectively.

The cube-list $P_S.L$, denoted as $(\langle c_{x1, y1}, w_1 \rangle, ..., \langle c_{xk, yk}, w_k \rangle)$, is used to store the cubes in which the instances of the features in S occur, and all the cubes in the cube-list must be neighbors. In other words, the ith cube $\langle c_{xi, yi}, w_i \rangle$ contains the instances of the ith feature $f_i \in S$, $1 \leq i \leq k$. With the cube-list, we could obtain the instances' count of a feature participating in pattern S, and approximate the number of instances of S.

The feature-list $P_S.Rp$ stores the features that are related to the pattern S and the cubes where the features' instances occur. Each element in the feature-list has the format $(f_r : \langle c_{xm, ym}, w_m \rangle)$, where $f_r \geq f_k$, $f_k \in S$, and the cube $\langle c_{xm, ym}, w_m \rangle$ that contains the instances of the feature f_r, is a neighboring cube of the cube-list $P_S.L$. The feature-list stores the potential features that can be used to combine with S to generate longer patterns. Figure 7.8(a) shows an example of the projected database of f_1.

The projected database of a topological pattern can be obtained from the summary structure directly. Consider the construction of the projected database of pattern f_i. First, we obtain the cube-lists of f_i by scanning FCI. For example in Figure 7.6(a), we get two cube-lists of f_1 by scanning FCI in Figure 7.4, that is $L_1 = (\langle c_{1,5}, w_5 \rangle)$ and $L_2 = (\langle c_{5,5}, w_1 \rangle)$.

Figure 7.5. Example of S-projected database

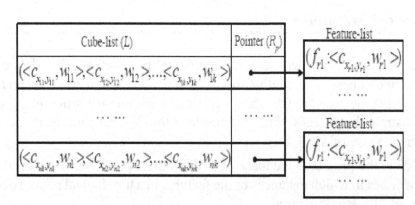

For each cube-list L in P_{fi}, we obtain its neighbor-set N_L. Then, for each cube in the neighbor-set N_L, we get the set of related features (i.e., RF) from CFI. With the related features and the neighboring cubes, we generate new entries for the feature-list R_p in P_{fi}. Figure 7.7(a) shows sample feature-lists in P_{f1}. Initially, for the cube-list $L_1 = (\langle c_{1,5}, w_5 \rangle)$, there is only one valid neighboring cube, that is, neighbor-set $N_{L1} = \{\langle c_{1,5}, w_5 \rangle\}$. From $c_{1,5}$, we obtain the set of related features of f_1, i.e., RF $= \{f_2\}$. Finally, we add the entry $(f_2: \langle c_{1,5}, w_5 \rangle)$ into the feature-list R_{p1}. Similarly, for the cube-list L_2, we obtain two entries for the feature-list R_{p2}, that is, $(f_2: \langle c_{6,5}, w_1 \rangle)$ and $(f_3: \langle c_{6,5}, w_2 \rangle)$.

The projected database of a length-k pattern $S_k = \{f_1, f_2, ..., f_{k-1}, f_k\}$ $(k \geq 2)$ can be derived from the projected database of its prefix $(k-1)$-sub-pattern $S_{k-1} = \{f_1, f_2, ..., f_{k-1}\}$. Note that the feature f_k is a related feature of the pattern S_{k-1} and $f_k \geq f_{k-1}$. We construct P_{Sk} from P_{Sk-1} as follows: For each entry $\langle L, R_p \rangle$ of P_{Sk-1} where the feature-list $P_{Sk-1}.R_p$ contains an element of the feature f_k, e.g., $(f_k: \langle c, w_m \rangle)$, we yield a new entry $\langle L, R_p \rangle$ for P_{Sk}, where $P_{Sk}.L = P_{Sk-1}.L \cup \{\langle c_{xm, ym}, w_m \rangle\}$ and the feature-list $P_{Sk}.R_p$ is a subset of the feature-list $P_{Sk-1}.R_p$, that is each element $(f_r, \langle c_{xs,ys}, w_s \rangle)$ in the feature-list $P_{Sk}.R_p$, where $f_r \geq f_k$ and $\langle c_{xs,ys}, w_s \rangle$ is a neighbor of the cube $\langle c_{xm,ym}, w_m \rangle$.

Figure 7.6(b) shows the projected database of the pattern $\langle f_1, f_2 \rangle$, which is derived from P_{f1}. In Figure 7.6(a), we know that the feature f_2 is contained in both entries of P_{f1}. Hence, we generate two entries for $P_{\langle f1, f2 \rangle}$, that is $L_1 = (\langle c_{1,5}, w_5 \rangle, \langle c_{1,5}, w_5 \rangle)$ and $L_2 = (\langle c_{5,5}, w_1 \rangle, \langle c_{6,5}, w_2 \rangle)$. Since the feature f_3 is only contained in $P_{f1}.R_{p2}$ and $\langle c_{6,5}, w_2 \rangle$ is a neighbor of $\langle c_{6,5}, w_1 \rangle$, we add the entry $(f_3: \langle c_{6,5}, w_2 \rangle)$ into the feature-list $P_{\langle f1, f2 \rangle}.R_{p2}$.

Figure 7.6. Construction of projected database

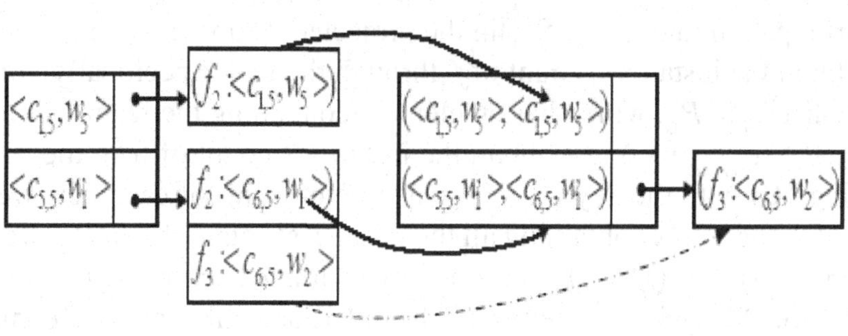

(a) f_1-projected database   (b) $\langle f_1, f_2 \rangle$-projected database

Mining Projected Databases

Let S_k be a frequent length-k topological pattern and P_{Sk} be constructed already. Now, we see the process to mine topological patterns from the projected database of S_k.

Mining Star-Like Patterns

To get star-like patterns, we directly mine the projected database of the features, that is, 1-topological patterns. For a feature f_i, the feature f_j is said to be a frequent related feature of f_i if and only if $pr(f_i, \langle f_i, f_j \rangle) \geq minprev$. All the frequent related features of f_i form a star-like pattern $S = \{f_i : \langle f_{r1}, \dots, f_{rm} \rangle\}$. For example in Figure 7.7(a), since $pr(f_1, \langle f_1, f_2 \rangle)$ and $pr(f_2, \langle f_1, f_2 \rangle)$ are greater than 0.3, we can generate a star-like pattern $S_1 = \langle f_1 : \{f_2, f_3\} \rangle$.

Mining Clique Patterns

The process to discover clique patterns is a little complicated. Our main idea is to check whether a related feature f_r of S_k can be combined with S_k to generate a longer clique pattern $S_{k+1} = S \cup \{f_r\}$ ($f_r \geq f_k$). To achieve this, we need to determine whether the prevalence of S_{k+1}, which is the minimum participation ratio among all features in S_{k+1}, is equivalent to or greater than $minprev$. In other words, we not only need to compute the participation ratio of related feature f_r w.r.t. S_{k+1}, but also the participation ratio of the features in S_k w.r.t. S_{k+1}. This is due to the incorporation of the feature f_r in S_k, $pr(f_i, S_{k+1}) = pr(f_i, S_k)$ for each $f_i \in S_k$.

Suppose the set RF contains all the related features of S_k, The features in RF are ordered according to $\prec_f$. For each feature f_r in RF, we first compute the participation ratio $pr(f_r, S_{k+1})$ in the projected database S_k. The main step is to obtain the instances' count of f_r through the FCI. Specifically, for each feature-list R_p in P_{Sk}, which has an element containing the feature f_r, for example, $(f_r : \langle c_{xm,ym}, w_m \rangle)$, we obtain the instance's count of fr in the cube by indexing FCI with the key $(f_r, \langle c_{xm,ym}, w_m \rangle)$. Note that for each key, we only query FCI once. After obtaining all the instances' count of f_r in P_{Sk}, we compute $pr(f_r, S_{k+1})$. If $pr(f_r, S_{k+1}) \geq minprev$, we continue to compute $pr(f_i, S_{k+1})$ for each $f_i \in S$. Otherwise, we remove f_r from RF, since it cannot be combined with the pattern S_k to generate any frequent topological pattern.

The process to compute the participation ratio $pr(f_i, S_{k+1})$ for each feature $f_i \in S_k$ proceeds as follows. For each entry $\langle L, R_p \rangle$ in P_{Sk} such that the feature-list $P_{Sk}.R_p$ contains the feature f_r, we get the cube $\langle c_{xi,yi}, w_i \rangle$ in L because it contains the instances of feature $f_i \in S_k$. We obtain the instances' count of f_i through FCI with the key $(f_i, \langle c_{xi,yi}, w_i \rangle)$. After scanning all entries in P_{Sk}, we compute $pr(f_i, S_{k+1})$. Once there is a feature in S_k whose participation ratio with respect to S_{k+1} is less than *minprev*, we stop the process because the prevalence of S_{k+1} cannot be greater than *minprev*. Only when $prevalence(S_{k+1}) \geq minprev$, we output the pattern S_{k+1}, construct the projected database of S_{k+1}, and mine it recursively.

Figure 7.7 shows the process of finding topological patterns with *minprev* = 0.3. In P_{f1}, the features f_2 and f_3 are related features of f_1. To determine whether f_2 is a frequent related feature of f_1, we need to compute $prevalence(f_1, f_2)$. In other words, we need to compute the participation ratios $pr(f_2, \langle f_1, f_2 \rangle)$ and $pr(f_1, \langle f_1, f_2 \rangle)$. As we know, there are in total six instances of f_2 in the spatio-temporal database, and only two instances of f_2 participate in the instances of $\langle f_1, f_2 \rangle$, i.e., one instance in cube $\langle c_{1,5}, w_5 \rangle$ and one in cube $\langle c_{6,5}, w_1 \rangle$. Hence, $pr(f_2, \langle f_1, f_2 \rangle) = 0.33$. Since all instance of f_1 participate in the instances of the pattern $\langle f_1, f_2 \rangle$, we have $pr(f_1, \langle f_1, f_2 \rangle) = 1$. Finally, prevalence $(\langle f_1, f_2 \rangle) = \min\{0.33, 1\} = 0.33 > 0.3$. Hence, f_2 is a frequent related feature of f_1 and can be combined with f_1 to generate a longer frequent pattern $\langle f_1, f_2 \rangle$. Similarly, we have the $prevalence(f_1, f_3) = 0.5 > 0.33$, and hence, f_3 is also a frequent related feature of f_1. After mining the f_1-projected database, we construct the $\langle f_1, f_2 \rangle$-projected database and mine it recursively. Figure 7.8 shows the corresponding mining process.

Figure 7.7. The projected database of f_1

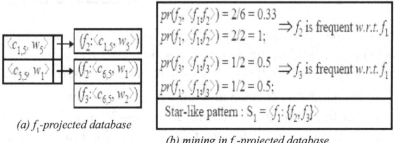

(a) f_1-projected database

(b) mining in f_1-projected database

Figure 7.8. The projected databases of $\langle f_1, f_2 \rangle$

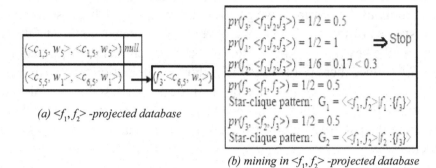

(a) $<f_1, f_2>$ -projected database

$pr(f_3, <f_1 f_2 f_3>) = 1/2 = 0.5$

$pr(f_1, <f_1 f_2 f_3>) = 1/2 = 1$ ⟹ Stop

$pr(f_2, <f_1 f_2 f_3>) = 1/6 = 0.17 < 0.3$

$pr(f_3, <f_1, f_3>) = 1/2 = 0.5$
Star-clique pattern: $G_1 = \langle\langle f_1, f_2\rangle| f_1 : \{f_3\}\rangle$

$pr(f_3, <f_2, f_3>) = 1/2 = 0.5$
Star-clique pattern: $G_2 = \langle\langle f_1, f_2\rangle| f_2 : \{f_3\}\rangle$

(b) mining in $<f_1, f_2>$ -projected database

Mining Star-Clique Patterns

Finally, we examine the process to get star-clique patterns. The mining of star-clique patterns is invoked after a clique pattern S_k is yielded. A star-clique pattern is generated by combining the clique pattern S_k with the star-like pattern of the features f_i, $f_i \in S_k$. Specifically, for each feature $f_i \in S_k$, denoted as $S_k | f_i$, we first obtain the set of cubes in which f_i occurs. In other words, we do the projection of P_{Sk} on the feature f_i, denote it as $P_{Sk}|f_i$. Next, with the cubes in $P_{Sk}|f_i$, we recompute the participation ratio $pr(f_r, \langle f_i, f_r \rangle)$ for each related feature f_r in the star-like pattern of the feature f_i. If $pr(f_r, \langle S_k|f_i, f_r \rangle) \geq minprev$, f_r is said to be a frequent related feature of $S_k|f_i$. All the frequent related features of $S_k|f_i$ form a star-clique pattern with respect to $S_k|f_i$. For example in Figure 7.8(b), we can generate two star-clique patterns, i.e., $G_1 = \langle\langle f_1, f_2\rangle|f_1 : \{f_3\}\rangle$ and $G_2 = \langle\langle f_1, f_2\rangle|f_2 : \{f_3\}\rangle$.

Algorithm TopologyMiner

Algorithm TopologyMiner takes as input the spatio-temporal database D, the distance threshold R, the time window threshold W, and the prevalence threshold *minprev*, and outputs the set of frequent topological patterns.

Line 1 scans the database once and constructs the summary structure. We then discover the topological patterns at lines 4-25. Line 5 constructs the projected database for each feature f_i in D with CFI. Lines 7-17 discover the star-like patterns with respect to f_i by scanning P_{fi}. For each feature f_i in D, lines 19-25 calls the procedure MiningPDB to find the longer frequent topological patterns.

The procedure MiningPDB works as follows: For each related feature f_r of S, line 2 computes the participation ratio $pr(f_r, S \cup \{f_r\})$ using FCI. If it is equivalent to or greater than *minprev*, lines 5-11 are executed to compute the participation ratio $pr(f_i, S \cup \{f_r\})$for each feature $f_i \in S$. If there is a feature fp such that $pr(f_p, S \cup \{f_r\})$ is less than *minprev*, the procedure terminates with the extension f_r (lines 8-10). If the participation ratios of all the features in S are greater than or equivalent to *minprev*, a new clique pattern $S' = S \cup \{f_r\}$ is generated. This is followed by a search for its geographical features, the construction of the projected database S' using CFI, invoking the procedure GenGenricPtn to find star-clique patterns, and then mining the projected database S' recursively (lines 13-19). The process continues until there are no more frequent topological patterns.

Algorithm TopologyMiner

Input: Spatio-temporal database D;

Distance threshold R;

Time window threshold W;

Prevalence threshold minprev;

Output: A set of frequent star-like S;

A set of clique patterns C;

A set of star-clique patterns G;

1. *Scan database D and construct summary structures CFI and FCI with R and W;*

2. $RF = \{all\ the\ features\ in\ D\}$;

3. $\forall f_i \in D,\ F_{si} = \phi$;

4. *FOR each feature $f_i \in RF$ do*

5. *Construct the projected database of f_i;*

6. $RF_i = \{related\ features\ in\ P_{fi}\}$;

7. *FOR each related feature $f_i \in RF_i$ do*

8. $pr_j = pr\ (f_p, <f_p f_j>)\ and\ pr_i = pr\ (f_p, <f_p f_j>)$

9. *Compute pr_j and pr_i through CFI and FCI;*

10. *IF $(pr_j < minprev \| pr_j < minprev)$ THEN*

11. $RF_i = RF_i \setminus \{f_j\}$;

12. *IF $(pr_j \geq minprev)$ THEN $F_{si} = F_{si} \cup \{f_j\}$;*

13. *IF $(pr_i \geq minprev)$ THEN $F_{sj} = F_{sj} \cup \{f_i\}$;*

14. *ENDFOR*

15. $s = <f_i : F_{si}>;$

16. $S = S \cup \{s\};$

17. ENDFOR

18. FOR each feature $f_i \in RF$ do

19.   FOR each feature $f_j \in RF_i$ do

20. $S' = <f_p f_j>;$

21. $C = C \cup \{S'\};$

22.   Construct $P_{S'}$ based on P_{fi};

23. $RF_{s'} = \{related\ features\ in\ P_{S'}\};$

24.   Call MiningPDB ($P_{S'}$, $RF_{s'}$, minprev);

25.   ENDFOR

26. ENDFOR

End Algorithm TopologyMiner

Procedure MiningPDB (P_S, RF_S, minprev)

1. FOR each feature $f_r \in RF$ do

2.   Compute $pr(f_p S \cup \{f_r\})$;

3.   IF ($pr(f_p S \cup \{f_r\}) < minprev$) THEN Continue

4.   ELSE

5.   flag = 1;

6.   FOR each $f_i \in S$ do

7.   Compute $pr(f_p S \cup \{f_r\})$;

8.   IF ($pr(f_p S \cup \{f_r\}) < minprev$)

9.   flag = 0;

10.   break;

11.   ENDFOR

12.   IF (flag) THEN

13. $S' = S \cup \{f_r\};$

14. $C = C \cup \{S'\};$

15.   Construct $P_{S'}$ based on P_S;

16. $RF_{s'} = \{related\ features\ in\ P_{S'}\};$

17.   Call GenGenericPtns (S', minprev);

18.   Call MiningPDB ($P_{S'}$, $RF_{s'}$, minprev);

19.   ENDIF

20.   ENDIF

21. ENDFOR

End Procedure MiningPDB

Procedure GenGenericPtn (C, minprev)

1. $F_s = \phi;$

2. FOR each feature f_i in C do

3.   Get $s \in S$ such that $s.f_i = f_i$;

4.   *FOR each frequent related feature $f_r \in S.F_s$ do*
5.   *IF (pr(f_p <C | f_i , f_r>) ≥ minprev) THEN*
6. $F_s = F_s \cup \{f_r\};$
7. $g = \{C \mid f_i : F_s\};$
8. $G = G \cup \{g\};$
9. *ENDFOR*
End Procedure GenGenericPtn

We will show that Algorithm TopologyMiner is correct and complete.

Theorem 2: Topology Miner is correct and complete.

Proof: TopologyMiner initializes the length-1 topological patterns to all spatial features in the database and obtains the corresponding projected databases. This is correct and complete as the features' participation ratios are equivalent to 1.

Now let us suppose that TopologyMiner can correctly discover all the length-k topological patterns.

Let α be a length-k topological pattern and $\{\beta_1, \beta_2,..., \beta_m\}$ be the set of all length-(k+1) topological patterns having prefix α. The complete set of topological patterns having prefix α is divided into m disjoint subsets. The jth subset ($1 \leq j \leq m$) is the set of topological patterns having prefix β_j. Each subset of topological patterns can be further divided when necessary. To mine the subsets of topological patterns, TopologyMiner constructs the corresponding projected databases. In other words, TopologyMiner can correctly discover all the frequent length-(k+1) topological patterns.

The completeness of the mining in the projected database of a topological pattern can be argued as follows. The projected database of a topological pattern S_k consists of cube-lists and feature-lists. With the cube-lists, we can obtain the instances of the features participating in S_k. With the feature-lists, we can get all the related features and the cubes containing the instances of the related features. This means we can determine the complete set of the frequent related features of the pattern using the projected database. In other words, we can find all frequent topological patterns.

Experimental Study

In this section, we evaluate the effectiveness and efficiency of Topology-Miner by comparing it with the Apriori-like algorithm in Shekhar and Huang (2001), which is implemented by incorporating the temporal aspect into the mining process for finding patterns in spatiotemporal databases. The algorithms are implemented in C++, and run on a Pentium 4, 3GHZ, 1G main memory PC.

Synthetic Data Generation

We extend the synthetic data generator described in Zhang, Mamoulis, and Cheung (2004) to spatio-temporal databases. Table 7.1 summarizes the parameters used in the data generator.

First, we set L features, which we call non-noise features and which can appear in the longest collocation pattern generated. We also set n noise features. The number of points for noise features is $r \times N$. We assign these points to the noise features uniformly. The remaining points are assigned to non-noise features uniformly.

The participation ratio of a feature in the longest pattern which has a participation ratio larger than the confidence threshold is $\delta_{max} + \theta$. The number of points N_i, which must appear in the instances of the longest pattern of a feature f_i is $(\delta_{max} + \theta) \times \dfrac{N \times (1-r)}{L}$. For other features, the participation ratios are $\delta_{min} + \theta$ and the number of points in instances of the longest pattern is $(\delta_{min} + \theta) \times \dfrac{N \times (1-r)}{L}$.

We generate instances of the longest pattern as follows. We divide the space into regular cells by dividing the map using a regular grid of cell-side length R and dividing the time using a regular window of length λ. At first, we generate a point randomly. We use the point as the center and generate points for a feature in the longest pattern around a cube, where r_s is the radius of a circle in space and r_t is the radius in time. The coordinates for the ith point of the feature f_j is Because r_s is in $(0, \dfrac{R}{2})$ and r_t is in $(0, \dfrac{\lambda}{2})$, we can assign r_s and r_t the values $\sigma(\dfrac{R}{2L})$ and $\sigma(\dfrac{\lambda}{2L}2L)$, $(1 \leq \sigma \leq L)$. In this way, any point in the cube can participate in an instance of the longest pattern. After selecting the first center point, we mark the cubes that intersect the cube centered at it such

Table 7.1. Data generation parameters

Parameter	Meaning	Default
N	Number of points on the map (x 1000)	200,000
L	Number of features in the longest pattern	10
m	Number of prevalent features in the longest pattern	8
n	Number of noise features	2
r	Percentage of points with noise features	0.1
d	Number of longest pattern instances generated	1500
θ	Minimum prevalence threshold	0.05
δ_{min}	Minimum difference between the prevalence of the longest pattern and θ	-0.023
δ_{max}	Maximum difference between the prevalence of the longest pattern and θ	0.08
R	Distance threshold	200
λ	Time window threshold	20
map	x- and y- extent of the map	8000x8000
T	Extend of the time dimension	1000

that no other longest pattern instances can be generated in them. Next, we continue to generate pattern instances from random points whose extended cube does not intersect the used cubes. After generating pattern instances d times, the process ends. The remaining points of the features which appear in the longest pattern are generated randomly on the map. Finally, we generate the points of noise features randomly on the map.

The generator described earlier generates instances of a long pattern with length L. The number of features which have participation ratios larger than the prevalence threshold is set to *m*.

Effect of Prevalence Threshold

We first evaluate TopologyMiner by varying the prevalence threshold. The results are shown in Figure 7.9.

Compared to the Apriori-like algorithm, TopologyMiner needs less time and space to find the topological patterns. This is expected because when the prevalence threshold decreases, more topological patterns become frequent and the length of the frequent patterns tends to be longer. As a result, the

Figure 7.9. Runtime vs. prevalence threshold

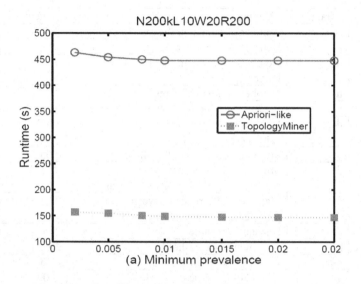

(a) Minimum prevalence

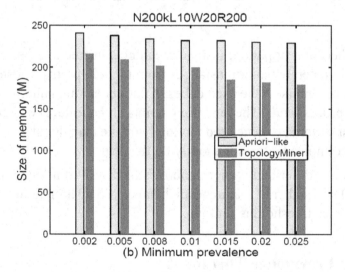

(b) Minimum prevalence

Apriori-like algorithm needs more time to compute the instances of topological patterns and count their frequency. In contrast, TopologyMiner uses the summary structure to approximate instances' count of a topological pattern and eliminate the generation and computation of the instances, which is very costly.

Effect of Database Size

Next, we study the effect of number of points N in a dataset. Figure 7.10 shows the results by varying N from 20k to 1000k.

Figure 7.10. Runtime vs. number of points

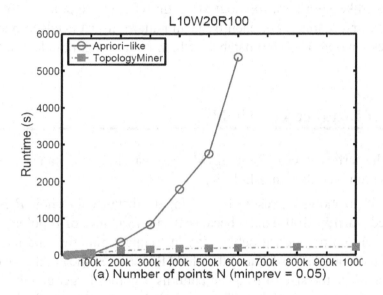

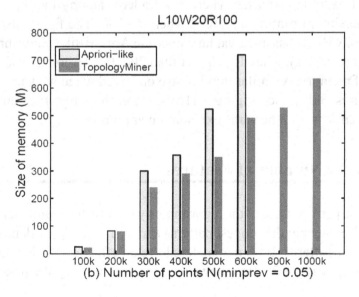

Figure 7.10(a) indicates that TopologyMiner scales linearly with number of points. Compared to the Apriori-like algorithm, TopologyMiner requires less time to find frequent topological patterns with the increase of N. Note that the Apriori-like algorithm runs out of memory when N is greater than 600k. This is because Apriori-like algorithm needs to generate many candidates and maintain their instances in the main memory. As N increases, the size of candidates and the number of the instances of the frequent patterns become larger. As a result, the Apriori-like algorithm needs much time and memory to compute and maintain the instances (see Figure 7.10(b)). Unlike the Apriori-like algorithm, TopologyMiner finds frequent topological patterns in a depth-first manner. For each frequent pattern, it just needs to maintain the corresponding projected database which reduces with the length of the patterns.

Effect of Distance Thresholds

We test the performance of TopologyMiner of varying the distance threshold R and the time window threshold W.

Figure 7.11(a) shows the results by varying the distance threshold R. A peak is reached when $R = 100$. This is because the performance of TopologyMiner is dependent on number of cubes, size of frequent patterns, and length of frequent patterns. As the distance threshold R increases, the number of cubes decreases while the size of frequent patterns becomes larger and the length of frequent patterns increases. There is a tradeoff among the three factors with the maximum runtime recorded when $R = 100$. The figure also shows that TopologyMiner has an advantage over the Apriori-like algorithm. Note that in Figure 7.11(a), when R is larger than 200, the Apriori-like algorithm runs out of memory. A similar trend is also observed when we vary the time window threshold W (see Figure 7.11(b)). Here, the longest runtime is recorded when $W = 20$. The same explanation applies here.

Effect of the Number of Features

We study the performance of the algorithms by varying the parameters L (i.e., number of features in the longest pattern) and m (i.e., the prevalent features in the longest pattern). Both parameters have an effect on the length of frequent patterns. Figure 7.12(a) shows the results of varying the parameter L

Figure 7.11. Runtime vs. distance thresholds

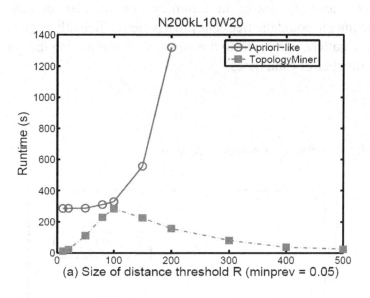

(a) Size of distance threshold R (minprev = 0.05)

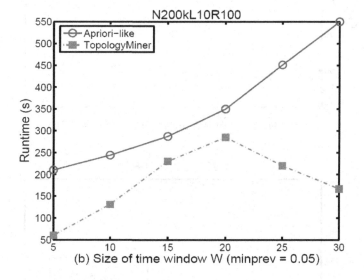

(b) Size of time window W (minprev = 0.05)

with values ranging from 10 to 40. We observe that TopologyMiner scales linearly with number of features in the longest pattern and outperforms the Apriori-like algorithm by a few orders of magnitude.

Similarly, Figure 7.12(b) shows the results of the algorithm when the parameter m is varied with values ranging from 5 to 18. As expected, the parameter

m has little effect on TopologyMiner. This is because the advantage of TopologyMiner lies in the use of the summary structure that not only enables
TopologyMiner to count the frequency of a pattern efficiently but also allows
it to find the pattern in a depth-first manner, thus eliminating the generation
of a huge number of candidates.

Figure 7.12. Runtime vs. number of features

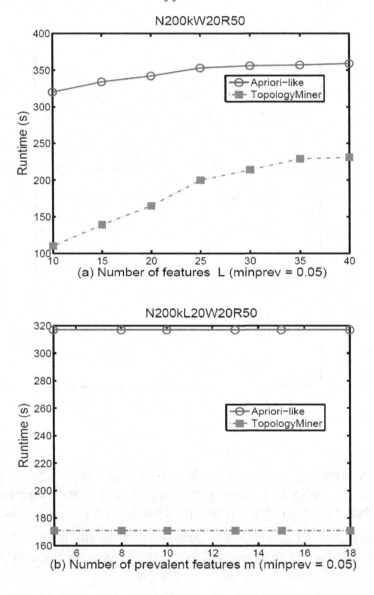

Summary

In this chapter, we have described an algorithm called TopologyMiner for finding topological patterns in spatio-temporal databases. We have presented a summary structure that summarizes spatio-temporal databases by recording instances' count information of a feature in a cube. Based on the summary structure, TopologyMiner finds topological patterns in a depth-first manner and eliminates the generation of too many candidates and frequency tests. The experimental studies indicate that TopologyMiner is effective and scalable in finding topological patterns and outperforms Apriori-like algorithms in a few orders of magnitude. In the next chapter, we will examine another class of useful spatio-temporal patterns called spatial sequence patterns.

References

Agrawal, R., & Srikant, R. (1994). Fast algorithms for mining association rules in large databases. In *Proceedings of the 20th International Conference on Very Large Data,* Santiago de Chile, Chile, September 12-15 (pp. 487-499). San Francisco, CA: Morgan Kaufmann Publishers.

Guha, S., Rastogi, R., & Shim, K. (1998). CURE: An efficient clustering algorithm for large databases. In *Proceedings of ACM SIGMOD International Conference on Management of Data,* Seattle, Washington, USA, June 2-4 (pp. 73-84). New York: ACM Press.

Han, J., Pei, J., & Yin Y. (2000). Mining frequent patterns without candidate generation. In *Proceedings of the ACM SIGMOD Conference on Management of Data,* Dallas, Texas, USA, May 16-18 (pp. 1-12). New York: ACM Press.

Huang, Y., Xiong, H., & Shekhar, S. (2003). Mining confident co-location rules without a support threshold. In *Proceedings of the ACM Symposium on Applied Computing,* Melbourne, Florida, USA, March 9-12 (pp. 497-501). New York: ACM Press.

Koperski, K., & Han, J. (1995). Discovery of spatial association rules in geographic information databases. In *Proceedings of the International Symposium on Large Spatial Databases,* Portland, Maine, USA, August 6-9 (pp. 47-66). Berlin/Heidelberg: Springer.

Koperski, K., Han, J., & Stefanovic, N. (1998). An efficient two-step method for classification of spatial data. In *Proceedings of the International Symposium on Spatial Data Handling,* Vancouver, Canada, July 12-15 (pp. 45-54). Berlin/Heidelberg: Springer.

Morimoto, Y. (2001). Mining frequent neighboring class sets in spatial databases. In *Proceedings of the ACM SIGKDD International Conference on Knowledge Discovery and Data Mining,* San Francisco, California, USA, August 26-29 (pp. 353-358). New York: ACM Press.

Ng, R. T., & Han, J. (1994). Efficient and effective clustering methods for spatial data mining. In *Proceedings of the International Conference on Very Large Databases,* Santiago de Chile, Chile, September 12-15 (pp. 144-155). San Francisco, CA: Morgan Kaufmann Publishers.

Sander, J., Ester, M., & Kriegel, H. P. (1998). Density-based clustering in spatial databases: A new algorithm and its applications. *Data Mining and Knowledge Discovery, 2*(2), 169-194.

Shekhar, S., & Huang, Y. (2001). Discovery of spatial co-location patterns. In *Proceedings of the International Symposium on Advances in Spatial and Temporal Databases,* Redondo Beach, California, USA, July 12-15 (pp. 236-256). Berlin/Heidelberg: Springer.

Zhang, X., Mamoulis, N., & Cheung, D. W. (2004). Fast mining of spatial collocations. In *Proceedings of ACM SIGKDD International Conference on Knowledge Discovery and Data Mining,* Seattle, Washington, USA, August 22-25 (pp. 384-393). New York: ACM Press.

Chapter VIII

Mining Flow Patterns in Spatio-Temporal Data

Besides topological patterns, another class of useful spatio-temporal patterns is spatial sequence patterns. In Chapter VI, we introduce the topological patterns to find the intra-relationships of events in a time window. These events may relate to each other in a star, clique, or star-clique manner within the given time window. However, the patterns cannot disclose the inter-relationships of events in different time windows. For example,

"Forest fire always occurs at region R_1 prior to the occurrence of haze in nearby region R_2." or

"Forest fire always occurs at a region prior to the occurrence of haze in its Northeastern nearby regions."

Here, we link the event "fire at R_1" to the event "haze in R_2". Such information cannot be obtained by spatial patterns, temporal patterns, or topological patterns alone. In other words, the focus of spatial sequence patterns is to describe how the observation of one event in some location implies the occurrence of another event in a second location, or how changes of events in one location can affect the events in another location. Such insights are critical for decision markers.

Further investigation reveals that this "flow" of events can be described in terms of the absolute location coordinates (region R_2), or the relative location coordinates (Northeastern regions). We call the absolute location patterns the *flow pattern;* and the relative location patterns the *generalized spatio-temporal patterns*.

The discovery of spatial sequence patterns is challenging because of the potentially large search space and the large number of candidates. Naïve incorporation of spatial information into existing sequence mining algorithms does not work. This calls for new spatial sequence pattern mining algorithms.

In this chapter, we describe flow patterns and the design of the algorithm called *FlowMiner* to find such flow patterns. FlowMiner incorporates a new candidate generation algorithm and employs various optimization techniques for better efficiency. The discovery of generalized spatio-temporal patterns will be described in the next chapter.

The rest of the chapter is organized as follows. We first give the notations and terminologies used, and define the problem of mining flow patterns. Then we illustrate the concept of flow patterns and the design of a new candidate generation algorithm which generates candidates by utilizing only length-2 sequences, instead of length k-1 sequences. By combining this with a depth-first search strategy and taking into account some spatial constraints, we are able to eliminate the need to generate large number of candidates. We introduce a disk-based algorithm called FlowMiner that incorporates the new candidate generation algorithm and employs various optimization techniques to improve its efficiency. Performance study shows that FlowMiner is both scalable and efficient, and experiments on real-life datasets also reveal some interesting flow patterns.

Notations and Terminologies

Spatio-temporal databases capture both the time and space dimensions. First, we divide time into disjoint time windows of length W. Each time window denotes a time period. Time t_1 and t_2 are said to be close if they are in the same time period, that is, $(t_1, t_2) \in W$.

Next, we divide the space into a set of disjoint grid cells, $S = \{l_1, l_2, ..., l_q\}$, where each grid cell represents a location, denoted as $l_i = (x, y)$. Let R be a *neighbor relation* over the locations in S. Location l_1 and l_2 are said to be neighbors if $(l_1, l_2) \in R$. The *neighborhood* of a location l is defined as a set of locations $N(l) = \{l_1, ..., l_k\}$ such that each l_j in $N(l)$ is a neighbor of l.

A *location-based event*, or *event* for short, denoted as $e(l, t)$, is a spatial feature e (such as drought, rain) occurring in location l at time t. Two events $e_1(l_1, t_1)$ and $e_2(l_2, t_2)$, $t_1 \leq t_2$, are said to be *related* or *CloseNeighbors* if and only if $(l_1,$

Figure 8.1. Example of a spatio-temporal database

(a) Space-time view

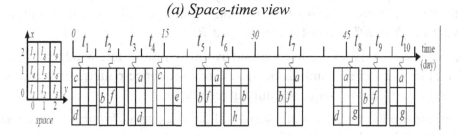

(b) Dataset sorted by window id and time

window id (wid)	time	eventsets
1	t_1	$d(l_1), c(l_7)$
	t_2	$b(l_4), f(l_5)$
	t_3	$d(l_2), a(l_8)$
	t_4	$e(l_6), c(l_7)$
2	t_5	$b(l_4), f(l_5), a(l_9)$
	t_6	$h(l_2), b(l_6)$
3	t_7	$b(l_4), f(l_5), a(l_9)$
4	t_8	$d(l_1), g(l_3), a(l_8)$
	$t_9 t_{10}$	$b(l_4), f(l_5)$
		$g(l_2), a(l_8)$

(c) Sequences for time windows

wid	Sequences
1	$\langle d(l_1), c(l_7) \rangle \rightarrow \langle b(l_4), f(l_5) \rangle \rightarrow \langle d(l_2), a(l_8) \rangle \rightarrow \langle e(l_6), c(l_7) \rangle$
2	$\langle b(l_4), f(l_5), a(l_9) \rangle \rightarrow \langle h(l_2), b(l_6) \rangle$
3	$\langle b(l_4), f(l_5), a(l_9) \rangle$
4	$\langle d(l_1), g(l_3), a(l_8) \rangle \rightarrow \langle b(l_4), f(l_5) \rangle \rightarrow \langle g(l_2), a(l_8) \rangle$

$l_2) \in R$ and t_1 is near t_2. For convenience, we simply write the location-based event as $e(l)$ when the sequential context is clear.

A set of location-based events that occur at the same time is called an *eventset*, denoted as $E = \langle e_1(l_1), ..., e_m(l_m) \rangle$. Two eventsets E_1 and E_2 are said to be *CloseNeighbors* if and only if every event in E_1 is related to every event in E_2. An eventset E_p at time t_1 is said to *flow* to an eventset E_q at time t_2, $t_1 \le t_2$, if and only if E_p and E_q are CloseNeighbors. We denote it as $E_p \to E_q$. In addition, an eventset E_t is said to be *reflexive* if and only if E_t flows to itself.

Figure 8.1 shows an example of a spatio-temporal database, where time is divided into four time windows (i.e., $W = 15$ days), and space is divided into nine locations, and the literals $\{a, b, ..., h\}$ represent some spatial features.

Suppose R is the unit length of a square and $R = 1$, then we could see that the two events $d(l_1, t_1)$ and $b(l_4, t_2)$ are CloseNeighbors, that is $d(l_1, t_1)$ and $b(l_4, t_2)$ are related. The eventset $E_1 = \langle b(l_4), f(l_5) \rangle$ at time t_2 and the eventset $E_2 = \langle d(l_2), a(l_8) \rangle$ at time t_3 are CloseNeighbors. Moreover, E_1 flows to E_2. In particular, the eventset $\langle b(l_4), f(l_5) \rangle$ at time t_2 is a reflexive eventset, but the eventset $\langle d(l_2), a(l_8) \rangle$ is not since $(l_2, l_8) \notin R$.

A *sequence* is a list of eventsets sorted by time within a time window. Figure 8.1(c) shows some examples of the various sequence patterns that can be found using existing sequence mining techniques.

Suppose we are given a spatio-temporal database as in Figure 8.1, we can observe at least three types of sequence patterns:

1. Global sequence patterns

    This class of patterns describes the global behavior of spatial features. For example, cities congestion $\to$ traffic jam $\to$ highway construction. Such patterns are not location specific. We can observe similar patterns in all the developed and developing countries. We denote the global sequence as

    $$s = \{(s_1 \to ... \to s_t) :: (L)\},$$

    where s_i $(1 \le i \le t)$ is a set of spatial features and L is a set of locations and, $L \subseteq S$ is a frequently occurring pattern if there are at least *sup* different locations containing s.

2. Local sequence patterns

    This class of patterns describes a local behavior of spatial features. For example, in country X, we have observed repeatedly the following sequence: rain → mosquito → dengue fever. A local sequence is a sequence $s = \{(s_1 \to ... \to s_t) :: (l_k)\}$, where s_i $(1 \leq i \leq t)$ is a set of spatial features and $l_k \in S$. Given a time window with width W, we say that s is frequent if there are at least *sup* different windows at location l_k containing s.

3. Location-sensitive sequence patterns

    A location-sensitive sequence pattern describes the behavior of location-specific spatial features over time. For example, forest fire in Indonesia → haze in Malaysia → haze in Singapore. It consists of a list of events sorted by time, denoted as $s = (E_1 \to ... \to E_t)$, where E_i $(1 \leq i \leq t)$ is an eventset. Given a time window with width W, s is said to be frequent if there are at least *sup* different windows containing s.

We can discover these three types of sequence patterns with existing association rule mining techniques or sequence mining techniques.

Flow Patterns

We have presented three types of sequence patterns that can be discovered in spatio-temporal databases. Although these three types of sequence patterns can reveal some interesting information of the events, that is the spatial relationships or the temporal relationships of the events, none of them can be used to link the changes in one location to the changes in a nearby location. In this section, we introduce the concept of flow patterns that are intended to describe the changes of events over space and time. We design a disk-based algorithm, called *FlowMiner*, which utilizes temporal relationships and spatial relationships amid events to generate flow patterns. The concept of the flow pattern is defined as follows:

Definition (Flow Pattern): A flow pattern is a sequence of reflexive eventsets sorted by time such that for any two consecutive eventsets, E_p at time t_i and E_q at time t_{i+1}, E_p flows to E_q.

Figure 8.2. Example of flow patterns

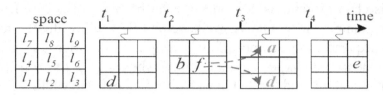

Consider Figure 8.1. To simplify the discussion, we define R as the unit length of a square. Let $R = 1$, then $d(l_1) \rightarrow \langle b(l_4), f(l_5) \rangle \rightarrow a(l_8)$ at time window 1 is a flow pattern, but $\langle b(l_4), f(l_5), a(l_9) \rangle$ at time window 3 is not since $(l_4, l_9) \notin R$.

We limit flow patterns to reflexive eventsets to provide a more meaningful interpretation of the patterns discovered. This is because a reflexive eventset guarantees that all the events within the set are related to each other. For example, in Figure 8.2, $d(l_2)$ and $a(l_8)$ are not related in the pattern $d(l_1) \rightarrow \langle b(l_4), f(l_5) \rangle \rightarrow \langle d(l_2), a(l_8) \rangle \rightarrow e(l_6)$. Thus, we will consider $d(l_1) \rightarrow \langle b(l_4), f(l_5) \rangle \rightarrow a(l_8) \rightarrow e(l_6)$, and $d(l_1) \rightarrow \langle b(l_4), f(l_5) \rangle \rightarrow d(l_2) \rightarrow e(l_6)$ as two independent patterns since they indicate two opposite trends.

A flow pattern with k events is called *k-flow*. A *k-flow* pattern is frequent if there are at least *minsup* different occurrences of the pattern over time, where *minsup* is a user-specified threshold. Let $P = E_{P1} \rightarrow ... \rightarrow E_{Ps}$ and $Q = E_{Q1} \rightarrow ... \rightarrow E_{Qt}$ be two flow patterns. P is called a *sub-flow* of Q, and Q a *super-flow* of P, denoted as $P \subseteq Q$, if there exist integers $1 \le j_1 < j_2 < ... < j_n \le t$ such that $E_{P1} \subseteq E_{Qj1}$, $E_{P2} \subseteq E_{Qj2}$, ..., $E_{Ps} \subseteq E_{Qjn}$. A flow pattern, P, is *maximal* if there does not exist any flow pattern Q such that $P \subseteq Q$.

Lemma 1: Flow patterns satisfy Apriori property: Any sub-flow of a frequent flow pattern must be frequent.

Proof: The set of flow patterns is a subset of sequences that satisfy the additional neighborhood constraint. We know that if a sequence is frequent, all its sub-sequences must be frequent. Since the set of flow patterns is a subset of sequences, we conclude that flow patterns also satisfy the Apriori property.

With these definitions, we can now define the problem to find flow patterns as follows: Given a spatio-temporal database D, a temporal window of length W, a neighbor relation R, and a user specified threshold minsup, the problem of mining flow patterns in spatio-temporal databases is equivalent to finding the set of all frequent flow patterns.

Mining Flow Patterns

The first step to discover flow patterns is to scan the database to find all frequent events (i.e., 1-*flows*). These events are sorted according to their support in descending order. Next, based on the sorted event order, we proceed from left-to-right to find all frequent length-2 sequences. Following that, we mine the frequent k-*flows (k > 2)* in a depth-first manner. This involves two main sub-tasks: candidate generation and support counting.

Candidates Generation

A key observation in mining flow patterns is that a length-2 sequence specifies a temporal relationship that must be maintained in the higher-order sequences.

Let $\{d(l_1) \to b(l_4)\}$, $\{d(l_1) \to f(l_5)\}$ and $\{d(l_1) \to a(l_8)\}$ be three frequent length-2 sequences. Suppose we want to extend $\langle b(l_4), f(l_5) \rangle \to a(l_8)$ by inserting event $d(l_1)$. An enumeration-based candidate generation method will generate five length-4 sequences as shown in Figure 8.3 (column 1). Note that an eventset corresponds to only one insert position because adding an event in different positions of an eventset only indicates the same fact that all the events occur at the same time. We assume that the events in an eventset are sorted alphabetically.

However, if we take into consideration the temporal constraints implied by the frequent length-2 sequences, then it is clear that $d(l_1)$ can only be inserted into $\langle b(l_4), f(l_5) \rangle \to a(l_8)$ at the position before $\langle b(l_4), f(l_5) \rangle$ in order to generate valid sequence candidates, that is, $d(l_1) \to \langle b(l_4), f(l_5) \rangle \to a(l_8)$. Moreover, with the neighborhood constraints of flow patterns, we can further remove sequence candidates which are not flow patterns.

Figure 8.3. Candidates validation with length-2 sequences and neighbourhood constraints

enumerated candidates	length-2 sequences			neighborhood constraints
	$\{d(l1) \rightarrow b(l4)\}$	$\{d(l1) \rightarrow f(l5)\}$	$\{d(l1) \rightarrow a(l8)\}$	
$d(l_p) \rightarrow \langle b(l_q), f(l_y) \rangle \rightarrow a(l_g)$	√	√	√	√
$\langle b(l_q), d(l_p), f(l_y) \rangle \rightarrow a(l_g)$	×	×	√	×
$\langle b(l_q), f(l_y) \rangle \rightarrow d(l_p) \rightarrow a(l_g)$	×	×	√	×
$\langle b(l_q), f(l_y) \rangle \rightarrow \langle a(l_g), d(l_p) \rangle$	×	×	×	×
$\langle b(l_q), f(l_y) \rangle \rightarrow a(l_g) d(l_p)$	×	×	×	×

These example indicates that it is possible to avoid generating infrequent and invalid candidate flow patterns by taking into consideration the temporal relationships specified by length-2 sequences and the spatial constraints specified by flow patterns.

Summary Tree

We devise a *summary tree* to keep track of all frequent flow patterns that have been generated and to capture the temporal relationships of length-2 sequences. The structure of a summary tree is as follows:

1. A *root* node, at level 0 of the tree, is denoted as *null*. This node has no incoming edge, and corresponds to the initial state.

2. Each node *n* at level *k*, consists of *a set of frequent k-flows*, and is associated with an *extension set*, denoted as *Ext(n)*, which stores events that can be combined with *k*-flows to form the children of node *n*.

Figure 8.4 shows the summary tree that has been constructed from the dataset in Figure 8.1(b) with *sup* = 50%, *W* = 15 days and *R* denoting a square of unit length 1. Node 0 is the root node and its extension set consists of all the frequent events, that is, $\{b(l_4), f(l_5), a(l_8), a(l_9), d(l_1)\}$. The nodes at level 1 in the tree are the frequent events that are 1-*flows*. A frequent event is included in the extension set of node *n* if this event occurs on the right of node n in the tree.

The children of a level *k* node *n*, $(k \geq 1)$, are generated by combining all frequent flow patterns in node n with the events in *Ext(n)*. For example, the children of node 1, that is, node 6, node 7, node 8, node 9 and node 10, are generated by combining 1-*flow* $b(l_4)$ with its extension set elements $b(l_4)$, $f(l_5)$, $a(l_8)$, $a(l_9)$ and $d(l_1)$ respectively.

Methodology

When we have found all the frequent events and length-2 sequences (i.e., level 1 and 2 nodes), we move on to the next step. Based on the level 1 and level 2 nodes in the summary tree, we can now construct the level *k* nodes, $k > 2$, by extending the level *k - 1* nodes with extension elements. This consists of four main steps which we will illustrate using node 24 in Figure 8.4.

Step 1. Determine Relevant Temporal Constraints

When extending a node *n* at level *k - 1* with the extension element β, we need to limit the number of sequences generated by eliminating infeasible sequences through the use of relevant temporal constraints. These temporal constraints are in the form of length-2 sequences that involve events in node n and the extension element β.

In Figure 8.4, node 24 is generated by extending node 21 with $d(l_1)$. The events in node 21 are $\{b(l_4), f(l_5), a(l_8)\}$. Hence, the relevant temporal constraints are those length-2 sequences involving an event in $\{b(l_4), f(l_5), a(l_8)\}$ with $d(l_1)$. They are contained in nodes 10, 14, and 17.

Figure 8.4. Summary tree for the dataset in Figure 8.1

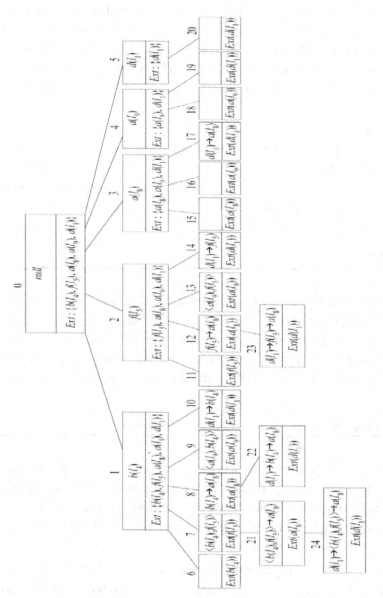

Step 2. Find Feasible Insert Positions Based on Temporal Constraints

Given a *(k-1)-flow* consisting of *t* eventsets $\alpha_1 \rightarrow \ldots \rightarrow \alpha_t$ where $\alpha_i = \langle e_{i1}, e_{i2}, \ldots, e_{im} \rangle$ $(1 \le i \le t)$ $(e_{ij}, 1 \le j \le m$, is an event) and an extension element β, there is a total of *2t+1* insert positions in which the extension element β can be inserted as an explicit eventset or as an element of the eventset α_i ($1 \leq i \leq t$) to form a *k-flow* (see Figure 8.5).

Not all the *2t+1* insert positions are feasible. To determine the feasible insert positions, we use the relevant length-2 sequences to determine the set of insert positions that do not violate the corresponding temporal constraints. Let us examine how the temporal relationships of length-2 sequences can be used to obtain the feasible insert positions.

A careful study reveals that there are seven ways in which a temporal constraint can affect the insert positions. Figure 8.5 summarizes the seven cases. Note that the position of β relative to e_{ij} is the position of β relative to eventset α_i where $e_{ij} \in \alpha_i$. Since an eventset corresponds to an insert position, we say that the temporal relationship between the events e_{ij} and β is also the temporal relationship between the eventset α_i and β.

Case 1: β occurs at the same time as e_{ij} .

> In this case, we only have one possible insert position. That is, β must be inserted at the same position as e_{ij} .

Case 2: β occurs before e_{ij} .

> Here, all the insert positions before e_{ij} are feasible. In other words, we have 2i - 1 insert positions.

Case 3: β occurs after e_{ij} .

> This is similar to Case 2 except in this case, all the insert positions after e_{ij} are feasible. In total, there are *2(t-i)+1* insert positions.

Case 4: β occurs before or at the same time as e_{ij} .

> This is a combination of Cases 1 and 2. In this case, there are *2i* possible insert positions for β to be inserted into α.

Case 5: β occurs at the same time as or after e_{ij} .

> This is a combination of Cases 1 and 3. In this case, we have a total of 2(t-i) + 2 insert positions.

Case 6: β occurs before or after e_{ij} .

> This is a combination of Cases 2 and 3. It has 2t insert positions.

Case 7: Combination of Cases 1, 2, and 3.

> In this case, none of the insert positions can be eliminated, and we have to generate all *2t+1* sequences (see Figure 8.5).

Figure 8.5. Temporal relationships of length-2 sequences

(k-1) -flow : $\alpha_1 \to \cdots \to \alpha_i \to \cdots \to \alpha_t$ with β insert positions: 1 2 3 $\quad$ 2i-1 2i 2i+1 $\quad$ 2t-1 2t 2t+1		
Cases	**Node$[e_{ij} + \beta]$**	**k-flows**
1	$\{\langle e_{ij}, \beta \rangle\}$	$\alpha_1 \to \alpha_2 \to \ldots \to \alpha_i\beta \to \ldots \to \alpha_t$
2	$\{\beta \to e_{ij}\}$	$\beta \to \alpha_1 \to \alpha_2 \to \ldots \to \alpha_i \to \ldots \to \alpha_t$ $\alpha_i\beta \to \alpha_2 \to \ldots \to \alpha_i \to \ldots \to \alpha_t$ $\ldots$ $\alpha_1 \to \alpha_2 \to \ldots \to \beta \to \alpha_i \to \ldots \to \alpha_t$
3	$\{e_{ij} \to \beta\}$	$\alpha_1 \to \alpha_2 \to \ldots \to \alpha_i \to \beta \to \ldots \to \alpha_t$ $\ldots$ $\alpha_1 \to \alpha_2 \to \ldots \to \alpha_i \to \ldots \to \beta \to \alpha_t$ $\alpha_1 \to \alpha_2 \to \ldots \to \alpha_i \to \ldots \to \alpha_t\beta$ $\alpha_1 \to \alpha_2 \to \ldots \to \alpha_i \to \ldots \to \alpha_t \to \beta$
4	$\langle e_{ij}, \beta \rangle$ $\beta \to e_{ij}$	$\beta \to \alpha_1 \to \alpha_2 \to \ldots\ldots \to \alpha_i \to \ldots \to \alpha_t$ $\alpha_i\beta \to \alpha_2 \to \ldots \to \alpha_i \to \ldots \to \alpha_t$ $\ldots$ $\alpha_1 \to \alpha_2 \to \ldots \to \beta \to \alpha_i \to \ldots \to \alpha_t$ $\alpha_1 \to \alpha_2 \to \ldots \to \alpha_i\beta \to \ldots \to \alpha_t$
5	$\langle e_{ij}, \beta \rangle$ $e_{ij} \to \beta$	$\alpha_1 \to \alpha_2 \to \ldots \to \alpha_i\beta \to \ldots \to \alpha_t$ $\alpha_1 \to \alpha_2 \to \ldots \to \alpha_i \to \beta \to \ldots \to \alpha_t$ $\ldots$ $\alpha_1 \to \alpha_2 \to \ldots \to \alpha_i \to \ldots \to \beta \to \alpha_t$ $\alpha_1 \to \alpha_2 \to \ldots \to \alpha_i \to \ldots \to \alpha_t\beta$ $\alpha_1 \to \alpha_2 \to \ldots \to \alpha_i \to \ldots \to \alpha_t \to \beta$
6	$\beta \to e_{ij}$ $e_{ij} \to \beta$	$\beta \to \alpha_1 \to \alpha_2 \to \ldots \to \alpha_i \to \ldots \to \alpha_t$ $\alpha_i\beta \to \alpha_2 \to \ldots \to \alpha_i \to \ldots \to \alpha_t$ $\ldots$ $\alpha_1 \to \alpha_2 \to \ldots \to \beta \to \alpha_i \to \ldots \to \alpha_t$ $\alpha_1 \to \alpha_2 \to \ldots \to \alpha_i \to \beta \to \ldots \to \alpha_t$ $\ldots$ $\alpha_1 \to \alpha_2 \to \ldots \to \alpha_i \to \ldots \to \beta \to \alpha_t$ $\alpha_1 \to \alpha_2 \to \ldots \to \alpha_i \to \ldots \to \alpha_t\beta$ $\alpha_1 \to \alpha_2 \to \ldots \to \alpha_i \to \ldots \to \alpha_t \to \beta$
7	$\langle e_{ij}, \beta \rangle$ $\beta \to e_{ij}$ $e_{ij} \to \beta$	$\beta \to \alpha_1 \to \alpha_2 \to \ldots \to \alpha_i \to \ldots \to \alpha_t$ $\alpha_i\beta \to \alpha_2 \to \ldots \to \alpha_i \to \ldots \to \alpha_t$ $\ldots$ $\alpha_1 \to \alpha_2 \to \ldots \to \beta \to \alpha_i \to \ldots \to \alpha_t$ $\alpha_1 \to \alpha_2 \to \ldots \to \alpha_i\beta \to \ldots \to \alpha_t$ $\ldots$ $\alpha_1 \to \alpha_2 \to \ldots \to \alpha_i \to \ldots \to \beta \to \alpha_t$ $\alpha_1 \to \alpha_2 \to \ldots \to \alpha_i \to \ldots \to \alpha_t\beta$ $\alpha_1 \to \alpha_2 \to \ldots \to \alpha_i \to \ldots \to \alpha_t \to \beta$

After Step 1, nodes 10, 14, and 17 will store the relevant length-2 sequences for node 24. The summary tree will capture the corresponding temporal con-

Figure 8.6. Example of insert positions

3-flow $\langle b(l_x), f(l_y)\rangle \to a(l_z)$ with ext $d(l_p)$		
Length 2-sequences	insert position by temporal constraints	insert position by spatial constraints
Node 10 = $\{d(l_p) \to b(l_x)\}$	1	1
Node 14 = $\{d(l_p) \to f(l_y)\}$	1	1
Node 17 = $\{d(l_p)\ a(l_z)\}$	1, 2, 3	1

straints. Since these constraints fall under Case 2, we can determine the feasible insert positions of event $d(l_p)$ in node *21* (see column 2 in Figure 8.6).

Step 3. Reduce Feasible Insert Positions Based on Spatial Constraints

Having decided on the insert positions based on temporal constraints, we can further optimize the set of insert positions based on the spatial constraint specified by flow patterns. This is realized by considering the neighborhood constraints between the extension element and the corresponding eventsets.

Let p be the position in α where event β may be inserted, $1 \leq p \leq 2t + 1$. The position p is said to be a valid insert position if:

1. β is inserted into α as an explicit eventset such that $(\beta, \alpha_{\lceil p/2 \rceil}) \in R$ and $(\beta, \alpha_{\lfloor p/2 \rfloor}) \in R$ hold, or;

2. β is inserted into α as an element of the eventset $\alpha_{\lceil p/2 \rceil}$ where $(\beta, \alpha_{\lceil p/2 \rceil}) \in R$, $(\beta, \alpha_{\lceil p/2 \rfloor - 1}) \in R$ and $(\beta, \alpha_{\lceil p/2 \rfloor + 1}) \in R$ hold.

Insert positions that do not satisfy these two conditions can be removed. Figure 8.6 (column 3) shows the final insert positions obtained for node 24.

Step 4. Generate New Flow Patterns

Step 3 yields a list of possible insert positions in which an extension element β can be inserted into an existing *(k-1)-flow* to form a new *k-flow*. If a *(k-1)-*

flow includes *m* unique events, then there are *m* level 2 nodes that can be used to decide *m* sets of feasible insert positions in α. The actual insert positions are determined by finding the intersection of these m sets of feasible insert positions. This process is repeated for a node until all the *(k-1)-flows* in the node have been examined.

In our running example, we have obtained the insert positions based on three nodes: nodes 10, 14, and 17. The intersection of these insert positions results in only one final insert position {1}, i.e., a new 4-*flow* $d(l_f) \rightarrow \langle b(l_d), f(l_s) \rangle \rightarrow a(l_g)$ being generated as node 24. Since all the 3-*flows* in node 21 have been checked, the candidate generation process for node 24 terminates.

Procedure FlowCandGen
Input: Node N at level k-1 in the Summary tree;
             Extension element β;
             Case table of two events Tbl;
Output: Child N' of node N at level k
1. $C_k = \phi$;
2.   *Cases* = *{Tbl[e_{ij}][β] | $e_{ij} \in N$};*
3.   *FOR each (k-1)-flow* $\alpha \in N$ *DO*
4.   *FOR each $c_i \in$ Cases DO*
5.   *pos_i is the set of insert positions imposed by c_i;*
6.   *finalpos$_i$ = ϕ;*
7.   *FOR each $p \in pos_i$ DO*
8.   *IF (β is an explicit eventset) && (β, $\alpha_{\lfloor p/2 \rfloor}$) $\in R$ && (β,*
                 $\alpha_{\lceil p/2 \rceil}$) $\in R$ || *(β is an element of $\alpha_{\lfloor p/2 \rfloor}$) && ($\beta$, $\alpha_{\lfloor p/2 \rfloor}$) $\in R$ &&*
                 (ext, $\alpha_{\lfloor p/2 \rfloor-1}$) $\in R$ && (ext, $\alpha_{\lfloor p/2 \rfloor+1}$) $\in R$
9.   *finalpos$_i$ = finalpos$_i$ $\cup$ {p};*
10.   *ENDIF*
11.   *ENDFOR*
12.   *FinalPos = $\cap_i$ finalpos$_i$;*
13.   *ENDFOR*
14. $C_k = C_k \cup$ *{k-flow generated using FinalPos};*
15. *ENDFOR*
16. *return C_k*
End Procedure FlowCandGen

The input to the candidate generation algorithm includes node N at level *k-1*, a upper triangle Tbl, where we store the case number of length2 sequences, and the extension element β. The child of the node *N*, *N'* (i.e., Node[N + ext]) at level *k+1*, is the output.

Initially, the cases of the relevant length-2 sequences are obtained from the Tbl (line 2). Then, we find the initial insert positions using the Cases for each *(k-1)-flow* in node *N* (lines 4-5), and further optimize the insert positions using the neighborhood constraints at lines 6-9. The final positions are decided at line 12. The process is continued until all *(k-1)-flows* in node *N* are examined. Finally, the *k-flows* in node *N'* regenerated.

Support Counting

Having generated the candidate patterns, we need to determine the frequencies of these candidates. Our algorithm makes use of a hash tree. Each node in the hash tree is associated with a hash table, where items of a candidate are hashed via some standard hash function. Each entry of the hash table is a list of *(item, pointer)*, where item denotes the item that has been hashed to this entry, and pointer points to the node containing the next item in the candidate.

When we add a candidate, we start from the root and descend the hash tree. At each depth *p* of the interior node, we apply the hash function to the *p*th item of the candidate and insert the corresponding *(item, pointer)* to the hash entry. The depth of the root node is 1 and the node at depth *p* points to the node at depth *p+1*.

In conventional algorithms (Agrawal & Srikant, 1996), a hash tree is built for the candidates of each level *k*, that is, the leaf nodes are of the same depth. In our case, flow patterns of different lengths are found simultaneously. To allow for this difference in lengths, we augment some interior nodes of the hash tree with a list to store flow patterns. Figure 8.7 shows an example of the construction of a hash tree for two different flow pattern lengths.

After constructing the hash tree for all the candidate flow patterns, we scan the database to count the number of occurrences of these candidate flow patterns. For each sequence found in the database, we check whether the sequence S is a superflow of any of the candidate flow patterns as follows:

For each event in S, we start at the root node, and recursively apply the hash function to determine the corresponding hash table entry with a pointer to the child node. Once we reach a leaf node or an augmented node, we check if S is a superflow of one of the flow patterns stored in the leaf node/augmented node. If it is, we increment the support count of the corresponding flow pattern.

Figure 8.7. Hash tree for varying flow patterns length

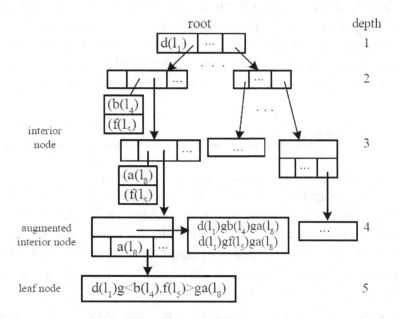

Pruning Techniques

In this section, we will discuss various optimization techniques that can be used to improve the efficiency of FlowMiner. These techniques include pruning infrequent candidates, eliminating non-promising events, and delaying database scans.

Prune Infrequent Candidates

The summary tree is constructed in a depth-first manner. As we expand a node to generate its children, some of the children may turn out to be unpromising as none of their flow patterns are frequent. Thus, we can immediately prune off their descendants.

For example, if node 10 in Figure 8.4 is infrequent, that is to say the combination of events $b(l_4)$ and $d(l_1)$ is infrequent. Hence, all the nodes in the summary tree that contain the two events $b(l_4)$ and $d(l_1)$ can be pruned, for example, node 22 and node 24. This is accomplished by removing $d(l_p)$ from the extension set of node 1.

To realize this pruning strategy efficiently, we associate a vertical bitmap with each node n in the summary tree, denoted as *bitmap(n)*. Each bit in the vertical bitmap indicates the occurrence of flow patterns in node n in each time window in the database, that is, if a flow pattern α appears in time window j, then bit j of *bitmap(n)* is set to one; otherwise, it is set to zero.

With the vertical bitmap, we can quickly eliminate the unpromising nodes from being generated by updating the appropriate extension set. When generating a new node by extending node n with the extension item β, we only need to check whether there is *minsup* ones in the result bitmap of *bitmap(n)* $\cap$ *bitmap(β))*. If the sum of ones is less than *minsup*, then we can conclude that the combination of events in node n with β is infrequent. Hence, we can eliminate β from subsequent extensions of node n.

Eliminate Hashing Non-Promising Events

Another optimization lies in the support counting process. We observe that certain events do not need to be hashed in the hash tree because they cannot be flow patterns, and will not be able to contribute to the support counts of any of the flow patterns in the hash tree. Suppose we have $S = \langle d(l_p), g(l_3),$ $a(l_8) \rangle \rightarrow \langle b(l_4), f(l_5) \rangle \rightarrow \langle g(l_7), a(l_8) \rangle$ in Figure 8.1. It is clear that $g(l_7), a(l_8)$ are not related to $d(l_p)$, that is, their locations are not neighbors of each other. Thus, we do not need to search the corresponding hash tree entries for them since there is no flow pattern involving these events. Based on this observation, we introduce a check prior to an event being hashed to ensure that this event satisfies both the reflexive and flow conditions in the flow pattern definition.

Delay Database Scans

A database scan is typically needed to determine whether a flow pattern α is frequent. However, if we know that a superset of α is frequent, then we can immediately conclude that α is frequent. This allows us to delay database scan, which ultimately minimizes the number of database scans needed.

To achieve this, we store a list of the maximal frequent flow patterns, called *MaxFilter* in the main memory. When a new node n is generated, we first check whether a flow pattern in n is a *sub-flow* of some of the flow patterns in MaxFilter. If it is, then it is frequent and we keep it in node *n*; otherwise, instead of scanning the database immediately to decide its frequency, we keep its pointer in a list. A database scan is carried out only when the number of flow patterns in the list exceeds the memory threshold, or all descendants of node n have been generated.

In real-life applications, we may have thousands of maximal frequent flow patterns which makes the *sub-flow* check expensive. In order to reduce the cost, instead of storing all the maximal flows in MaxFilter, we only store the maximal sets that can potentially be supersets of candidates generated from node *N*. We call this list *the local maximal frequent flow patterns, $LMFS_N$*. In this way, we can eliminate many comparisons with the maximal sets that are not super-or sub-flows of node *N*.

Algorithm FlowMiner

In the FlowMiner framework, the database *D* is sorted first by time, then by location. Lines 2-3 find all the frequent 1-*flows* and extend them to 2-*flows* in a left-to-right order. Lines 6-11 call the procedure DFS-PathScan to generate *k-flows* (*k>2*).

The procedure DFS-PathScan generates nodes in a depth-first manner: Lines 2-3 generate node *N*'s child *N'* and prune it using $LMFN_N$. We delay the counting of flow patterns and minimize the number of database scans needed at Lines 5-14. Line 15 updates $LMFS_{N'}$ with those maximal sets in $LMFN_N$ who contains all the events in node *N'*. Then we prune those unpromising extension events in *Ext(N')* at line 16 accordingly. Finally, we call DFS PathScan recursively to generate *N'* descendants at lines 17-18. This process is continued until all the nodes in the summary tree are generated or no additional frequent flow patterns are found.

Algorithm FlowMiner
Input: Database D;
*   Spatial relation R;*
*   Temporal relation W;*
*   Minimum support;*
Output: Set of frequent flow patterns M;

1. $M = \phi;$
2. $F_1 = \{all\ frequent\ location\text{-}based\ events,\ that\ is,\ 1\text{-}flow);$
3. $F_2 = \{all\ frequent\ 2\text{-}flow\};$
4. Fill Tbl with frequent length-2 sequences;
5. $i = 1;$
6. FOR each level 2 node N and $N \neq \phi;$
7. $LMFN_N = \phi;$
8. $F_i = DFS\text{-}PathScan\ (N,\ LMFN_N,\ Tbl,\ minsup);$
9. $M = M \cup F_i;$
10. $i ++;$
11. ENDFOR
12. Answer = M;
End Algorithm FlowMiner

Procedure Ext-combine (N', ext_i, N, minsup)
1. $C = \phi;$
2. FOR each $ext_j \in Ext(ext_i)$ DO
3.   IF ($ext_j \in Ext(N)$) && ($bitmap(ext_j) \cap bitmap(N') \geq minsup$))
4.   THEN $C = C \cup ext_j;$
5. ENDFOR
6. Return C
End Procedure Ext-combine

Procedure DFS-PathScan (N, $LMFS_N$, Tbl, minsup)
Pre-condition: $F = \phi;$
1. FOR each $ext_i \in Ext(N)$ DO
2. $N' = FlowCandGen\ (N,\ ext_i,\ Tbl);$
3.   Prune N' using $LMFS_N;$
4. $LMFS_N = \phi;$
5.   IF (k-flow $\in N'$ need to count)
6.   THEN Add these k-flow to path;
7.   IF (k-flow in path $\geq$ memory threshold)
8.   THEN Scan database for path;
9.   FOR each $\alpha \in$ path DO
10.   IF ($sup(\alpha) \geq minsup$)
11.   THEN $F = F \cup \{\alpha\};$
12.   IF ($\exists\ \beta \in N,\ \beta \leq \alpha$)
13.   THEN Update $LMFN_N$ s.t. $\{\gamma \in LMFN_N \mid \gamma \leq \alpha,\ \alpha \leq \gamma\};$
14.   ENDFOR
15. $LMFN_{N'} = LMFN_N \cup \{\alpha \in LMFN_N \mid ext_i \in \alpha\};$
16. $Ext(N') = Ext\text{-}combine\ (N',\ ext_i,\ N,\ minsup);$
17.   IF there are frequent or uncertain flows in N'

18.   *THEN DFS-PathScan (N', LMFN$_N$, Tbl, minsup);*
19. *ENDFOR*
20. *Return F;*
End Procedure DFS-PathScan

Performance Study

In this section, we present the results of experiments to evaluate the effectiveness and efficiency of FlowMiner on both synthetic and real-life datasets. The experiments are carried out on a Pentium 4, 1.6 GHZ processor with 256MB memory running Windows XP. The algorithm is implemented in C++.

Synthetic Dataset

We augment the Quest synthetic dataset generator in Agrawal and Srikant (1995) to include spatial information by generating N item using F spatial features and L locations. We generate synthetic datasets by setting N=10,000, F=1000 and L=100. The other parameters used in the experiments are listed in Table 8.1.

Real-Life Datasets

We also evaluate our algorithm on the following two real-life datasets. The characteristics of the datasets are shown in Table 8.2.

1. **Meteorological dataset.** We retrieve two years' worth of standard meteorological data for eight closely located stations from the Nation Data Buoy Center (http://www.ndbc.noaa.gov/rmd.shtml). The data consists of 10 continuous features being recorded at an hourly interval. We first discretize the features and then divide the space into grids for the locations to distribute uniformly.

2. **Forest Fire dataset.** Two years of forest fire satellite images, which include 2,495,097 forest fire occurrences, are obtained from a remote imaging center. We divide the region into 49 grids whereby each region

Table 8.1. Parameters used in the experiments

Parameters	Meaning	Range
|D|	Number of time windows (x10,000)	1, 2, 4, 6, 8, 10
|C|	Average number of eventsets per time window W	5, 10, 15, 20
|T|	Average number of events per Eventset	2, 4, 6, 8

Table 8.2. Characteristics of real-life dataset

Dataset	Number of locations	Number of features	Average length of eventsets	Number of eventsets
Meteorological	8	30	20	17520
Forest Fire	49	10	13	16650

is 10 degrees in the longitudinal direction and 10 degrees in the latitudinal direction.

Experiments on Synthetic Datasets

We first examine how the various parameters listed in Table 8.1 affect the performance of FlowMiner. Figure 8.8, Figure 8.9, Figure 8.10, and Figure 8.11 show the results for the synthetic dataset. In general, we observe that the runtime of FlowMiner increases when the minimum support is small. This is because many flow patterns become frequent and the length of the frequent flow patterns tends to be long when minimum support is small.

Figure 8.8 shows the effect when the parameter C (i.e., time window length W) varies from 5 to 20. The runtime of FlowMiner grows as C increases. This is expected as an increase in time window length implies a longer data sequence, which in turn implies longer flow patterns.

Figure 8.9 shows the runtime of FlowMiner for varying values of T. We observe that the runtime of FlowMiner grows as T increases because the size of an eventset and the length of the sequences in the databases become large. Hence, many flow patterns tend to be frequent and longer.

Figure 8.8.Effect of varying parameter C (synthetic dataset)

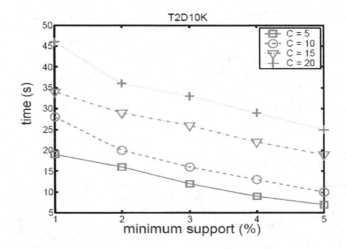

Figure 8.9. Effect of varying parameter T (synthetic dataset)

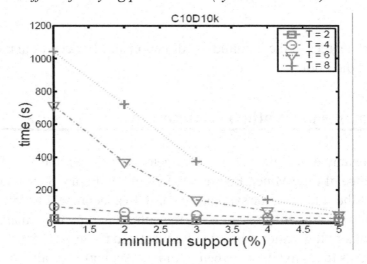

Figure 8.10 shows the performance of FlowMiner when the size of neighbor-hood relation R (i.e., length of a unit square) varies from 1 to 7. We observe that the runtime of FlowMiner remains almost constant, and grows slightly when R is 7. The explanation is: As the size of R increases, more events qualify as belonging to the spatial neighborhood of an event. As a result, the

length of frequent flow patterns tends to increase, and the number and size of candidates grow rapidly.

Finally, we evaluate the performance of FlowMiner by varying the parameter D that is the number of time windows from 20,000 to 100,000. Figure 8.11 shows that the time taken by FlowMiner scales well with the increase in number of time windows.

Figure 8.10. Effect of varying parameter R (synthetic dataset)

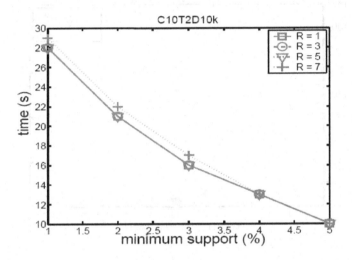

Figure 8.11. Varying parameter D (synthetic dataset)

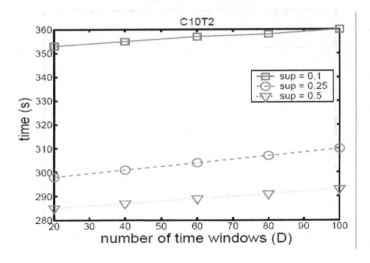

Experiments on Real-life Datasets

Next, we examine the performance of FlowMiner on real-life datasets. Figure 8.12 shows the results on the meteorological dataset for time window length of 6, 9, and 12 time units respectively, Figure 8.13 shows the results

Figure 8.12. Runtime vs. parameter minsup (real-life dataset)

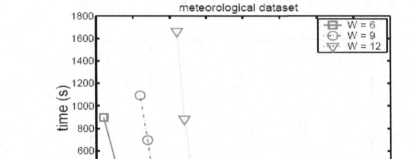

Figure 8.13. Runtime vs. spatial neighbor relation R

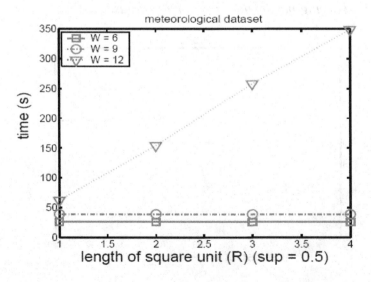

Figure 8.14. Scalability (real-life dataset)

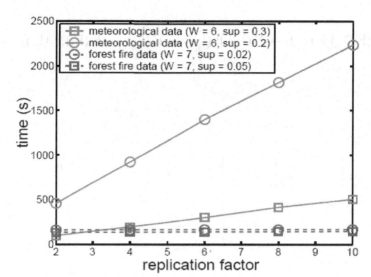

when the spatial neighbor relation R is varied, and Figure 8.14 shows the results when the size of the database is varied. The results are consistent with those obtained on the synthetic dataset. Note that in Figure 8.14, the replication factor is a value to inflate the database size to test the scalability of our algorithms.

We also discovered meaningful flow patterns in the real-life datasets. Figures 8.15 and 8.16 show samples of the flow patterns found in the forest fire dataset. These patterns have been cross-matched with weather maps. The events related to the *fire* in the patterns are indicated as the rectangle floated in the space according to time, and the corresponding locations are indicated using the white color in the space. The fire spots depict two distinct spread patterns: the first is from West to East as shown in Figure 8.16(a), which occurs mostly in March and the beginning of April; and the second is from South to Northwest as shown in Figure 8.16(b), which happens mostly in April and May.

Figure 8.15. Flow patterns [Trend 1: From West to East in March and April]

$$\langle F\,(l_{29}), F\,(l_{30})\rangle \rightarrow \langle F\,(l_{30}), F\,(l_{32})\rangle \rightarrow F\,(l_{38}) \rightarrow \langle F\,(l_{37}), F\,(l_{38})\rangle$$

(a)

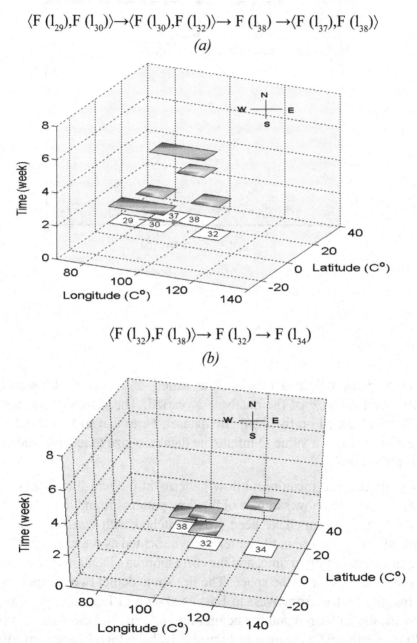

$$\langle F\,(l_{32}), F\,(l_{38})\rangle \rightarrow F\,(l_{32}) \rightarrow F\,(l_{34})$$

(b)

Figure 8.16. Flow patterns [Trend 2: From South to Northwest in April and May]

$$\langle F\,(l_{31}), F\,(l_{32})\rangle \rightarrow F\,(l_{38}) \rightarrow \langle F\,(l_{37}), F\,(l_{38})\rangle \rightarrow F\,(l_{37}) \rightarrow F\,(l_{29})$$

(a)

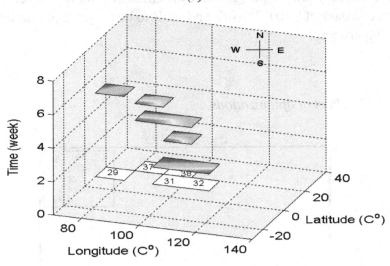

$$F\,(l_{6}) \rightarrow \langle F\,(l_{26}), F\,(l_{27})\rangle \rightarrow F\,(l_{32}) \rightarrow F\,(l_{38})$$

(b)

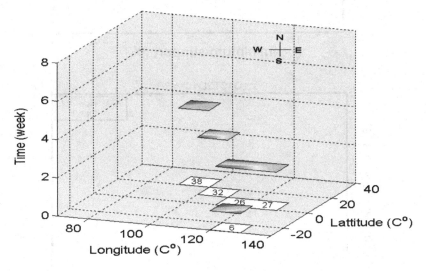

Evaluation of Optimization Techniques

Finally, we investigate how the three optimization techniques, namely, prune infrequent candidates (Opt1), eliminate hashing non-promising events (Opt2), and delay database scan (Opt3) enhance the efficiency of FlowMiner. We use the synthetic dataset C10T 2D10K, and set R to be a square of unit length 3 for this experiment.

Figure 8.17. Effect of optimizations

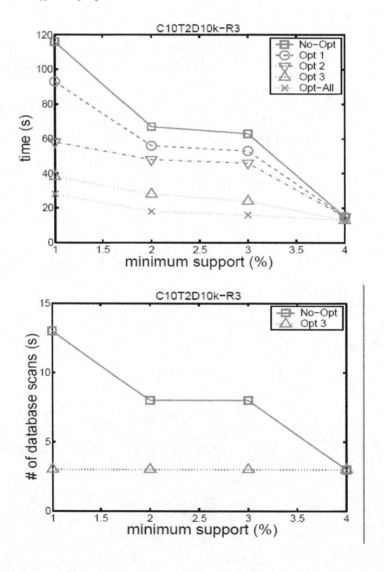

Figure 8.17 shows that the greatest gain is obtained by delaying database scans. This is to be expected because FlowMiner is a disk-based algorithm and the number of database scan plays an important role in its performance.

Comparative Study

We observe that FlowMiner reduces to a sequence mining algorithm when the spatial relation R is the whole space. This allows us to compare FlowMiner with existing sequence mining algorithms. Since FlowMiner is disk-based, we compare it with *GSP* and disk-based *PrefixSpan*, where instead of retrieving the projection databases of all the frequent items in one database scan, we divide them into multi-groups and get one group in a database scan. We implement GSP and PrefixSpan according to Agrawal and Srikant (1996), and Pei, Han, and Mortazavi-Asl (2001).

Figure 8.18 shows the results for the synthetic dataset C10T 2D10k. Figure 8.18(a) gives the runtime when the minimum support is varied, and Figure 8.18(b) records the amount of memory used by the three algorithms. We observe that FlowMiner outperforms GSP. PrefixSpan outperforms Flow-Miner when minimum support is large; but when minimum support is low, FlowMiner outperforms PrefixSpan. The amounts of memory used by both FlowMiner and GSP are much smaller than that used by PrefixSpan.

The results confirm that FlowMiner is more scalable as compared to Pre-fixSpan. When minimum support is large, the set of frequent sequences is small. Hence, PrefixSpan runs slightly faster than FlowMiner. However, when minimum support is low, we have many longer candidate sequences. As a result, PrefixSpan needs more time and memory to obtain and store the large number of projection databases. In contrast, FlowMiner, with its small set of candidates generated and its optimization techniques, is able to save much time and memory. Hence, FlowMiner excels at finding frequent sequences when minimum support is small.

We also compare the candidate generation of FlowMiner with the Apriori-like candidate generation such as GSP (Agrawal & Srikant, 1996), and the enumeration-based candidate generation f such as DFS Mine (Tsoukatos & Gunopulos, 2001) and SPADE (Zaki, 1998). Table 8.3 shows the results based on the synthetic dataset C10T 2D10k. We observe that the total number of candidates generated by FlowMiner is comparable to that by GSP algorithm, but much fewer than that by the enumeration-based process. Moreover, we see

Figure 8.18. Comparative study (sequence patterns)

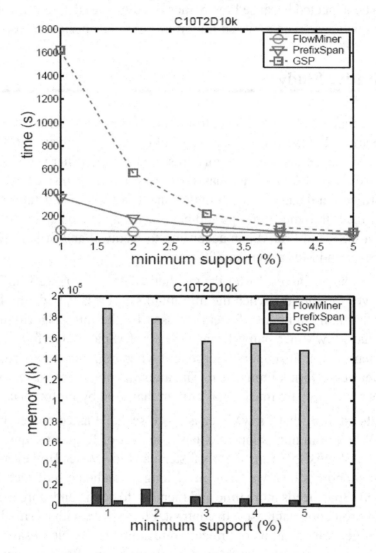

that the size of candidates really needed for counting support in FlowMiner is much smaller. This is due to FlowMiner's adoption of a depth-first search strategy, which could find long frequent patterns quickly. Another reason is the further improvement realized through using the filter *LMFN*, which helps decide the frequency of candidates quickly.

Table 8.3. Comparison of number of candidates generated

Algorithm	Support threshold					
	1	2	3	4	5	6
FlowMiner	15679	7573	3731	1832	891	428
FlowMiner (support)	515	62	35	33	31	29
GSP	15648	7543	3719	1820	879	416
enumeration-based	60926	30251	14962	7347	3582	1699

Summary

In this chapter, we have studied the problem of mining spatial sequence patterns. We have presented a new spatial sequence pattern called *flow patterns* to describe the changes of events over space and time. We have developed a depth-first algorithm FlowMiner to find flow patterns. We have also designed a new candidate generation algorithm that could quickly remove infeasible candidates by using both temporal and spatial relationships among events. In addition, we have proposed some optimization techniques to enhance the efficiency of FlowMiner. A comprehensive performance study shows that FlowMiner is able to discover the complete set of flow patterns efficiently with linear scalability.

References

Agrawal, R., & Srikant, R. (1995). Mining sequential patterns. In *Proceedings of the IEEE International Conference on Database Engineering,* Taipei, Taiwan, March 6-10 (pp. 3-14). Los Alamitos, CA: IEEE Computer Society Press.

Agrawal, R., & Srikant, R. (1996). Mining sequential patterns: Generalizations and performance improvements. In *Proceedings of the International Conference on Extending Database Technology,* Avignion, France, March 25-29 (pp. 3-17). Berlin/Heidelberg: Springer.

Pei, J., Han, J., & Mortazavi-Asl, B. (2001). PrefixSpan: Mining sequential patterns efficiently by prefix-projected pattern growth. In *Proceedings of the IEEE International Conference on Data Engineering,* Heidelberg, Germany, April 2-6 (pp. 215-224). Los Alamitos, CA: IEEE Computer Society Press.

Tsoukatos, I., & Gunopulos, D. (2001). Efficient mining of spatiotemporal patterns. In *Proceedings of the International Symposium on Advances in Spatial and Temporal Databases,* Redondo Beach, California, USA, July 12-15 (pp. 425-443). Berlin/Heidelberg: Springer.

Zaki, M. (1998). Efficient enumeration of frequent sequences. In *Proceedings of the International Conference on Information and Knowledge Management,* Bethesda, Maryland, USA, November 3-7 (pp. 68-75). New York: ACM Press.

Chapter IX

Mining Generalized
Flow Patterns

In the previous chapter, we describe *flow patterns* in spatio-temporal data-bases to capture the evolution of events in neighboring regions over time. While flow patterns can clearly capture the flow of events to some degree, they rely heavily on the assumption that these events will repeat themselves in exactly the same locations. However, in some applications, the absolute locations in which an event *e* has occurred are not important. Rather, it is the relative locations of events with respect to event *e* that are interesting. For example, an increase of rainfall at location *x* is followed by an increase of dengue fever cases in the Northeastern neighbourhood of *x*.

In this chapter, we investigate an efficient method to discover this class of relative-location sensitive flow patterns. These generalized flow patterns aim to summarize the sequential relationships between events that are prevalent in sharing the same topological structures. We adopt the pattern growth approach and develop an algorithm called GenSTMiner to discover these patterns. In order to increase the efficiency of the mining process, we also present two optimization techniques. The first is the use of conditional projected databases to prune infeasible events and sequences, and the second is pseudo projection to reduce memory requirement.

This chapter is organized as follows. We will extend the notations in the previous chapter for generalized flow patterns. We will discuss the concept of generalized flow patterns and present the algorithm GenSTMiner. The performance study indicates that GenSTMiner is highly efficient and out-performs PrefixSpan.

Notations and Terminologies

We denote a location as $l = (x, y)$, and a location-based event as $e(x, y, t)$. Figure 9.1 shows an example of a spatio-temporal database which records the various locations where cyclones and storms occur over time. The space (shown in Figure 9.1(b)) is partitioned into 25 disjoint locations, and the time is divided into three disjoint time windows. Figure 9.1(a) shows the events *{a, b, c, d, etc}* that are observed at various locations over time.

Some sequences in Figure 9.1(a) that satisfy the *flow pattern* definition are as follows:

$$<a (0, 0), f (0, 1)> \rightarrow d (1, 1)$$
$$<a (1, 2), f (1, 3)> \rightarrow d (2, 3)$$
$$<a (1, 1), f (1, 2)> \rightarrow d (2, 2)$$
$$<a (0, 2), f (0, 3)> \rightarrow d (1, 3)$$

Each of these flow patterns occurs only once and will be discarded by most mining algorithms. However, a closer examination reveals that these patterns actually convey some interesting behavior of the cyclones, that is, "*Event a in an area that has been hit by the storm always leads to event f in its Northern neighbors and event d in its Northeastern neighbors.*" In other words, the absolute locations in which event *a* have occurred are not important. Rather, it is the relative locations of event *d* or *f* with respect to the event *a* that are interesting.

We observe that relative addresses play an important role in capturing the invariant topological relationships of a pattern. In order to incorporate the

Figure 9.1. Example spatio-temporal database (W = 15 days, R = 1)

(a) Space-time view

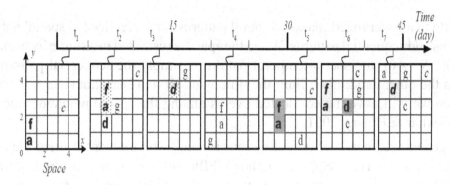

(b) Datasets of events

Window ID	Time	Eventsets
1	t1	a(0, 0), c(3, 2), f(0, 1)
	t2	a(1, 2), c(4, 4), d(1, 1), f(1, 3), g(2, 2)
	t3	d(2, 3), g(3, 4)
2	t4	a(1, 1), f(1, 2), g(0, 0)
3	t5	a(1, 1), c(4, 3), d(3, 0), f(1, 2)
	t6	a(0, 2),c(2, 1),c(3, 4),d(2, 2),f(0, 3),g(3, 3)
	t7	a(0, 4), c(2, 2), c(4, 4), d(1, 3), g(2, 4)

concept of relative addresses, we first select a *reference location* denoted as $l_{ref} = (x_{ref}, y_{ref})$. We map each occurring event $e_1(x_1, y_1)$, $e_2(x_2, y_2)$, ..., $e_m(x_m, y_m)$ to its corresponding relative occurring location as $e_1(x_1 - x_{ref}, y_1 - y_{ref})$, $e_2(x_2 - x_{ref}, y_2 - y_{ref})$, ..., $e_m(x_m - x_{ref}, y_m - y_{ref})$.

A *RelativeEventset* is a set of mapped events that occur at the same time t, denoted as $\hat{E} = E \langle e_1(x_1 - x_{ref}, y_1 - y_{ref}), e_2(x_2 - x_{ref}, y_2 - y_{ref}), ..., e_m(x_m - x_{ref}, y_m - y_{ref}) \rangle$. We assume that all events in a RelativeEventset are listed alphabetically. A RelativeEventset $\hat{E}_p$ is a *CloseNeighbor* of a RelativeEventset $\hat{E}_q$ if every event in $\hat{E}_p$ is a *CloseNeighbor* of every event in $\hat{E}_q$, denoted as $(\hat{E}_p, \hat{E}_q) \in (R, W)$.

Definition (Generalized Spatio-Temporal Pattern): A generalized spatio-temporal pattern is a sequence of RelativeEventsets, and all the RelativeEventsets are CloseNeighbors of each other, denoted as, $\hat{E}_1 \to \hat{E}_2$ $\to ... \to \hat{E}_m$, such that $(\hat{E}_i, \hat{E}_j) \in (R, W)$, $i, j \in (1..m)$.

Note that generalized spatio-temporal patterns can be reduced to spatial patterns and sequential patterns. When the space is restricted to a single location (i.e., $S \to 0$), the spatio-temporal pattern is simply the sequential pattern. On the other hand, if we limit the time window to a snapshot (i.e., $t \to 0$), then we will have the co-located events among the spatial neighborhoods (Shekhar & Huang, 2001).

A generalized spatio-temporal pattern is said to be frequent if there are at least *t-minsup* (i.e., temporal support) different occurrences of the pattern over time, and in each time window, there are at least *s-minsup* (i.e., spatial support) patterns occurring in the space. A generalized spatio-temporal pattern involving k different events is called a k-generalized spatio-temporal pattern.

Given two generalized spatio-temporal patterns, $P = \hat{E}_1 \to \hat{E}_2 \to ... \to \hat{E}_m$, and $Q = \hat{E}_1' \to \hat{E}_2' \to ... \to \hat{E}_m'$. Let P' be generated by concatenating P with Q, denoted as $P' = P \cdot Q$. P is called the *prefix* of P', and Q the *suffix* of P'. Q can be concatenated with P in two ways, namely Q is an *eventset extension*, that is, $\hat{E}_1 \to \hat{E}_2 \to ... \to (\hat{E}_m \cup \hat{E}_1') \to \hat{E}_2' \to ... \to \hat{E}_m'$, or Q is a *sequence extension*, that is, $\hat{E}_1 \to \hat{E}_2 \to ... \to (\hat{E}_m \to \hat{E}_1') \to \hat{E}_2' \to ... \to \hat{E}_m'$.

Suppose there is a lexicographic ordering $\leq$ among the set of events in the spatio-temporal database. For example, given two events $e_1(x_1, y_1)$ and $e_2(x_2, y_2)$, $e_1(x_1, y_1) \leq e_2(x_2, y_2)$ if and only if (1) $e_1 \leq e_2$, or (2) $e_1 = e_2$, $x_1 \leq x_2$, or (3) $e_1 = e_2$, $x_1 = x_2$, $y_1 \leq y_2$.

Here, we will focus on finding frequent generalized spatio-temporal patterns by exploiting their similarity to sequence patterns. Among many sequence mining algorithms, we focus on the pattern growth method because it has been shown to be one of the most effective methods for frequent pattern mining and is superior to the candidate-maintenance-test approach, especially on a dense database or where there is low minimum support threshold (Han, Pei, & Yin, 2000). As a divide-and-conquer method, the pattern growth method partitions the database into subsets recursively, but does not generate candidate sets. It also makes use of the Apriori property to prune the search space and count the frequent patterns in order to decide whether it can assemble longer patterns.

Generalized ST Patterns

The pattern growth approach in PrefixSpan utilizes a set of locally frequent items to grow patterns. We can adapt PrefixSpan to discover generalized spatio-temporal patterns.

First, we find all the frequent sequential patterns that satisfy *t-minsup*. Next, we scan each time window and check if there are *s-minsup* spatial-sequences which are instances of frequent sequential patterns, and all the eventsets in a spatial-sequence are CloseNeighbors, and add these sequences into the candidate sets. Finally, all the frequent generalized spatio-temporal patterns are obtained by mapping the spatial-sequences in the candidate sets into their relative addresses, where their support is larger than or equal to *s-minsup*.

Although PrefixSpan could find all the frequent generalized spatio-temporal patterns, it is neither efficient nor scalable as it needs to generate a set of candidates before pruning the infrequent ones. This requires the maintenance of a large number of candidates (sequences and spatial sequence patterns) in memory, and scanning the database at least two times.

In this section, we describe an efficient algorithm called GenSTMiner that follows the framework of pattern growth methods and finds the complete set of generalized spatio-temporal patterns directly without maintaining a large number of candidates. We also devise optimization techniques that eliminate redundant candidates, and reduce the size of the projected database so that it fits into the memory. The GenSTMiner algorithm consists of the following three steps:

First, find the set of frequent events F_1 (1-general spatial-sequences) by scanning the database once, and sort them according to their lexicographic order.

Next, divide the set of frequent patterns into $|F_1|$ partitions and retrieve the projected database PDB_e of each event $e \in F_1$ from the database D. Then, for each sequence in PDB_e, choose its reference location and map events in it into their relative locations. The transformed PDB_e is called the generalized projected database, denoted as GDB_e.

Finally, based on GDB_e, find all frequent k-generalized spatio-temporal patterns prefixed with e by constructing and mining the projected databases of the length-k generalized spatio-temporal patterns recursively.

The spatial support of an event in a time window can be determined by the number of different locations where it occurs, that is, an event is frequent in a time window if it occurs in at least *s-minsup* locations. The temporal support of an event is decided by the number of different time windows where it is spatially frequent. Only when the temporal support of an event is larger than *t-minsup*, it is considered frequent.

Note that in the second step, we use all the instances of an event e regardless of their locations in an input sequence in the database to retrieve the projection database of the event e. For the same instances of the event e (same location), we only consider the first occurrence of it. This differs from PrefixSpan which considers only the first occurrence of the event e in an input sequence.

Consider Figure 9.1. Suppose R = 1, W = 15 days, and the input sequence s1 = $\langle$a(0, 0), c(3, 2), f(0, 1)$\rangle$ → $\langle$a(1, 2), c(4, 4), d(1, 1), f(1, 3), g(2, 2)$\rangle$ → $\langle$d(2, 3), g(3, 4)$\rangle$. Suppose we want to retrieve the projection of s1$_a$. Since there are two instances of a in s1, namely a(0, 0) and a(1, 2), the projection of s1$_a$ consists of two sub-sequences: $\langle \ddagger$, c(3,2), f(0,1)$\rangle$ → $\langle$a(1,2), c(4,4), d(1,1), f(1,3), g(2,2)$\rangle$ → $\langle$d(2,3), g(3,4)$\rangle$ and $\langle \ddagger$, c(4,4), d(1,1), f(1,3), g(2,2)$\rangle$ → $\langle$d(2,3), g(3,4)$\rangle$. Figure 9.2 shows the *a*-projected database obtained from Figure 9.1.

Having obtained the projected database of the frequent events, we need to choose the reference locations of the sequences, and then map events in a

Figure 9.2. Projected database of event a

Wid	Sid	Sequences	Prefix
1	1	$\langle \ddagger$, c(3,2), f(0,1)$\rangle$ → $\langle$a(1,2), c(4,4), d(1,1), f(1,3), g(2,2)$\rangle$ → $\langle$d(2,3), g(3,4)$\rangle$	a(0, 0)
	2	$\langle \ddagger$, c(4,4), d(1,1), f(1,3), g(2,2)$\rangle$ → $\langle$d(2,3), g(3,4)$\rangle$	a(1, 2)
2	1	$\langle \ddagger$, f(1, 2), g(0, 0)$\rangle$	a(1, 1)
	1	$\langle \ddagger$, c(4, 3), d(3, 0), f(1, 2)$\rangle$ → $\langle$a(0, 2), c(2, 1), c(3, 4), d(2, 2), f(0, 3), g(3, 3)$\rangle$ → $\langle$a(0, 4), c(2, 2), c(4, 4), d(1, 3), g(2, 4)$\rangle$	a(1, 1)
3	2	$\langle \ddagger$, c(2, 1), c(3, 4), d(2, 2), f(0, 3), g(3, 3)$\rangle$ → $\langle$a(0, 4), c(2, 2), c(4, 4), d(1, 3), g(2, 4)$\rangle$	a(0, 2)
	3	$\langle \ddagger$, c(2, 2), c(4, 4), d(1, 3), g(2, 4)$\rangle$	a(0, 4)

sequence into their relative locations. Here, the problem is how to choose the reference location.

Choice of Reference Location

We can either use the location of the event e or the base location of a sequence as the reference location. The base location of a sequence s is given by $\{(x, y)|\forall x_{ij} \in s, y_{ij} \in s, x = min(x_{ij}), y = min(y_{ij})\}$. If we use the base location of a sequence as the reference location, then we may change the center of the topological structure to another event since the base locations of the sequences in the projected database may not be the locations of the event e.

For example, the a-projected database consists of two sequence $s_1 = d(0, 1) \rightarrow \langle a(1, 2), g(2, 2)\rangle$ and $s_2 = a(1, 2) \rightarrow \langle f(1, 3), g(2, 2)\rangle$, and $base(s_1) = (0, 1)$, $base(s_2) = (1, 2)$. If we choose the base locations of the sequences as the reference locations, then the center of the topological structure of s_1 is changed to the event d, instead of a.

Hence, to keep all the events in the generalized spatio-temporal patterns consistent in their topological structure, we use the location of the event e as the reference location. Figure 9.3 shows the generalized projected database of the event a.

Figure 9.3. Generalized projected database of event a

Wid	Sid	Sequences	LF
1	1	$\langle \sharp, c(3, 2), f(0, 1)\rangle \rightarrow \langle a(1, 2), c(4, 4),$ $d(1, 1), f(1, 3), g(2, 2)\rangle \rightarrow \langle d(2, 3),$ $g(3, 4)\rangle$	$\langle \sharp, c(3, 2)\rangle,$ $\langle \sharp, f(0, 1)\rangle,$ $d(1, 1),$
	2	$\langle \sharp, c(3, 2), d(0, -1), f(0, 1), g(1, 0)\rangle \rightarrow$ $\langle d(1, 1), g(2, 2)\rangle$	$g(2, 2)$
2	1	$\langle \sharp, f(0, 1), g(-1, -1)\rangle$	
3	1	$\langle \sharp, c(3, 2), d(2, -1), f(0, 1)\rangle \rightarrow$ $\langle a(-1, 1), c(1, 0), c(2, 3), d(1, 1),$ $f(-1, 2), g(2, 2)\rangle \rightarrow \langle a(-1, 3), c(1, 1),$ $c(3, 3), d(0, 2), g(1, 3)\rangle$	
	2	$\langle \sharp, c(2, -1), c(3, 2), d(2, 0), f(0, 1),$ $g(3, 1)\rangle \rightarrow \langle a(0, 2), c(2, 0), c(4, 2),$ $d(1, 1), g(2, 2)\rangle$	
	3	$\langle \sharp, c(2, -2), c(4, 0), d(1, -1), g(2, 0)\rangle$	

k-Generalized Spatio-Temporal Patterns

Having obtained the generalized projected database of an event e, we proceed to discover the frequent k-generalized spatio-temporal patterns ($k \geq 2$) that are prefixed with it.

We first find the set of the locally frequent events LF_e. Then, for each valid event in LF_e, we generate the $(k+1)$-generalized spatio-temporal patterns, construct its projected database, and mine it recursively. Note that in the projected database of a length-k generalized spatio-temporal pattern, the spatial support of a local event at time window i is decided by the number of sequences in the projected databases that contain it, and the temporal support is up to the number of time windows where it is spatially frequent.

For example, let $R = 1$, $W = 15$ days, $s\text{-}minsup = 2$ and $t\text{-}minsup = 2$. We want to retrieve all the frequent generalized spatio-temporal patterns prefixed with a in Figure 9.3. First, by mining GDB_a, we can obtain the set of its locally frequent events, that is, $LF_a = \{\langle \ddagger, c(3, 2)\rangle, \langle \ddagger, f(0, 1)\rangle, d(1, 1), g(2, 2)\}$.

Note that $\langle \ddagger, c(3, 2)\rangle$ means $c(3, 2)$ is an eventset extension, and $d(1, 1)$ a sequence extension. With LF_a, we can generate the following four frequent patterns:

$$\langle a(0, 0), c(3, 2)\rangle$$
$$\langle a(0, 0), f(0, 1)\rangle$$
$$a(0, 0) \rightarrow d(1, 1)$$
$$a(0, 0) \rightarrow g(2, 2)$$

However, since $\langle a(0, 0), c(3, 2)\rangle$ are not neighbors and $\langle a(0, 0), g(2, 2)\rangle$ are also not neighbors, only $P_{21} = \langle a(0,0), f(0,1)\rangle$ and $P_{22} = a(0,0) \rightarrow d(1,1)$ are the frequent 2-generalized spatio-temporal patterns.

Next, the frequent generalized spatio-temporal patterns prefixed with event a can be further partitioned into two subsets: one prefixed with P_{21}, and the other prefixed with P_{22}. We can construct their projected database respectively and mine them recursively. The process continues until there are no more valid locally frequent events found.

In a similar way, we can find the k-generalized spatio-temporal patterns prefixed with the events $c, d, f,$ and g respectively. The final set of frequent generalized spatio-temporal patterns is the collection of patterns found in the above recursive mining process.

Algorithm GenSTMiner

The GenSTMiner algorithm first scans the database once to find the frequent 1-generalized spatio-temporal patterns F_1 (line 2), treats each $e_k \in F_1$ as a prefix, builds its projected database PDB_{ek}, and then transforms PDB_{ek} into GDB_{ek} (lines 3-5). Next, it calls the sub-routine Ptngrowth method (line 6). The sub-routine Pattern-growth method recursively calls itself and works as follows: For prefix e, it scans its projected database once to find its locally frequent events (line 9), it grows e with each valid locally frequent event to get a new prefix e', it builds the projected database for the new prefix, and it calls itself recursively (lines 12-16).

Algorithm GenSTMiner
Input: Spatio-temporal database D;
          Size of spatial neighbour relation R;
          Size of time window W;
          Minimum spatial support s-minsup;
          Minimum temporal support t-minsup
Output : Set of generalized spatio-temporal patterns M ;
1. M = φ;
2. F_1 = {all the frequent events};
3. FOR each $e_k \in F_1$ do
4. PDB_{ek} = projected database (D, e_k);
5.   Convert PDB_{ek} into generalized format GDB_{ek};
6.   Call Ptn-growth (e_k, GDB_{ek}, s-minsup, t-minsup);
7. Return M;
End Algorithm GenSTMiner

Procedure Ptn-growth(α, $PDB_{α}$, s-minsup, t-minsup)
8.   M = M ∪ α;
9. $PDB_{α}$ once to get all the frequent LF;
10. IF LF is empty THEN
11.   RETURN;
12. FOR each β ∈ LF DO
13.   IF ∀ e_i ∈ in α, (e_i, e_j) ∈ (R,W) THEN

14. $\alpha' = \alpha \cdot e_j$;
15. $PDB_{\alpha'} = projected\ database\ (PDB_{\alpha'},\ \alpha')$;
16. $Call\ Ptn\text{-}growth\ (\alpha',\ PDB_{\alpha'},\ s\text{-}minsup,\ t\text{-}minsup)$;
17.   *Return*
End Procedure Ptn-growth

Compared to PrefixSpan, the algorithm GenSTMiner can find the complete set of generalized spatio-temporal patterns by generating a much smaller set of candidates. The following section describes optimization techniques to reduce further the number of candidates generated and the memory requirement.

Conditional Projected Database

We observe that not every event or eventset in the sequence in the database participates in generalized spatio-temporal patterns. In order to eliminate those events or eventsets that are not promising in the projected database of an event, we introduce the concept of the conditional database with respect to an event e.

Given an input sequence s in the database D, the conditional spatial-sequences with respect to an event e of s is the set of sub-sequences of s prefixed with e, and each of them is a spatial-sequence and all the eventsets in these sub-sequence are CloseNeighbors of the event e.

For example, suppose we are given an input sequence $s = \langle a(0,\ 0),\ c(3,\ 2),\ f(0,\ 1)\rangle \rightarrow \langle a(1,\ 2),\ c(4,\ 4),\ d(1,\ 1),\ f(1,\ 3),\ g(2,\ 2)\rangle \rightarrow \langle d(2,\ 3),\ g(3,\ 4)\rangle$, and $R = 1$, $W = 15$ days. We want to retrieve the conditional spatial sequence of the event a. Notice that there are only two instances of a in s, i.e., $a(0,\ 0)$ and $a(1,\ 2)$. First, for the instance $a(0,\ 0)$, there are only two events $f(0,\ 1)$ and $d(1,\ 1)$ in s that can form a conditional spatial sequence together with $a(0,\ 0)$; for the instance $a(1,\ 2)$, the events $d(1,\ 1), f(1,\ 3), g(2,\ 2)$ and $d(2,\ 3)$ are valid. Hence, the final s_a consists of two sequences $\langle a(0,\ 0), f(0,\ 1)\rangle \rightarrow d(1,\ 1)$ and $\langle a(1,\ 2),\ d(1,\ 1),\ f(1,\ 3),\ g(2,\ 2)\rangle \rightarrow d(2,\ 3)$.

The collection of all the conditional spatial-sequences with respect to an event e in the database D forms the conditional database with respect to the event e. All the conditional spatial-sequences are ordered according to their time.

The algorithm GenSTMiner obtains the projected database of an event e from its conditional database, instead of database D. This effectively filters off unpromising events from the projected databases of the event e. For simplicity, we call the projected databases of an event e retrieved from the conditional database as the *conditional projected databases* with respect to the event e or *e-conditional projected databases*.

For example, Figure 9.4 shows the a-conditional projected database retrieved from Figure 9.1 by setting $R = 1$. Clearly, the a-conditional projected database is much more compact than the a-projected database in Figure 9.2.

While the conditional database can be used to remove events that are not promising from the event e-projected database, there remain other non-promising events when we further construct the projected database of length-k ($k>2$) generalized spatio-temporal patterns. We use the Apriori checking as in Pei, Han, and Mortazavi-Asl (2001) to prune events during the construction of the projected databases of length-k generalized spatio-temporal patterns.

In order to construct the P-conditional projected database, where P is a length-l generalized spatio-temporal pattern, let E be the last element of P and P' be the prefix of P such that $P = P' \cdot E$.

If $P' \cdot x$ is not frequent, then event x can be excluded from projection. For example, if we know that $a(0, 0) \rightarrow g(0, 1)$ is not frequent, then event $g(0, 1)$ can be excluded from the construction of "$a(0, 0) \rightarrow d(1, 1)$"-conditional projected databases.

However, if $P' \cdot x$ is frequent, but there exists $e \in P$, such that $\langle e, x \rangle \notin R$, then event x can be excluded from the projection. For example, let $R = 1$ and $\langle a(0, 0), g(-1, -1) \rangle$ is frequent, but since $\langle f(0, 1), g(-1, -1) \rangle \notin R$, we can remove $g(-1, -1)$ from the construction of $\langle a(0, 0), f(0, 1) \rangle$-conditional projected database.

Moreover, let E' be formed by substituting any item in E by x. If $P' \cdot E'$ is not frequent, then event x can be excluded. For example, suppose $a(0, 0) \rightarrow \langle b(0,$

Figure 9.4. a-conditional projected database

Wid	Sid	Conditional spatial-sequences	Prefix
1	1	$\langle \sharp, f(0, 1) \rangle \rightarrow \langle d(1, 1) \rangle$	$a(0, 0)$
	2	$\langle \sharp, d(1, 1), f(1, 3), g(2, 2) \rangle \rightarrow d(2, 3)$	$a(1, 2)$
2	1	$\langle \sharp, f(1, 2), g(0, 0) \rangle$	$a(1, 1)$
3	1	$\langle \sharp, f(1, 2) \rangle \rightarrow \langle a(0, 2), c(2, 1), d(2, 2) \rangle \rightarrow c(2, 2)$	$a(1, 1)$
	2	$\langle \sharp, f(0, 3) \rangle \rightarrow d(1, 3)$	$a(0, 2)$
	3	$\langle \sharp, d(1, 3) \rangle$	$a(0, 4)$

1), $f(1, 1)\rangle$ is not frequent. To construct $a(0, 0) \rightarrow \langle b(0, 1), c(0, 1)\rangle$-projected database, the conditional spatial-sequence $a(0, 0) \rightarrow \langle (b(0, 1), c(0, 1), f(1, 1), g(1, 1)\rangle \rightarrow d(0, 1)$ should be projected to $\langle \ddagger, g(1, 1)\rangle \rightarrow d(0, 1)\rangle$.

Pseudo Projection

In general, we obtain projected databases by scanning the sequences at each time window in the databases. However, after scanning the projected databases, we have known the time windows in which the locally frequent event e is not spatially frequent. Hence, there is no need to scan such time windows to get the projection sequences of the event e.

For example in Figure 9.1, we know that event a is not spatially frequent at time window 2. Hence, we can stop retrieving projection of sequences prefixed with a at time window 2.

This optimization can be realized as follows. For each locally frequent event e, we use a bitmap to record the time windows in which it is frequent. We only retrieve the projection of the sequences from the time windows where its corresponding value in the bitmap is set to 1. In addition, we could get the frequent period of a generalized spatio-temporal pattern by scanning the bitmap once.

When we retrieve the conditional projected database with respect to an event e, we observe that an event e_k in the sequence in the database may appear many times in the e-conditional projected database. The cost of the projection (constructing the conditional projected database recursively) becomes a major cost in GenSTMiner. We can use the pseudo projection technique in PrefixSpan to reduce the cost of the projection.

In PrefixSpan, pseudo projection is used to avoid physically copying suffixes. When the database can be held in main memory, instead of constructing a physical projection by collecting all suffixes, pseudo projection uses pointers referring to the sequences in the database. Every projection consists of two pieces of information $\langle pointer, offset\rangle$, where *pointer* points to the sequence in the database and *offset* indicates the start position of the suffix in the sequences.

Unlike PrefixSpan where only the first occurrence of an item is considered, GenSTMiner needs to consider the suffixes in an input sequence prefixed with different instances of the event e. Hence, the problem of pseudo projection becomes more complicated.

Figure 9.5. Example of pseudo projection

s=⟨a(0,0), c(3,2), f(0,1)⟩ → ⟨a(1,2), c(4,4), d(1,1), f(1,3), g(2,2)⟩ → ⟨d(2, 3), g(3, 4)⟩			
	prefix	physical projection	pseudo projection
s_a	a(0, 0)	⟨‡, f (0, 1)⟩ → d(1, 1)	⟨*pointer to s, 3, 10010000, (0,0)*⟩
	a(1, 2)	⟨‡, d(1, 1), f(1, 3), g(2, 2)⟩ → d(2, 3)	⟨*pointer to s, 6, 11110, (1,2)*⟩

In GenSTMiner, every projection consists of four pieces of information: ⟨*pointer, offset, bitmap, refloc*⟩, where *pointer* points to the sequence in the database, *offset* indicates the start position of the suffixes in the sequence, *bitmap* indicates the appearance of the events in the suffixes of the sequence in the conditional spatial sequence with respect to the event *e*, size of *bitmap* is equivalent to the number of events in the suffixes of the sequence, and *refloc* stores the reference location of the conditional spatial sequence. Figure 9.5 shows an example of the pseudo projection of a sequence in the database.

Performance Evaluation

We implemented the algorithms in C++ and evaluated their performance on both synthetic and real-life datasets. The experiments were carried out on a Pentium 4, 1.6 GHZ processor with 256MB memory running Windows XP.

Experiments on Synthetic Dataset

We augment the IBM Quest synthetic data generator (http://www.almaden. ibm.com/software/quest) to include spatial information by generating N items using F spatial features and L locations. We generate datasets by setting N=10,000, F=1,000, L=100. The other parameters are D, number of sliding windows (= size of Database); C, average number of eventsets in a sliding window; and T, average number of events in an eventset.

We evaluate the performance of GenSTMiner on the synthetic dataset C10T 10D10k by varying the parameters *R*, *t-minsup*, and *s-minsup*. We test the performance of GenSTMiner with and without optimization techniques and compare it with PrefixSpan. The results are shown in Figure 9.6, Figure 9.7,

Figure 9.6. Runtime vs. parameter R

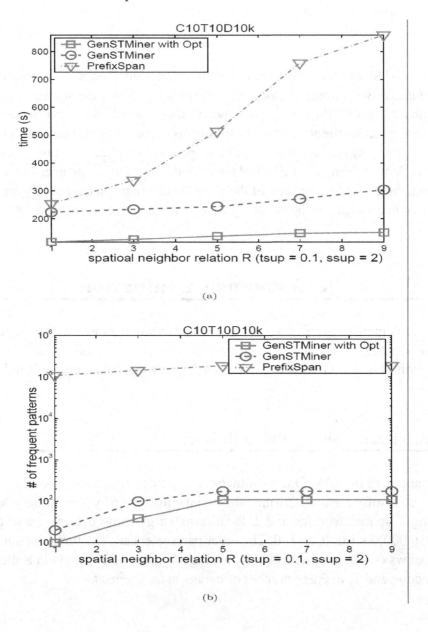

Figure 9.7. Runtime vs. parameter t-minsup

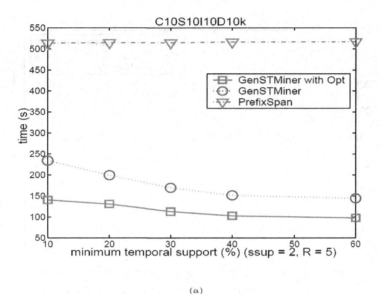

(a)

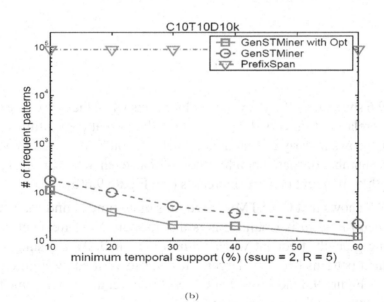

(b)

and Figure 9.8. The results indicate that GenSTMiner outperforms PrefixS-pan, especially when it uses optimization techniques. This is expected as the pruning techniques we use in GenSTMiner not only reduce the size of the projected databases, but also eliminate infeasible events and sequences.

Figure 9.8. Runtime vs. parameter s-minsup

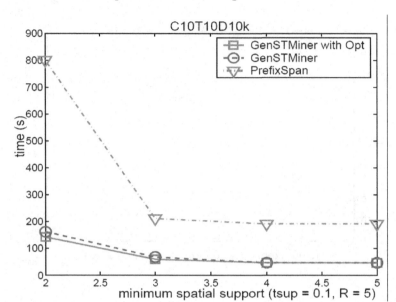

Figure 9.6 shows the efficiency of the algorithms when the size of the spatial neighbor relation R is varied. Figure 9.6(a) shows that the runtime of Gen-STMiner grows linearly as spatial neighbor relation R increases. When R is large, the number of spatial neighborhoods of an event tends to be large, and the length of frequent patterns increases (see Figure 9.6(b)).

Figure 9.7 shows that GenSTMiner requires more time to find frequent patterns when *t-minsup* is small. This is due to more local frequent patterns becoming globally frequent when *t-minsup* is small. As a result, the size of frequent patterns becomes larger. This is also verified by Figure 9.7(b). Similarly, Figure 9.8 indicates that GenSTMiner requires more time to find frequent patterns when *s-minsup* is small.

We also investigate the scalability of GenSTMiner in terms of database size. Figure 9.9 shows the runtime of GenSTMiner when the parameter D (i.e., number of sliding windows) is varied from 20k to 100k. Figure 9.9 indicates that GenSTMiner grows linearly with database size. In other words, GenST-Miner is able to scale well for large datasets.

Figure 9.9. Scalability

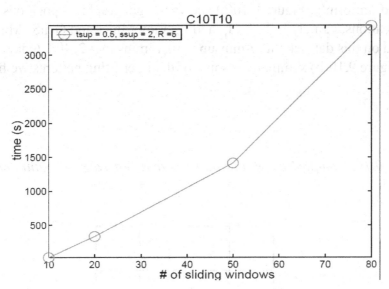

Comparative Study

This set of experiments aims to show the usefulness of generalized spatio-temporal patterns as compared to flow patterns using a real-life dataset. We obtain three years of standard meteorological data from five stations that are closely located in space from the Nation Data Buoy Center. The dataset has 10 features that are recorded hourly. After discretization, the final dataset contains 30 features. With these 30 features, we define a set of meteorological events. A sample of the events defined is as follows:

$A{\uparrow}(l_a)$ (or $A{\downarrow}(l_a)$): denote the event that the air temperature at location l_a has increased (or decreased);

$S{\uparrow}(l_a)$ (or $S{\downarrow}(l_a)$): denotes the event that the wind speed at location l_a has increased (or decreased); and

$G{\uparrow}(l_a)$ (or $G{\downarrow}(l_a)$): denotes the event that the gust speed at location l_a has increased (or decreased).

We divide the whole space into 4×4 grids so that the five locations are distributed uniformly. Figure 9.10(a) shows the geographical positions of the five locations, namely l_2, l_7, l_{10}, l_{12} and l_{15}. FlowMiner and GenSTMiner are applied on this dataset with t-minsup = 10, s-minsup = 2, $W = 6$ days and $R = 2$. Figure 9.10(b) summarizes some of the interesting patterns we find.

Figure 9.10. Comparison of flow patterns and generalized spatio-temporal patterns

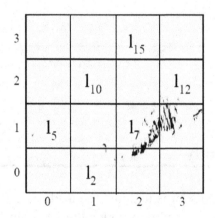

(a) Neighbor relations

Flow Patterns
$A \uparrow (l_2) \rightarrow G \uparrow (l_7), S \uparrow (l_7) \langle \rightarrow \langle G \downarrow (l_{10}), S \downarrow (l_{10}), G \downarrow (l_{12}), S \downarrow (l_{12}) \rangle$
$\langle A \uparrow (l_{10}), A \uparrow (l_{12}) \rangle \rightarrow \langle G \uparrow (l_{15}), S \uparrow (l_{15}) \rangle$
$\langle G \uparrow (l_{10}), S \uparrow (l_{10}) \rangle \rightarrow A \uparrow (l_{15})$
$\langle G \uparrow (l_7), S \uparrow (l_7) \rangle \rightarrow \langle A \uparrow (l_{10}), A \uparrow (l_{12}) \rangle$
$\langle G \uparrow (l_{10}), S \uparrow (l_{10}) \rangle \rightarrow \langle G \downarrow (l_{15}), S \downarrow (l_{15}) \rangle$

Generalized Spatio-Temporal Patterns
$A \uparrow (0,0) \rightarrow \langle G \uparrow (1,1), S \uparrow (1,1) \rangle$
$\langle G \uparrow (0,0), S \uparrow (0,0) \rangle \rightarrow A \uparrow (1,1)$
$\langle G \uparrow (0,0), S \uparrow (0,0) \rangle \rightarrow \langle G \downarrow (1,1), S \downarrow (1,1) \rangle$

(b) Interesting frequent patterns

We observe that flow patterns are able to capture the flow of events such as: an increase in air temperature at location l_2 leads to an increase in wind speed and gust speed at location l_7; and an increase in air temperature at location l_{10} leads to an increase in wind speed and gust speed at location l_{15}. However, the usefulness of these flow patterns is rather limited as they are unable to provide a general trend.

On the other hand, the generalized spatio-temporal pattern reveals the trend that whenever there is an increase in air temperature at a specific location, we can expect an increase in wind speed and gust speed at the Northeastern neighbor of the location. By knowing the general trend, the meteorologist can perform more accurate forecast of the weather.

Summary

In the chapter, we have discussed another type of spatial sequence patterns, namely, *generalized spatio-temporal patterns*. We have shown that generalized flow patterns are able to summarize the sequential relationships between events that share the same topological structures. We have presented a pattern growth approach to discover such patterns and designed an algorithm called GenSTMiner. Two optimizations are used to improve the performance of GenSTMiner. Infeasible events and sequences are pruned using conditional projected databases, and pseudo projection are employed to reduce the memory requirement. We have evaluated the algorithm on both synthetic and real-life datasets. The results indicate that GenSTMiner is effective and scalable in mining frequent generalized spatio-temporal patterns.

In the next two chapters, we will present algorithms to discover arbitrary complex spatio-temporal patterns in the form of tree patterns and graph patterns.

References

Han, J., Pei, J., & Yin, Y. (2000). Mining frequent patterns without candidate generation. In *Proceedings of the ACM SIGMOD Conference on*

Management of Data, Dallas, Texas, USA, May 16-18 (pp. 1-12). New York: ACM Press.

Pei, J., Han, J., & Mortazavi-Asl, B. (2001). PrefixSpan: Mining sequential patterns efficiently by prefix-projected pattern growth. In *Proceedings of the IEEE International Conference on Data Engineering,* Heidelberg, Germany, April 2-6 (pp. 215-224). Los Alamitos, CA: IEEE Computer Society Press.

Shekhar, S., & Huang, Y. (2001). Discovery of spatial co-location patterns. In *Proceedings of the International Symposium on Advances in Spatial and Temporal Databases,* Redondo Beach, California, USA, July 12-15 (pp. 236-256). Berlin/Heidelberg: Springer.

Chapter X

Mining Spatio-Temporal Trees

Flow patterns and the generalized spatio-temporal patterns can easily be modeled as trees/graphs with each vertex representing a variable labeled by the event, and each edge representing a spatial relationship, temporal relationship, or both. Take the flow pattern $\langle F\,(l_{32}),\ F\,(l_{38})\rangle \to F\,(l_{32}) \to F\,(l_{34})$ as an example, the corresponding tree representation of the pattern is shown in Figure 10.1. In this tree representation, we model the "precede" temporal relationship as an edge.

Figure 10.1. Tree representation of a flow pattern

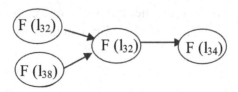

With suitable modeling, all spatio-temporal databases can be correspondingly transformed into a tree or graph database, and the problem of mining frequent spatio-temporal patterns then becomes the problem of finding frequent tree/sub-graphs. In this chapter, we examine the problem of mining spatio-temporal tree patterns.

We observe that many spatio-temporal trees patterns are both unordered and embedded. Unordered refers to the condition that the sequence between children of the same parent is not important (for example, the tree with bedroom1 as the left son and bedroom2 as the right son is the same as the tree with bedroom2 as the left son and bedroom 1 as the right son) while embedded suggests that it is not necessary to strictly keep the parent-child relations among nodes.

Existing tree mining algorithms treat data trees as either ordered or induced (Asai, Abe, & Kawasoe, 2002; Asai, Arimura, & Uno, 2003 ; Chi, Yang, & Muntz, 2003, 2004; Chi, Yang, & Xia, 2004; Miyahara, Shoudai, & Uchida, 2001; Nijssen & Kok, 2003; Wang, Hong, & Pei, 2004; Wang & Liu, 2000; Xiao, Yao, & Li, 2003; Yang, Lee, & Hsu, 2003; Zaki, 2002). In these cases, some candidates may not be correctly counted and interesting patterns may be lost. Compared to the other three classes of tree mining algorithms (i.e., the ordered induced sub-tree mining algorithms, the ordered embedded sub-tree mining algorithms, and the unordered induced sub-tree mining algorithms), the unordered embedded sub-tree mining algorithms usually have much higher complexities for two reasons. First, they require more complicated matching functions which have been proven to be NP-complete (Kilpeläinen, 1992). Second, they generate a larger candidate set which significantly increases the number of matches and database traversals.

To address these issues, we present a divide-and-conquer method called WTIMiner to efficiently mine unordered embedded sub-tree patterns. We introduce the notion of mapping equivalent class, and develop a framework for mining frequent sub-trees via frequent itemset mining. The new algorithm suffers less from combinatorial explosion as compared to normal candidate-generate-and-test methods, with the number of database scans strictly bounded by the number of frequent itemsets generated. The proposed algorithm discovers the complete set of unordered and embedded sub-trees patterns, and can be easily modified to mine other types of sub-tree patterns. Experimental results confirm the efficiency of WTIMiner in both time and space.

Preliminaries

A *tree* is an acyclic connected graph. A *forest* is a collection of trees. A *rooted tree* is a tree in which a particular vertex is designated as the *root*. A *labeled tree* is a tree each of whose nodes is associated with a label. For any node $u \in N$, $L(u)$ is the label of u. An *edge labeled tree* is a tree whose edges are labeled. A labeled and rooted tree can be denoted as $T(r, N, L, E)$, where $r \in N$ is the root node; N is the set of nodes; L is the set of node labels; and E is the set of edges in the tree. In this chapter, we assume that all the trees are labeled and rooted unless specifically indicated. A *leaf* of a tree refers to the non-root node that has the degree of 1. The *size* of a tree T is the number of nodes in the tree, which is denoted as $|T|$.

For any two nodes u and v of a rooted tree T, if u is on the unique path from the root to v, u is called an *ancestor* of v and v is called a *descendent* of u, denoted as $u <_n v$ or $v >_n u$ (n is a non-negative integer which indicates the number of nodes between u and v); if $u <_0 v$ or $v >_0 u$, u is also called the *parent* of v and v a *child* of u. Further, if u and v have the same parent, we say that they are *siblings*; if neither $u <_n v$ nor $v <_n u$ stands, we say that u and v are *embedded siblings*. The *level* of a node v is the length of the simple path from the root to v. The *height* of a rooted tree is the maximum level that occurs in the tree.

An *ordered tree* is a rooted tree in which all children of the same parent node are uniquely numbered. An *unordered tree* is a rooted tree in which the children of each node are not ordered. For any two siblings, u and v, of a rooted ordered tree T, if u appears before v in a prefix-order traversal of T, we denote $u < v$, or $v > u$.

Two labeled trees T_1 and T_2 are *isomorphic* to each other if and only if there is a one-to-one mapping f from the vertices of T_1 to the vertices of T_2 that preserves vertex labels, edges labels, and adjacency (Chi, Yang, & Muntz, 2003). An *automorphism* of is an isomorphism from a tree to itself.

A tree P is a *sub-tree* of another tree T if and only if P is included in T under certain inclusion rules: Given a data tree $T(r, N, L, E)$ and a pattern tree $P(r_p, N_p, L_p, E_p)$, f is a one-to-one mapping from nodes of P to nodes of T. We say that:

P is an *ordered sub-tree* of T if and only if (1) $N_p \subseteq N$; (2) $\forall \, u_p \subseteq N_p$, $L(u_p) = L(f(u_p))$; (3) $\forall \, u_p, v_p \subseteq N_p$, $u_p < v_p$ if and only if $f(u_p) < f(v_p)$. If the matching does not satisfy (iii), we say that P is an *unordered sub-tree* of T.

P is an *induced sub-tree* of T if and only if (1) $N_p \subseteq N$; (2) $\forall \, u_p \in N_p$, $L(u_p) = L(f(u_p))$; (3) $\forall \, u_p, v_p \in N_p$, $u_p <_0 v_p$ if and only if $f(u_p) <_0 f(v_p)$. If we change (3) into: $\forall \, u_p, v_p \in N_p$, if $u_p <_0 v_p$, $f(u_p) <_n f(v_p)$, P is called an *embedded sub-tree* of T.

In other words, P is an ordered sub-tree of T if and only if P can be obtained by deleting nodes and edges of T; P is an unordered sub-tree of T if and only if P is isomorphic to an ordered sub-tree of T. An induced sub-tree of T strictly preserves the parent-child relations between nodes, whereas an embedded sub-tree of T only follows the ancestor-descendent relations.

Sub-tree matching refers to the process of finding a required sub-tree structure P in T. We denote $Match(P, T) = 1$ if P is a sub-tree of T, and $Match(P, T) = 0$ if otherwise.

Sub-Tree Categorization

Given a data tree T and a pattern tree P, if we consider whether the sub-tree matching involved is ordered or unordered, embedded or induced, then we have the following four categories of sub-trees (see Figure 10.2):

P is a *strong sub-tree* of T if and only if P is both an ordered and induced sub-tree of T.

P is a *permutable sub-tree* of T if and only if P is both an unordered and induced sub-tree of T.

P is a *reducible sub-tree* of T if and only if P is both an ordered and embedded sub-tree of T.

P is a *weak sub-tree* of T if and only if P is both an unordered and embedded sub-tree of T.

Figure 10.2. Examples of four categories of sub-trees: (a) strong; (b) permutable;(c) reducible; (d) weak

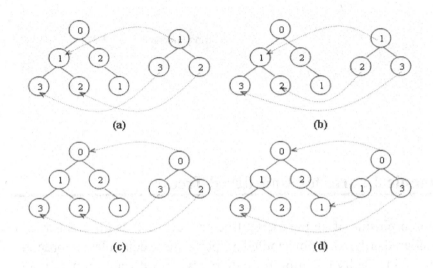

(a)   (b)

(c)   (d)

DFS String Encoding

This method was first introduced by Zaki (2002). It encodes an ordered tree with a string by following Depth First preorder Search (DFS) of the tree, adding the current node's label to the string. A unique backtrack label "-1" is also added whenever tracing from a child to its parent. Figure 10.3 illustrates an example tree and its DFS encoding.

Since the total number of backtrack items is exactly the same as the number of edges in the tree, the space cost for DFS encoding is $O(2|T|)$. Encoding a tree can be completed within a pre-order traversal with a time complexity of $O(|T|)$, whereas constructing a tree from DFS encoding takes $O(2|T|)$ time. Several variations of this representation include depth-labeled-sequence (Asai, Arimura, & Uno, 2003), DFCS (Chi, Yang, & Xia, 2004), l-sequence and l^2-sequence (Wang, Hong, & Pei, 2004).

Figure 10.3. Examples of DFS string encoding

DFS String Encoding: 0 1 3 -1 2 -1 -1 2 1 -1 -1

Canonical Form for Unordered Trees

Automorphisms of an unordered tree are regarded as different trees when considered ordered. If not handled properly, these equivalent unordered trees may lead to faulty counting for patterns when we want to mine unordered trees. Hence, it is important to select one as the representative, which is called the *canonical form*.

In contrast to works that use canonical forms for unique enumeration of unordered candidate trees (Asai, Arimura, & Uno, 2003; Chi, Yang, & Muntz, 2004; Chi, Yang, & Xia, 2004; Nijssen & Kok, 2003), we use our canonical form definition to achieve a uniform encoding of trees since tree enumeration is avoided in our work. The definition of our canonical form is as follows:

Label Ordering: Node labels are in the same order as we commonly use. We use the "$<_c$" symbol to represent the "less than" relation between node labels, and the "$=_c$" symbol to represent the "equal to" relation. The backtrack symbol "-1" of the DFS encoding is smaller than any node labels.

String Ordering: For two arbitrary nodes N_1 and N_2, $s(N_1)$ and $s(N_2)$ are DFS string encodings of sub-tree rooted at N_1 and N_2 respectively. Then $s(N_1)$ $<_c s(N_2)$ if and only if $s(N_1)$ is smaller than $s(N_2)$ in a string comparison, and $s(N_1) =_c s(N_2)$ if and only if $s(N_1)$ and $s(N_2)$ are equal in a string comparison.

Sibling Ordering: For two arbitrary nodes N_1 and N_2 of the same parent, N_1 is the left sibling of N_2 if and only if $L(N_1) <_c L(N_2)$ or $L(N_1) =_c L(N_2)$.

The problem of mining frequent sub-trees can be stated as follows:

Given a tree database TDB and a minimum support threshold σ ∈ [0,1], let P be a pattern tree and T be any tree in TDB. The occurrence of P in TDB: occ(P) = $\Sigma_{T \in TDB}$ Match(P, T) and the support of P in D: support(P) = occ(P)/|TDB|. A pattern P is considered frequent (or σ-frequent) in TDB if and only if support(P) ≥ σ. A frequent sub-tree mining problem is the problem that finds all frequent sub-trees of TDB.

Related Work

Many tree mining algorithms have been proposed, with wide applications in semi-structured document mining (Termier, Rousset, & Sebag, 2002), query pattern mining (Yang, Lee, & Hsu, 2003), Web usage mining (Wang & Liu, 2000; Zaki, 2002), Web access mining (Chi, Yang, & Muntz, 2004; Xiao, Yao, & Li, 2003), RNA topology mining (Zaki, 2002), and so forth.

Zaki (2002) and Asai, Abe, and Kawasoe (2002) presented TreeMiner and FREQT to mine reducible and strong sub-trees. These algorithms utilized the rightmost path expansion method to efficiently and uniquely enumerate ordered trees. This approach was further applied in other tree mining algorithms (Chi, Yang, & Xia, 2004; Nijssen & Kok, 2003; Yang, Lee, & Hsu, 2003). Chi, Yang, and Muntz (2004) used a breadth-first method to uniquely grow candidates along the lower borders and handle permutable trees. Wang and Liu (2000) and Xiao, Yao, and Li (2003) adopted Apriori itemset algorithms to mine frequent path sets in permutable trees. Wang, Hong, and Pei (2004) devised two pattern growth methods, Chopper and XSpanner, to mine reducible sub-trees via frequent sequences.

The only algorithm that mines weak sub-tree patterns is TreeFinder (Termier, Rousset, & Sebag, 2002) which avoided the costly candidate-generation-and-test process by first using an Apriori clustering algorithm to group similar data trees, then followed by using the LGG operation and Θ-subsumption to generate maximal common patterns from each class. However, TreeFinder is not a complete miner and may lose patterns because of over-clustering. Further, the LGG operation is expensive and NP-complete.

Other research works generalize trees as graphs and treat tree mining as graph mining (Dehaspe, Toivonen, & King, 1998). This approach has two drawbacks. First, a general graph mining algorithm may not be efficient in dealing with tree mining tasks. Trees are considered to be more specific and have more structural constraints as compared to graphs. Many problems would become easier if graphs are tree structured. Second, a general-purpose graph mining algorithm may not be able to discover certain sub-tree patterns. For instance, a common graph mining algorithm typically matches sub-patterns by isomorphism (e.g., the FFSM algorithm proposed by Huan, Wang, & Prins, 2003) which strictly preserves edges and does not allow skipping node matching. Such graph mining algorithms cannot find embedded sub-trees which matches skipping-level ancestor-descendent relations.

Frequent Weak Sub-Tree Mining

In this section, we describe *WTIMiner*, a divide-and-conquer algorithm for efficient discovery of frequent weak sub-trees. We introduce the notion of *mapping equivalent class*, and develop a framework for mining frequent sub-trees via frequent itemset mining. The proposed algorithm *WTIMiner (Weak Tree Inclusion Miner)* reduces the problem of *combination explosion* since the number of database traversals is strictly bounded by the number of frequent itemsets generated.

The algorithm *WTIMiner* has three main steps. First, the tree database is converted into an itemset database by flattening out the tree structure. Consider the example database in Figure 10.4. The corresponding itemset database is shown in Table 10.1.

Second, a function called *FPGEx* finds all potentially frequent itemsets and maps them to the equivalent classes of trees. Third, the *FindTree* function discovers all frequent sub-trees. For each frequent itemset discovered, the *FindTree* function discovers the corresponding frequent sub-trees. Lines 2-16 in algorithm *FindTree* scans the database to count all sub-trees that can be mapped to the itemset. If there is no duplication, the algorithm correctly counts all frequent sub-trees. Otherwise, lines 17-35 is called to make up the miss-counts caused by duplication. Finally, lines 36-37 prunes the infrequent patterns.

Table 10.1. Conversion into itemset database

Tree		Itemset Mapping	Frequent Itemset (Ordered)
(a)		**A B D C E**	**B C A D E**
	(b)	A C B D	B C A D
	(c)	B C F D	B C D
	(d)	A B C E	B C A E
	(e)	A G E	A E
	(f)	B H C D	B C D

Figure 10.4. An example database of trees

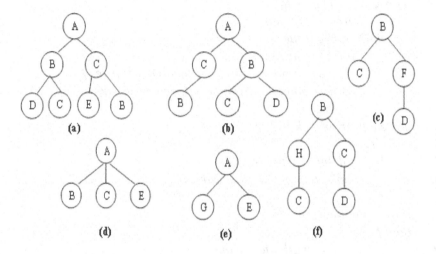

Algorithm WTIMiner

Input: The forest database file, a minimum support threshold σ.

Output: The complete set of frequent tree patterns P.

1. Construct an in-memory forest F from database, and build a sorted label frequency list L;

2. Regard each tree in F as an itemset, scan F once and build an indexed FP-tree T;

*3. Call **FPGEx(T, null, F, L, σ)** to get the frequent sub-trees.*

End Algorithm WTIMiner

Algorithm FindTree (α, F, L, σ)
Input: An indexed frequent itemset a
          Data forest F
          Sorted label frequency list L
          Minimum support threshold σ.
Output: $P_α$ (all the corresponding frequent tree patterns of α).

1. $P_α = \phi$; *has_duplicates = false;*
2. *for each tree T_i in occurence list of α, i is the unique tree id in F,*
3. *do{*
4.   *prune all nodes of T_i which is not in α, and get a forest F_i;*
5. $S = \phi$; *localDup = false;*
6.   *for each tree X_j of F_i do*
7.   *if ($X_j \in E[α]$) then*
8.   *if ($|X_j| > |α|$) then {*
9.   *has_duplicates = true; localDup = true; }*
10.   *get the canonical form of X_j; denoted as str_j;*
11. $str_j \rightarrow S$;
12.   *for each str_k of S, k = 1, 2 ... |S|*
13. $str_k \rightarrow P_α$;
14.   *if (localDup = true) then {*
15. $dupList(str_k) = dupList(str_k) \cup \{i\}$; }
16.   *}*
17.   *if (has_duplicates)*
18.   *then {*
19.   *sort $P_α$ in a length increasing order;*
20.   *for each pattern p in $P_α$ do*
21.   *if (p has duplicate labels)*
22.   *then {*
23.   *get all possible sub-trees of p in E[α], say p_1, p_2 ...;*
24.   *for j = 1, 2 ...*
25. s_j *is the canonical form of p_j;*
26.   *if ($s_j \notin P_α$) then {*
27. $s_j \rightarrow P_α$, *with s_j.support = p_j.support;*
28. $dupList(s_j)= dupList(p);$ }
29.   *else*
30. $s_j.support=s_j.support+ p_j.support;$
31.   *for each $l \in dupList(p)$ do*
32.   *if ($l \in dupList(s_j)$) then*
                                     $s_j.support=s_j.support - 1;$
33.   *else $dupList(s_j) = dupList(s_j) \cup \{l\}$;*

34.   *}*
35. *}*
36. *for each pattern p in P$_\alpha$*
37.   *if (p.support < σ) then prune p from P$_\alpha$;*
End Algorithm FindTree

ATMiner

ATMiner (stands for *Apriori Tree Miner*) servers as a naïve tree mining method to contrast *WTIMiner* with. It follows a common candidate-generate-and-test strategy and prunes infrequent patterns by the *Downward Closure Property*. The details of algorithm *ATMiner* is given in the following:

Algorithm ATMiner
Input: The forest database file, a minimum support threshold σ.
Output: The complete set of frequent tree patterns P.
1 . construct an in-memory forest Forest from database;
2. P = ϕ; F$_1$ = {frequent ancestor-descendent relations}; k = 0;
3. while (F$_k$ ≠ ϕ) do {
4.   P = P ∪ F$_k$, F$_{k+1}$ = ϕ;
5.   grow patterns on lower border of F$_k$ to get C$_{k+1}$;
6.   for each candidate tree t in C$_{k+1}$ do
7.   for each tree tree in Forest do
8.   if (MatchTree(t, tree) = true)
9.   then increment count for t;
10.   F$_{k+1}$ = { frequent k + 1 sub-trees in C$_{k+1}$};
11.   k = k + 1;
12. }
End Algorithm ATMine

Candidate Generation

ATMiner uses a strategy which uniquely enumerates a *k*-node candidate tree along the lower border of a (*k*-1)-node frequent pattern. The correctness of lower-border expansion can be found in Chi, Yang, and Muntz (2004) which introduces a hybrid candidate enumeration method and a breadth-first string encoding to mine permutable sub-trees.

Pattern Matching

The speed of sub-tree matching is an essential element that affects the performance of *ATMiner*. The *MatchTree* Algorithm in Kilpeläinen (1992) is a fast tree matching algorithm and has time complexity linear to the tree size when the pattern tree is small.

Candidate Pruning by Apriori

Before counting the occurrence of a $(k + 1)$-candidate, we make use of the Downward Closure Property to prune those who have infrequent k-patterns as sub-trees (realized in the *Prune* sub-function).

Experimental Evaluation

All the experiments were conducted on a Pentium IV 2.6 GHz with 1GB RAM, running Windows XP. We implemented the algorithms in C++. *WTIMiner* uses a variation of the FP-growth method to mine frequent itemsets (Han, Pei, & Yin, 2000).

We tested both algorithms on four synthetic databases. The SYN1 dataset is generated using the Zipfian distribution. In such a database, a few trees

Table 10.2. Characteristics of datasets

DataSets	Distribution	Ave. # of Nodes	Max. Depth	Max. Fanout	Size Range (K)
SYN1	zipfian	7.4	8	12	10-1000
SYN2	uniform	9.2	8	12	50-100
SYN3	uniform	7.5	6	9	50-200
SYN4	zipfian	7.4	8	12	10-100

occur very often while many others occur rarely. Thus the frequent items may vary sharply when the minimum support threshold changes. The SYN2 and SYN3 datasets are generated based on the uniform distribution. We also generate another dataset SYN4 with sizes varying from 10k to 100k at the step of 10k. The purpose is to minimize the influence of factors such as tree depth and fanout by different databases. The characteristics of the different datasets are shown in Table 10.2.

Response Time

We first evaluate the execution time of *WTIMiner* and *ATMiner* on SYN1 (80k) and SYN3 (50K) respectively by varying the minimum support threshold from 0.004 to 0.5. The results are shown in Figures 10.5 and 10.6. We observe that *WTIMiner* outperforms *ATMiner* in both datasets. The gap widens when the minimum support threshold decreases. At the support of 0.004, *WTIMiner* outperforms *ATMiner* by a magnitude on the dataset SYN3 (10.8 times).

We note that although SYN3 dataset is much smaller in size and contains fewer frequent labels than SYN1 dataset, it still costs *WTIMiner* more time on SYN3 (the numbers of frequent labels are 19 vs. 23-25 when σ is between [0.004, 0.05], and the number of frequent edges are 45 vs. 72 when σ is between [0.004, 0.01]). This is because SYN3 is evenly distributed and a

Figure 10.5. Time comparison on SYN3 (50K)

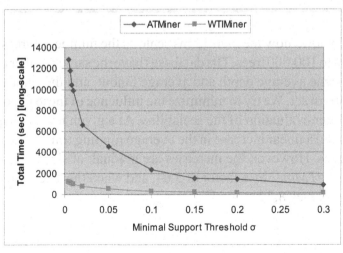

Figure 10.6. Scaleup comparison on SYN4

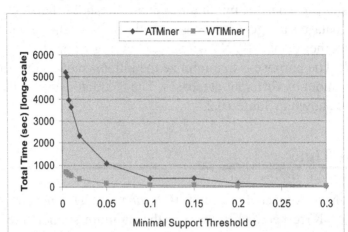

large pattern tends to be more frequent. As a consequence, SYN3 possibly has more frequent sub-tree patterns, which needs more time to discover. In fact, the patterns discovered reveal that SYN3 does contain 1-3 times more sub-trees than SYN1. From the time complexity analysis we conclude that *WTIMiner* performs even better in datasets with more frequent patterns.

Scalability

Figure 10.7 shows how the algorithms scale as the number of trees increases from 10,000 to 100,000 trees. The databases have the same number of frequent nodes, the same average depth and average fanout, and the same number of frequent pattern set. We try to minimize the influence of these factors in order to have a better evaluation of the scalability. At a given level of support (σ = 0.008), we find a linear increase in the average running time as the number of trees increases. However, the increases are gradual: at size 10K, *WTIMiner* is faster than *ATMiner* by a factor of 5.64, and when the size grows to 100K, the factor becomes 8.72.

Figure 10.7. Scaleup comparison on SYN4

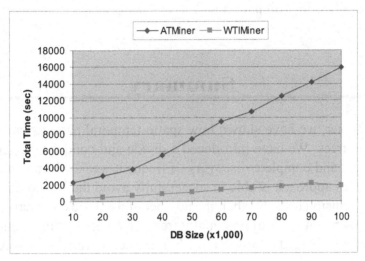

Space Requirement

We track the memory usage of the two algorithms with the help of Microsoft Windows Performance Monitor. Figure 10.8 shows the memory page file

Figure 10.8. Space comparisons on SYN2

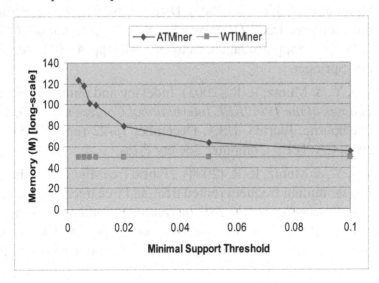

usage. *WTIMiner* requires almost constant memory at each level of σ while it successfully mines all patterns.

Summary

In this chapter, we have shown how spatio-temporal patterns can be modeled using trees. We have introduced a divide-and-conquer framework for the efficient and complete discovery of frequent weak sub-trees in tree databases. This approach is able to successfully avoid the NP-complete weak sub-tree inclusion tests. Further, the number of database traversals is strictly bounded by the number of potentially frequent mapping equivalent classes. The experimental study show that *WTIMiner* excels in all three aspects: time, space, and scalability.

References

Asai, T., Abe, K., & Kawasoe, S. (2002). Efficient substructure discovery from large semistructured data. In *Proceedings of the SIAM International Conference on Data Mining,* Arlington, Virginia, USA, April 11-13. Philadelphia, PA: SIAM Press.

Asai, T., Arimura, H., & Uno, T. (2003). Discovering frequent substructures in large unordered trees. *Discovery Science, 6th International Conference, DS 2003,* Sapporo, Japan, October 17-19 (pp. 47-61). Berlin/Heidelberg: Springer.

Chi, Y., Yang, Y., & Muntz, R. R. (2003). Indexing and mining free trees. In *Proceedings of the 19th IEEE International Conference on Data Mining,* Melbourne, Florida, USA, December 19-22 (pp. 509-512). Los Alamitos, CA: IEEE Computer Society Press.

Chi, Y., Yang, Y., & Muntz, R. R. (2004). HybridTreeMiner: An efficient algorithm for mining frequent rooted trees and free trees using canonical forms. In *Proceedings of the 16th Inernational Conference on Scientific and Statistical Database Management,* Santorini Island, Greece, June 21-23 (pp. 11-20). Los Alamitos, CA: IEEE Computer Society Press.

Chi, Y., Yang, Y., & Xia, Y. (2004). CMTreeMiner: Mining both closed and maximal frequent subtrees. In *Proceedings of the 8th Pacific-Asia Conference on Knowledge Discovery and Data Mining,* Sydney, Australia, May 26-28 (pp. 63-73). Berlin/Heidelberg: Springer.

Dehaspe, L., Toivonen, H., & King, R. D. (1998). Finding frequent substructures in chemical compounds. In *Proceedings of the ACM SIGKDD International Conference on Knowledge Discovery and Data Mining,* New York City, New York, USA, August 27-31 (pp. 30-36). Menlo Park, CA: AAAI Press.

Han, J., Pei, J., & Yin, Y. (2000). Mining frequent patterns without candidate generation. In *Proceedings of the ACM SIGMOD Conference on Management of Data,* Dallas, Texas, USA, May 16-18 (pp. 1-12). New York: ACM Press.

Huan, J., Wang, W., & Prins, J. (2003). Efficient mining of frequent subgraph in the presence of isomorphism. In *Proceedings of the IEEE International Conference on Data Mining,* Melbourne, Florida, USA, December 19-22 (pp. 549-552). Los Alamitos, CA: IEEE Computer Society Press.

Kilpeläinen, P. (1992). *Tree matching problems with applications to structured text databases.* PhD thesis, University of Helsinki.

Miyahara, T., Shoudai, T., & Uchida, T. (2001). Discovery of frequent tree structured patterns in semistructured Web documents. In *Proceedings of the 5th Pacific-Asia Conference on Knowledge Discovery and Data Mining,* Hong Kong, China, April 16-18 (pp. 47-52). Berlin/Heidelberg: Springer.

Nijssen, S., & Kok, J. N. (2003). Efficient discovery of frequent unordered trees. In *1st International Workshop on Mining Graphs, Trees and Sequences,* Cavtat-Dubrovnik, Croatia, September 22-23 (pp. 55-64).

Termier, A., Rousset, M. C., & Sebag, M. (2002). TreeFinder, a first step towards XML data mining. In *Proceedings of the IEEE International Conference on Data Mining,* Maebashi City, Japan, December 9-12 (pp. 450-457). Los Alamitos, CA: IEEE Computer Society Press.

Wang, C., Hong, M., & Pei, J. (2004). Efficient pattern-growth methods for frequent tree pattern mining. In *Proceedings of the 8th Pacific-Asia Conference on Knowledge Discovery and Data Mining,* Sydney, Australia, May 26-28 (pp. 441-451). Berlin/Heidelberg: Springer.

Wang, K., & Liu, H. (2000). Discovering structural association of semistructured data. *IEEE Transactions on Knowledge and Data Engineering, 12*(2), 353-371.

Xiao, Y., Yao, J. F., & Li, Z. (2003). Efficient data mining for maximal frequent subtrees. In *Proceedings of the IEEE International Conference on Data Mining,* Melbourne, Florida, USA, December 19-22 (pp. 379-386). Los Alamitos, CA: IEEE Computer Society Press.

Yang, L. H., Lee, M. L., & Hsu, W. (2003). Efficient mining of XML query patterns for caching. In *Proceedings of the International Conference on Very Large Databases,* Berlin, Germany, September 9-12 (pp. 69-80). San Francisco, CA: Morgan Kaufmann Publishers.

Zaki, M. J. (2002). Efficiently mining frequent trees in a forest. In *Proceedings of the ACM SIGKDD International Conference on Knowledge Discovery and Data Mining,* Edmonton, Alberta, Canada, July 23-26 (pp. 71-80). New York: ACM Press.

Chapter XI

Mining Spatio-Temporal Graph Patterns

In the previous chapter, we have described a method to find spatio-temporal tree patterns. A more general representation for patterns with arbitrary relationships is the graph model.

Data mining in graph databases has received much attention. We have witnessed many algorithms proposed for mining frequent graphs. Inokuchi, Washio, and Nishimura (2002) and Karpis and Kumar (1998) introduce the Apriori-like algorithms, AGM and FSG, to mine the complete set of frequent graphs. However, both algorithms are not scalable as they require multiple scans of databases and tend to generate many candidates during the mining process. Subsequently, Yan and Han (2002) and Nijssen and Kok (2004) propose depth-first graph mining approaches called gSpan and Gaston, respectively. These approaches are essentially memory-based and their efficiencies decrease dramatically if the graph database is too large to fit into the main memory.

Recognizing this problem, Wang, Wang, and Pei (2004) focus on the problem of mining graphs on large, disk-based databases. An effective index structure

ADI is proposed to facilitate major graph mining operations. However, this solution does not work well when the graph database is still evolving. This is because the ADI structure has to be rebuilt each time the graph database is updated.

In short, while previous studies have made excellent progress in mining graph databases, many of them assume that the graphs in the databases are relatively static and simple, that is, the number of possible labels in the graphs is small. They do not scale well for mining graphs in a dynamic environment. For example, a spatio-temporal database can contain millions of different structures and the number of different labels in the graphs is easily in the range of hundreds. Changes to spatio-temporal databases cause changes to the graph structures that model the relationships in the spatio-temporal data. Re-execution of the mining algorithm each time the graphs are updated is costly, and may result in an explosion in the demand for computational and I/O resources. Consequently, there is an urgent need to find an algorithm that is scalable and can incrementally mine from only those parts of the graph databases that have been changed.

We design a partition-based approach to graph mining. Our idea is to isolate update changes to a small set of sub-graphs and re-execute the graph mining algorithm only on the isolated sub-graphs. Instead of finding frequent graph patterns on large and complex graphs, we recursively partition complex graphs into smaller, more manageable sub-graphs until these sub-graphs can fit into the main memory. With this, existing memory-based graph mining algorithms can be utilized to discover frequent patterns in the sub-graphs. The discovered patterns are then joined via a merge-join operation to recover the final set of frequent patterns that exist in the original complex graphs.

In this chapter, we design a partition-based algorithm to divide graphs into k smaller sub-graphs (k is determined by the size of the main memory) with the goal of reducing connectivity among sub-graphs while localizing most, if not all, the updated nodes to a minimal number of sub-graphs. Once divided, we can utilize existing efficient memory-based graph mining algorithms to discover frequent patterns in these sub-graphs. We develop a merge-join operation to losslessly recover the complete set of frequent sub-graphs in the database from the set of sub-graphs found in the partitions. We also give a theoretical proof to ensure that mining of frequent sub-graphs in the partitions will be equivalent to mining in the original graph database. In the following, we present the details of our partition-based graph mining algorithm, called *PartMiner*. Here, we make use of the cumulative information obtained during the mining of previous sub-graphs to effectively reduce the number of candidate graphs. PartMiner is inherently parallel in nature and can be parallelized with minimal communication and synchronization among processing nodes. Finally, we extend PartMiner to handle updates in the graph database. The IncPartMiner, an extended version of PartMiner, makes use of the pruned results of the pre-updated database to eliminate the generation of unchanged candidate graphs, thus leading to tremendous savings.

The rest of the chapter is organized as follows. We will first discuss some preliminary concepts before presenting the partition-based graph mining approach. Then we will report the experimental results before concluding the chapter.

Related Work

Karpis and Kumar (1998) first investigate techniques to partition the graphs in the database and develop the software package METIS. The algorithms in METIS are based on multi-level graph partitioning and reduce the size of the graph by collapsing vertices and edges, partition the smaller graphs, and then uncoarsen it to construct a partition for the original graph, which allow METIS to quickly produce high-quality partitions for a large variety of graphs.

Research in graph mining includes Inokuchi, Washio, and Nishimura (2002); Kuramochi and Karypis (2004); Yan and Han (2002); Nijssen and Kok (2004); and Wang, Wang, and Pei (2004). The Apriori-like algorithms introduced by Inokuchi, Washio, and Nishimura (2002) and Kuramochi and Karypis (2004) are not scalable since they require multiple database scans and tend to generate many candidates during the mining process. The depth-first graph mining methods gSpan and Gaston are essentially memory-based. Wang, Wang, and Pei (2004) design a disk-based graph mining algorithm called ADIMINE. While their approach is effective, it does not work well when updates occurs. This is because the ADI structure has to be rebuilt each time the graph database is being updated.

Recent work also examines algorithms/methods to discover different types of patterns in graphs. Yan and Han (2003) investigate the mining of frequent closed graphs. Huan, Wang, and Prins (2004) introduce an algorithm SPIN to mine maximal frequent sub-graphs. Faloutsos, McCurley, and Tomkins (2004) propose algorithms to find the "connection graphs" which are small graphs that convey much information about the relationship of a pair of nodes. Yan, Yu, and Han (2004) further use frequent graph patterns to index graphs. As special cases of graphs, tree patterns have also been the focus of Zaki (2002); Chi, Yang, and Muntz (2003); Shasha, Wang, and Zhang (2004); and Termier, Rousset, and Sebag (2004).

Mining frequent patterns in databases using the partition-based approach is not new. As early as the 1990s, Savasere, Omiecinski, and Navathe (1995) introduced a partition-based method to find association rules. Since then, many partition-based algorithms have been developed to solve the various problems in data mining, such as classification (Hall, Chawla, & Bowyer, 1998; Shafer, Agrawal, & Mehta, 1996), clustering (Bradley, Fayyad, & Reina, 1998; Ng & Han, 2002), and incremental mining (Lee, Lin, & Chen, 2001b), and so forth. The data partitioning approach involves splitting a dataset into subsets, learning/mining from one or more of the subsets, and possibly combining the results. The advantage of the data partitioning approach is the ability to avoid thrashing by memory management systems which frequently occurs when algorithms try to process huge datasets in the main memory. To date, there has been no work on mining frequent sub-graphs using the partition-based method.

Preliminary Concepts

We represent a labeled graph by $G = (V, E, L_V, L_E)$ where V is the set of vertices, E is the set of edges denoted as pair of vertices, L_V is a set of labels associated with the vertices, and L_E is a set of labels for the edges. A graph G is connected if a path exists between any two vertices in V. The size of a graph is the number of edges in it, and a graph G with k edges is called a *k-edge graph* or a graph of size k.

A graph G_1 is *isomorphic* to a graph G_2 if there exists a bijective function f : $V_1 \rightarrow V_2$ such that for any vertex $u \in V_1$, $f(u) \in V_2$ and $L_u = L_{f(u)}$, and for any edge $(u, v) \in E_1$, $(f(u), f(v)) \in E_2$ and $L_{(u,v)} = L_{(f(u), f(v))}$. An *automorphism* of a graph G is an isomorphism from G to G. A *sub-graph isomorphism* from G_1 to G_2 is an isomorphism from G_1 to a sub-graph G_2, and G_1 is called a super-graph of G_2, denoted as $G_2 \subseteq G_1$.

A graph database is a set of tuples (*gid*, *G*), where *gid* is a graph identifier and *G* is an undirected labeled graph. Given a graph database *D*, the support of a graph *G* is the number of graphs in *D* that are supergraphs of *G*.

To find all frequent sub-graphs in a database, we need to encode the structure of a graph such that if two graphs have identical encoding, they are isomorphic. We use the method proposed in (Yan & Han, 2002) to encode a graph. The method in Yan and Han (2002) performs a depth-first search on a graph *G* to order the vertices and construct the *DFS-tree T* of *G*. An edge (v_i, v_j) is called a *forward edge* if $i < j$; otherwise, it is called a *backward* edge.

A linear order $\prec$ on the edges in *G* is defined as follows: Given two edges $e = (v_i, v_j)$ and $e' = (v_{i'}, v_{j'})$, $e \prec e'$ if either one of the following conditions is true:

1. both *e* and *e'* are forward edges, $j < j'$ or $(i > i' \land j = j')$;
2. both *e* and *e'* are backward edges, $j < j'$ or $(i > i' \land j = j')$;
3. *e* is a forward edge and *e'* is a backward edge, $j \leq i'$;
4. *e* is a backward edge and *e'* is a forward edge, $i < j'$.

By ordering the edges in a graph *G*, the structure of *G* can be encoded using the *DFS code*. Given a graph *G*, and a DFS-tree *T*, the DFS code of *G* w.r.t

Figure 11.1. Example of the DFS tree and DFS code

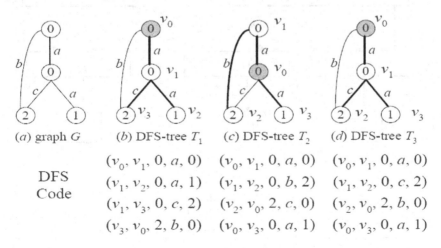

	(a) graph G	(b) DFS-tree T_1	(c) DFS-tree T_2	(d) DFS-tree T_3
DFS Code		$(v_0, v_1, 0, a, 0)$	$(v_0, v_1, 0, a, 0)$	$(v_0, v_1, 0, a, 0)$
		$(v_1, v_2, 0, a, 1)$	$(v_1, v_2, 0, b, 2)$	$(v_1, v_2, 0, c, 2)$
		$(v_1, v_3, 0, c, 2)$	$(v_2, v_0, 2, c, 0)$	$(v_2, v_0, 2, b, 0)$
		$(v_3, v_0, 2, b, 0)$	$(v_0, v_3, 0, a, 1)$	$(v_0, v_3, 0, a, 1)$

T, denoted by code(G, T), is a list of all edges E in the order of $\prec$, where an edge (v_i, v_j) is written as $(v_i, v_j, l_{vi}, l_{(vi,vj)}, l_{vj})$.

Since a graph can have many different DFS-trees, Yan and Han (2002) define the notion of the *minimum* DFS code, which is the minimum of all the DFS codes of a graph G, to encode the graph. Figure 11.1 shows a graph G, and three DFS trees of G, together with their corresponding DFS codes. The code(G, T_1) in Figure 11.1(b) is the minimum DFS code.

Partition-Based Graph Mining

Figure 11.2 shows the framework of the proposed partition-based graph mining approach. It consists of two phases. In the first phase, we iteratively call a graph partitioning algorithm to partition each of the graphs in the graph database into smaller sub-graphs. Then we group the sub-graphs into units.

Figure 11.2. Overview of partition-based graph mining

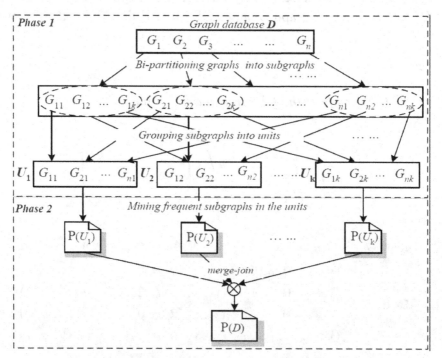

The second phase applies any existing memory-based graph mining algorithm to discover the frequent sub-graphs in each unit. The set of frequent sub-graphs in each unit are then merged via a merge-join operation to recover the complete set of frequent sub-graphs. The proposed framework can be easily extended to handle incremental mining when updates occur in the graph database.

Divide Graph Database into Units

The motivation for the proposed partition-based graph mining approach is to effectively deal with graphs in the presence of frequent updates. By partitioning the graphs, we can reduce graph complexity as well as size so that existing memory-based graph mining algorithms can be applied. However, the frequent sub-graphs obtained from each unit need to be combined using a merge-join operation which is costly.

In order to minimize the number of units involved in the merge-join operation, it is important to minimize connectivity (i.e., the number of connective edges) among sub-graphs in the units. Moreover, in the presence of updates, it is also important to isolate those vertices and edges that are changed frequently, and localize them in a minimal number of units to reduce the number of units that need to participate in the incremental mining process.

To achieve this goal of minimizing connectivity among units, each graph in the database must be carefully partitioned and organized into units. If we randomly partition the graphs and group them into units, then the connectivity among the sub-graphs in the units will not be clear, and a merge-join operation will be needed on each pair of units. Therefore, we adopt an approach that repeatedly bi-partitions each of the graphs in the database.

Figure 11.3 shows a graph G which is first divided into two sub-graphs G_1 and G_2. $G_1(G_2)$ is again further divided into two sub-graphs G_{11} and G_{12} (G_{21} and G_{22}). This bi-partitioning process yields a total of four sub-graphs for G. By applying this bi-partitioning procedure on each of the graphs G_i in the database, we have four sub-graphs G_{i1}, G_{i2}, G_{i3}, and G_{i4} for each G_i. Each of the sub-graphs G_{ij}, $1 \leq j \leq 4$, is grouped into one unit U_j.

The bi-partitioning approach facilitates the recovery of the complete set of graphs in a database from the sub-graphs in the units. In our example, we just need to combine the set of sub-graphs in U_1 and U_2 to get the set of sub-graphs in U_{12}, and the set of sub-graphs in U_3 and U_4 to get the set of sub-graphs in

Figure 11.3. Example of graph bi-partitioning

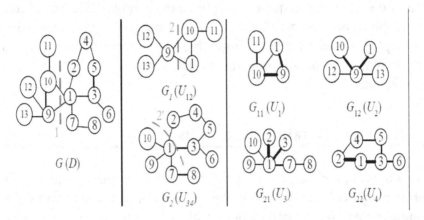

U_{34}. The set of sub-graphs in U_{12} and U_{34} are subsequently combined to obtain the original graph database. This also indicates the sequence of combining the frequent sub-graphs mined in each unit to obtain the final set of frequent sub-graphs for the database.

We use two criteria to carry out bi-partitioning. The first criterion minimizes the connectivity between sub-graphs, and the second criterion isolates frequently updated vertices to a sub-graph. Figure 11.4 illustrates how a graph G can be partitioned using these two criteria. Note that sub-graphs should include the connective edges between them so that we can recover the original graph later. For example, edges (v_1, v_2) and (v_3, v_4) in Figure 11.4(a), and edges (v_3, v_4), (v_4, v_6) and (v_6, v_7) in Figure 11.4(b) are connective edges.

We associate each vertex v in a graph G with a value *ufreq* to indicate its update frequency, denoted as $v.ufreq$. The vertices of G are sorted in descending order according to their update frequencies. Suppose that the vertex set V of the graph G is divided into two subsets V_1 and V_2, we define a weight function $w(V_1)$ to reflect the average update frequencies of the vertices in the vertex set V_1 and its connectivity to the vertex set V_2 (see Equation (1)).

$$w(V_1) = \lambda_1 \frac{\sum_{v_i \in V_1} v_i.ufreq}{|V_1|} - \lambda_2 |E_{V_1, V_2}| \tag{1}$$

where $E_{V1, V2}$ is the set of connective edges $e(v_i, v_j)$ between vertex sets V_1 and V_2, i.e., $v_i \in V_1, v_j \in V_2$ or $v_i \in V_2, v_j \in V_1$. The first term in $w(V_1)$ computes

Figure 11.4. Example of partitioning criteria

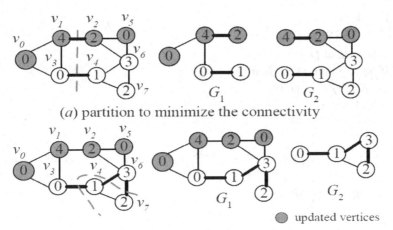

(*a*) partition to minimize the connectivity

(*b*) partition to isolate all updated vertices

the average update frequencies of the vertices in the subset V_1, and the second term counts the number of connective edges. We use two parameters λ_1 and λ_2 to set the weight between these two terms.

Algorithm *GraphPart* performs the partitioning of the graph. Line 1 sorts the vertex set V of the graph G according to their update frequency. Let v_c be the centroid of V. Then v_c divides V into two subsets V_1 and V_2, where V_1 contains the vertices $v_i \in V$ and $v_i.ufreq \geq v_c.ufreq$, and V_2 contains vertices $v_j \in V$ and $v_j.ufreq < v_c.ufreq$. For each vertex $v_i \in V_1$, we traverse the graph G in depth-first manner to construct the vertex subset V_i, and compute the weight function $w(V_i)$ (lines 4-12). The vertex set with the largest weight function is the final subset V^*. Note that when scanning unvisited neighbors of a vertex, the vertex with the highest frequency should be the next visited node (line 21). Finally, we obtain two sub-graphs G_1 and G_2. G_1 contains all vertices in V^*, and G_2 contains all vertices in V / V^*. Both G_1 and G_2 also include the connective edges (lines 13-14).

Algorithm GraphPart
Input: A graph G;
Output: Two sub-graphs of G: G1, G2;

1. V = {vertices sorted according to their update frequency};
2. V* = ϕ;

3. $\omega (V^*) = -\infty;$

4. For $(i = 0; i < |V| / 2; i++)$ {

5. $V_i = \phi;$

6.   Call DFSScan $(V, i, V_i);$

7.   Compute $\omega (V_i);$

8.   If $(\omega (V_i) > \omega (V^*)$ then

9. $\omega (V^*) = \omega (V_i);$

10. $V^* = V_i;$

11.   Endif

12. Endfor

13. $G_1 = \{e_{ij} = (v_i, v_j) \mid v_i \in V^*, v_j \in V^*\} \cup \{e_{ij} = (v_i, v_j) \mid v_i \in V^*, v_j \notin V^*\};$

14. $G_2 = \{e_{ij} = (v_i, v_j) \mid v_i \notin V^*, v_j \notin V^*\} \cup \{e_{ij} = (v_i, v_j) \mid v_i \in V^*, v_j \notin V^*\};$

End Algorithm GraphPar

Procedure DFSScan $(V, i, V_i);$

15. stack $= \phi; m = 0;$

16. stack.push(v_i);

17. while (stack $!= \phi$ and $m \le |V|/2$) do

18. $v = $ stack.pop();

19. $V_i = V_i \cup \{v\};$

20. $m++;$

21.   choose the neighbor vertex v_h such that $v_h.visited = 0$ and $\forall v_s,$ $v_s.visited = 0 \wedge (v, v_s) \in E, v_s.ufreq < v_h.ufreq;$

22.   stack.push(v_h);

End Procedure DFSScan

After partitioning each graph in the database into a set of sub-graphs, the next step is to group the sub-graphs into units such that each unit can fit into the main memory. Algorithm *DBPartition* divides the database into units. We use a parameter k to indicate the number of units that the database will be divided into. The value of k is determined by the availability of the main memory and the size of the database. For each graph in the database, we repeatedly call Algorithm *GraphPart* to partition it. The sub-graphs generated during the partitioning process are kept in the database $D_{i,j}$, $1 \le i \le \lceil log_2 k \rfloor$, $0 \le j \le 2^{i-1}$. Finally, the resulting k sub-graphs are then distributed to the k units, i.e., $U_1, U_2, ..., U_k.$

Procedure DBPartition (D, k)

//D is a graph database and k is the number of units

1. $D_{0,0} = D$;
2. $i = 1$;
3. $l = \lfloor log_2\, k \rfloor$;
4. while $(i \leq l)$ do
5.   for $(j = 0; j < 2^{i-1}; j++)$
6.   DivideDBPart $(D_{i-1,j},\, D_{i,2j},\, D_{i,2j+1})$;
7. $i++$;
8. endwhile
9. for $(j = 0; j < k - 2^l; j++)$
10.   DivideDBPart $(D_{i-1,j},\, U_{2j},\, U_{2j+1})$;
End Procedure DBPartition

Function DivideDBPart $(D_s,\, D_{1,0},\, D_{1,1})$
1. $D_{1,0} = \phi$;
2. $D_{1,1} = \phi$;
3. for each graph $G \in D_s$
4.   Call GraphPart(G) to obtain sub-graphs G_1 and G_2;
5. $D_{1,0} = D_{1,0} \cup \{G_1\}$;
6. $D_{1,1} = D_{1,1} \cup \{G_2\}$;
End Function DivideDBPart

Mine Frequent Sub-Graphs in Units

After dividing the graph database into k units such that each unit can fit into the main memory, we can now use any existing memory-based algorithms to find frequent sub-graphs in the units.

Many memory-based algorithms have been proposed to discover frequent graphs. In this work, we use the Gaston algorithm (Nijssen & Kok, 2004) to find the set of frequent graphs in the units. Gaston has been developed based on the observation that most frequent sub-structures in practical graph databases are actually free trees, and it employs a highly efficient strategy to enumerate frequent free trees first.

Algorithm Gaston
Input: A unit of the database U;
         Minimum support sup;
Output: Set of frequent sub-graphs in U, P(U);

1. F_1 = {frequent edges in U};
2. for each p ∈ F_1 do
3.   L = {allowable extended edges of p};
4.   for each allowable extended edge l ∈ L do
5.   G' = Add l to p;
6.   L' = {allowable extended edges of G'};
7.   If l is a node refinement Then
8.   If G' is a path Then
9.   Find paths with G' and L';
10.   Else
11.   Find trees with G' and L';
12.   EndIf
13.   Else
14.   Find cyclic graphs with G' and L';
15.   Endfor
16. Endfor
End Algorithm Gaston

Line 1 of the Gaston algorithm finds all frequent edges in the database. For each frequent edge p, the algorithm generates the descendants G' of p by extending it with the set of allowable extended edges L (lines 4-6). According to the types of G' and the extended edges, the algorithm will decide to find paths, trees, or cyclic graphs (lines 7-14).

Combine Frequent Sub-Graphs

When we have computed the set of frequent sub-graphs in the units, we need to recover the complete set of frequent sub-graphs in the original database. We design a **merge-join** operation to accomplish this. We first illustrate the idea behind the merge-join operation before presenting the algorithm. We also give theoretical proof to show the complete set of frequent sub-graphs in the database can be losslessly recovered by the merge-join operation on the set of frequent sub-graphs found in the units.

Suppose unit U is partitioned into two units U_1 and U_2. Let $P(U_1)$ and $P(U_2)$ be the set of frequent sub-graphs found in the units U_1 and U_2. We want to recover the set of frequent sub-graphs in the unit U, that is, $P(U)$. We first sort the frequent sub-graphs in each unit according to their number of edges. We shall use $P^k(U_i)$ to denote the set of sub-graphs of size k.

First, frequent 1-edge sub-graphs in the units U_1 and U_2 are simply merged since they do not share any common connective edges. We denote the resulting set of 1-edge sub-graphs by $P^1(U) = P^1(U_1) \cup P^1(U_2)$.

Next, we merge frequent 2-edge sub-graphs, that is $P^2(U) = P^2(U_1) \cup P^2(U_2)$, and join the 2-edge sub-graphs based on the common connective edges to produce a set of candidate 3-edge sub-graphs C^3. A sub-graph isomorphism check is then carried out to remove the infrequent 3-edge sub-graphs in C^3, resulting in the set of *frequent* 3-edge sub-graphs, that is, F^3.

For frequent k-edge sub-graphs, $k > 2$, we obtain the set of k-edge sub-graphs by merge $P^k(U_1)$, $P^k(U_2)$ and F^k, that is, $P^{k+1}(U) = P^k(U_1) \cup P^k(U_2) \cup F^k$. Then, the merge-join operation is applied to find the set of candidate $(k + 1)$-edge sub-graphs C^{k+1}. We obtain C^{k+1} in three steps:

Step 1. Join the sub-graphs in the set $P^k(U_1)$ with the sub-graphs in the set F^k to obtain the candidate set C_1^{k+1};

Step 2. Join the sub-graphs in the set $P^k(U_2)$ with those in the set F^k to obtain the candidate set C_2^{k+1};

Step 3. Join the sub-graphs in the set F^k with themselves to get the candidate set C_3^{k+1}.

The set of candidate sub-graphs C^{k+1} is the union of the set C_1^{k+1}, C_2^{k+1} and C_3^{k+1}, that is, $C^{k+1} = C_1^{k+1} \cup C_2^{k+1} \cup C_3^{k+1}$. We remove the infrequent $(k+1)$-edge sub-graphs from C^{k+1}, resulting in F^{k+1}. This process continues until all frequent sub-graphs in the original database are discovered. Figure 11.5 shows an example of the merge-join operation. Figure 11.5(a) shows the unit U with one graph G and its two sub-graphs G_1 in U_1 and G_2 in U_2. The process of recovering $P(G)$ from $P(G_1)$ and $P(G_2)$ is illustrated in Figure 11.5(b), where the left light grey region marks the set of sub-graphs of G_1, that is, $P(G_1)$, and the dark grey region marks the set of sub-graphs of G_2, $P(G_2)$.

Proof of Completeness

In this section, we prove that the complete set of frequent graphs in the database D can be recovered when the merge-join operation is performed on the set of frequent sub-graphs found in all the units. We first prove that it is possible to recover all sub-graphs of a graph G from its partitioned sub-graphs.

Figure 11.5. Example of the merge-join operation

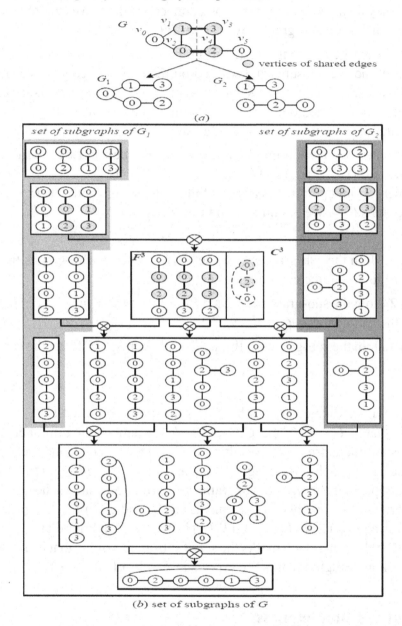

(b) set of subgraphs of G

Then we introduce the Apriori property of sub-graphs, and proceed to show that the complete set of frequent sub-graphs in the original database can be losslessly recovered even when the mining is performed on the individual smaller units.

Theorem 3: The set of sub-graphs of a graph G (that is, P(G)) with size of n, n ≥ 2, can be losslessly recovered when the merge-join operation is recursively applied on its bi-partitioned sub-graphs G_1 and G_2.

Proof: We prove this by induction. Let Hn denote the hypothesis that the set of sub-graphs of a graph G of size n can be losslessly recovered from its partitions G_1 and G_2, n ≥ 2

Base Case: n = 2. This is trivially true as shown in Figure 11.6 which shows the division of the graph G into two sub-graphs G_1 and G_2 and the process to recover $P(G)$ from $P(G_1)$ and $P(G_2)$.

Induction Step: Suppose H_n is true, we want to show that H_{n+1} is also true. If H_n is true, we know that we are able to recover all sub-graphs of a graph G of size n. Now we have a graph G' of size n + 1. We partition graph G' into two sub-graphs. Let G_1 denote the partition of size n, and let G_2 denote the partition of size i − 2 where 3 < i < n (see Figure 11.6). By our assumption, we know we can recover all sub-graphs from G_1 (because G_1 is of size n). Hence, the only missing sub-graphs are those involving the edge (v_1, v_2) in G_2. These sub-graphs are formed by the joining of the sub-graphs of G_1 and G_2, which share one of the common edges (v_2, v_3), ..., (v_2, v_i) marked as grey in Figure 11.6. This step is in fact included in the merge-join operation. In other words, if H_n is true, then H_{n+1} must be true.

Theorem 4 (Apriori Property): If a graph G is frequent, all of its sub-graphs are frequent.

Proof: A graph G is frequent implies the number of occurrences of G exceeds some minimum support threshold. A sub-graph of G must, by definition, occur in G. Hence, the number of occurrences of the sub-graph must be equal to or exceed G's occurrences. In other words, the sub-graph is frequent.

Theorem 5: Let D be a graph database that has been divided into k smaller units U_i, k ≥ 2, 1 ≤ i ≤ k. If we know the complete set of frequent sub-graphs P(Ui) in each unit U_i, 1 ≤ i ≤ k, we can determine the complete set of frequent sub-graphs P(D) in D.

Figure 11.6. Example used in the Proof of Theorem 3

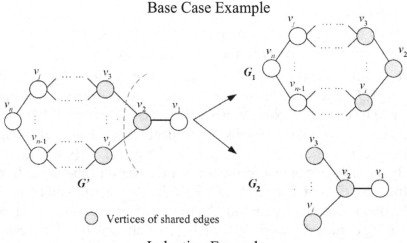

(*a*) division of *G*   (*b*) process to recover $P(G)$

Base Case Example

Induction Example

○ Vertices of shared edges

Proof: Let H_{k-1} denote the hypothesis that the complete set of frequent sub-graphs of the unit U can be losslessly recovered from the set of frequent sub-graphs in its k-1 subunits U_i ($1 \leq i \leq k-1$).

Base Case: $k = 2$, that is D is divided into two units U_1 and U_2. Given $P(U_1)$ and $P(U_2)$, according to the Theorem 1 and Theorem 2, we can losslessly recover the set of frequent sub-graphs in D, that is we can get the complete set of frequent graphs $P(D)$.

Induction Step: k > 2. Suppose Hk−1 is true, we want to show that Hk is also true. Given the unit U is divided into k subunits Ui ($0 \leq i \leq k$). If Hk−1 is true, we know that we are able to recover the complete set of frequent sub-graphs of the unit U' from the set of frequent sub-graphs in its k−1 subunits U_j ($0 \leq j \leq k-1$). Now we have the set $P(U')$ and $P(U_k)$. According to the base case, we know that we can losslessly recover $P(U)$ from $P(U')$ and $P(U_k)$. In other words, if H_{k-1} is true, then H_k must be true.

From Theorem 3, we note that the completeness of the frequent graphs in the database D depends on the completeness of the frequent sub-graphs in the units. Hence, we can reduce the support threshold used to discover frequent sub-graphs in units to get the complete set of frequent graphs in the units.

Algorithm PartMiner

Algorithm PartMiner takes as input the database D, the minimum support sup, and the number of units k, and outputs the set of frequent sub-graphs in D.

Algorithm PartMiner works in two phases. In the first phase, it divides the database D into set of units of proper and manageable size (line 1). In the second phase (lines 2-17), PartMiner first calls the algorithm Gaston to find the set of frequent sub-graphs in the k units with the support threshold sup/k (lines 2-17). The reason that we use the lower support threshold for mining the units is to guarantee that the sub-graphs that are frequent in the original database are also frequent in the units.

After mining the units, line 14 recursively calls the procedure *MergeJoin* to combine the results of $D_{i,j}$ and $D_{i,j+1}$ ($0 \le i \le log_2 k$, $0 \le j \le k$) together. The

Table 11.1. Meaning of symbols

Symbol	Meaning
U_i	original unit
U_i'	updated unit
$D_{i,j}$	set of intermediate sub-graphs generated during the graph partitioning process
$P(U_i)$	set of frequent sub-graphs in the unit U_i
$P^k(U_i)$	set of frequent k-edge sub-graphs in the unit U_i
C^{k+1}	set of candidate $(k+1)$-edge sub-graphs
F^{k+1}	set of frequent $(k+1)$-edge sub-graphs
P	difference between $P(U_i)$ and $P(U_i')$
P	prune set

process continues until the set of frequent sub-graphs of D (i.e., $P(D)$) is found. The symbols used in the algorithm are listed in Table 11.1.

Algorithm PartMiner

Input: *Graph database D;*
                   Minimum support sup;
                   Number of units k;
Output: P(D), the set of frequent sub-graphs in D;
// Phase 1: Divide the database into k units.
    1.   DBPartition (D, k);
// Phase 2: Combine the results of k units.
    2. $l = \lfloor log_2\, k \rfloor$;
    3.   i = l + 1;
    4.   For (j = 0; j < k − 2^l; j++) do
    5.   Call Algorithm Gaston to mine U_{2j} and U_{2j+1};
    6. $P(D_{i-1,j})$ = MergeJoin $(D_{i-1,j}, P(U_{2j}), P(U_{2j+1}), sup/k)$;
    7.   Endfor
    8.   i--;
    9.   While (i > 0) do
    10.   For (j = 0; j < 2^i; j = j + 2) do
    11.   If (i == $log_2\, k \wedge j > k - 2^l − 1$) Then
    12.   Call Algorithm Gaston to mine D_{ij} & $D_{i,j+1}$;
    13. $S = D_{i-1,j/2}$;
    14. $P(S)$ = MergeJoin $(S, P(D_{ij}), P(D_{i,j+1}), sup/2^i)$;
    15.   Endfor
    16.   i--;
    17. Endwhile
End Algorithm PartMiner

Procedure MergeJoin

Input: *Graph dataset S;*
                   $P(S_0)$, the set of frequent sub-graphs in S_0;
                   $P(S_1)$, the set of frequent sub-graphs in S_1;
                   Minimum support sup;
Output: P(S), the set of frequent sub-graphs in the dataset S;
    1. $P^1(S)$ = {frequent 1-edge sub-graphs in S};
    2. $P = P(S_0) \cup P(S_1) \setminus P^1(S)$;
    3.   Prune the graphs in $P(S_0)$ and $P(S_1)$ with P;
    4. $P^2(S) = P^2(S_0) \cup P^2(S_1)$;
    5. C^3 = Join $(P^2(S_0), P^2(S_1))$;
    6. F^3 = CheckFrequency (C^3, sup);

7.   *For (k = 3; $F^k \neq \phi$; k++) do*
8. $P^k(S) = P^k(S_0) \cup P^k(S_1) \cup F^k$;
9. $C_1^{k+1} = Join\ (P^k(S_0),\ F^k)$;
10. $C_2^{k+1} = Join\ (P^k(S_1),\ F^k)$;
11. $C_3^{k+1} = Join\ (F^k,\ F^k)$;
12. $C^{k+1} = C_1^{k+1} \cup C_2^{k+1} \cup C_3^{k+1}$;
13. $F^{k+1} = CheckFrequency\ (C^{k+1},\ sup)$;
14. *Endfor*
15. $P(S) = \cup\ P^k(S)$;
End Procedure MergeJoin

Incremental Mining Using PartMiner

The motivation for the proposed approach is to effectively deal with graphs in the presence of updates. It is important to isolate those vertices and edges that are changed frequently into a small set of sub-graphs so that the number of sub-graphs that need to participate in the incremental mining process is minimized. Recall that PartMiner finds the set of frequent sub-graphs by first partitioning the database into several units, then mining the set of frequent sub-graphs in each of these units, and finally merging the results of the units with the merge-join operation. If we are able to isolate the updated vertices and/or edges of a graph to a small set of sub-graphs, we will be able to focus only on this set of sub-graphs instead of mining on the entire database each time an update occurs. Patterns that are affected by updates can be classified into three categories:

1.   *UF* (unchange frequencies): the set of patterns whose frequencies remain unchanged;

2.   *FI* (frequent to infrequent): the set of previously frequent patterns that have become infrequent; and

3.   *IF* (infrequent to frequent): the set of previously infrequent patterns that have become frequent.

Algorithm PartMiner can be easily extended to discover *UF* and *IF*. The idea is as follows: When the database D is updated, for each updated unit U_i' (U_i

is the original unit before the updates), we re-execute the main memory algorithm to find the new set of frequent sub-graphs $P(U_i{}')$. We then compare the set $P(U_i{}')$ against the set $P(U_i)$. If they are different, we do the following:

1. We keep the sub-graphs that appear in the set $P(U_i)$ but not in the set $P(U_i{}')$ in the prune set P. For each sub-graph in the prune set P, we check to see if it exists in any other $P(U_j{}')$ ($0 \leq j \leq k$ and $j \neq i$). If it exists, we remove it from P. Otherwise, we do nothing. Note that P keeps track of all sub-graphs that may potentially change from frequent to infrequent.

2. Next, we check the set of sub-graphs in the pre-updated database D, i.e., $P(D)$ against the prune set P. We remove those sub-graphs in $P(D)$ that are the supergraphs of some graphs in P, and add them to the set FI. The pruned $P(D)$ is denoted as $P(D)'$.

When all of the updated units are checked, we perform a final merge-join operation to obtain the updated results. However, since there are some graphs whose frequencies are not changed during the updates, we do not need to check them. This can result in further optimization.

The *IncPartMiner* algorithm is designed to handle updates. Line 1 scans the updated database D' to get the set of frequent edges, that is, $P^l(D')$. Line 2 compares the set of frequent edges in the original database D, that is, $P^l(D)$ with the set $P^l(D')$, and add the sub-graphs that exist in $P^l(D)$ but not in $P^l(D')$ into the prune set P.

Next, for each unit $U_i{}'$ that consists of the updated vertices, we re-execute the Gaston algorithm to mine the set of frequent sub-graphs (i.e., $P(U_i{}')$), and compare it with the set of sub-graphs in the unit U_i, that is, $P(U_i)$. Those potentially infrequent sub-graphs are added to the prune set P (lines 3-9). Line 10 then prunes the sub-graphs in the set $P(D)$ with the prune set P, which results in the pruned set $P(D)'$. Then, lines 11-12 further use the pruned set $P(D)'$ to prune the candidate graphs when carrying out the merge-join operation on the updated results of the units (see Figure 11.13). Finally, the three sets of the sub-graphs, that is, UF, FI, and IF, are output (lines 13-15), where IF consists of the graphs in $P(D')$ but not in $P(D)$, UF is the set of graphs in $P(D')$ but not in IF, and FI contains all the graphs G in $P(D)$ such that there is a graph G' in P that is a sub-graph of G.

Algorithm IncPartMiner

Input: *Updated database D';*
          $P(U_i)$, *set of frequent sub-graphs in unit U_i ($0 \le i \le k$);*
          P(D), the old set of frequent sub-graphs in D;
          Minimum support sup;
          Setword to indicate the re-examined units set;
Output: *Three sets of patterns: UF, IF, FI;*
  1. *$P^1(D') = \{frequent\ 1\text{-}edge\ sub\text{-}graphs\ in\ D'\}$;*
  2. *$P = P^1(D) \setminus P^1(D')$;*
  3. *For (i = 0; i < k; i++) do*
  4.   *If (set(i) ≠ 1 Then Continue;*
  5.   *Call Gaston algorithm to mine the unit U_i; Result is stored in $P(U_i')$;*
  6.   *If ($P(U_i') \setminus P(U_i) \ne \phi$) Then recombine = 1;*
  7.   *$P' = P(U_i') \setminus P(U_i)$;*
  8.   *$P = P \cup \{G \in P' \mid \forall j = 0 \dots k \wedge j \ne I,\ G \notin P(U_j)\}$;*
  9. *Endfor*
  10. *$P(D') = \{G \in P(D) \mid \forall\ G' \in P,\ G' \preccurlyeq G\}$;*
  11. *If (recombine) Then*
  12.   *Call IncMergeJoin to join the units' results; Result is stored in P(D');*
  13. *IF = P(D') \ P(D);*
  14. *UF = P(D') \ IF;*
  15. *$FI = \{G \in P(D) \mid \exists\ G' \in P,\ G' < G\}$;*

End Algorithm IncPartMiner

Procedure IncMergeJoin (D', $P(S_0)$, $P(S_1)$, P(D))
  1. *$P^2(D') = P^2(S_0) \cup P^2(S_1)$;*
  2. *$C^3 = Join\ (P^2(S_0),\ P^2(S_1))$;*
  3. *For each $G \in C^3 \wedge G \in P(D')$ do*
  4.   *$C^3 = C^3 - \{G\}$;*
  5.   *$F^3 = F^3 \cup \{G\}$;*
  6. *Endfor*
  7. *$F^3 = F^3 \cup \{G \in C^3 \mid G.sup \ge sup\}$;*
  8. *For (k = 3; $F^k \ne \phi$; k++) do*
  9.   *$P^k(D') = P^k(S_0) \cup P^k(S_1) \cup F^k$;*
  10.   *$C_1^{k+1} = Join\ (P^k(S_0),\ F^k)$;*
  11.   *$C_2^{k+1} = Join\ (P^k(S_1),\ F^k)$;*
  12.   *$C_3^{k+1} = Join\ (F^k,\ F^k)$;*
  13.   *$C^{k+1} = C_1^{k+1} \cup C_2^{k+1} \cup C_3^{k+1}$;*
  14.   *For each $G \in C^{k+1} \wedge G \in P(D')$ do*
  15.   *$C^{k+1} = C^{k+1} - \{G\}$;*

16. $F^{k+1} = F^{k+1} \cup \{G\};$
17.   *Endfor*
18. $F^{k+1} = F^{k+1} \cup \{G \in C^{k+1} \mid G.sup \geq sup\};$
19.   *Endfor*
20.   *Return $\cup$ $P^k(D');$*
End Procedure IncMergeJoin

Experimental Study

In this section, we report the performance study of the proposed algorithms. The algorithms are implemented in C++. All the experiments are conducted on a P4 2.8GHZ CPU, 2.5GB RAM and 73GB hard disk. The operating system is Redhat Linux 9.0.

We use the synthetic data generator described in Wang, Wang, and Pei (2004). The data generator takes as input five parameters D, N, T, I, and L, whose meanings are shown in Table 11.2. For example, the dataset D50kT 20 N20L200I5 indicates that the dataset is made up of 50k graphs, the average number of edges in each graph is 20, and there are 20 possible labels and 200 potentially frequent kernels. The average number of edges in the frequent kernels is 5.

Table 11.2. Parameters of synthetic data generator

Parameter	Meaning	Range
D	total number of graphs in the data set	100k -1000k
N	number of possible labels	20, 30, 40, 50
T	average number of edges in graphs	10, 15, 20, 25
I	average number of edges in potentially frequent graph patterns	2, 3, 4, 5, 6, 7, 9
L	number of potentially frequent kernels	200

Experiments on Static Datasets

In this section, we study the performance of PartMiner in a static environment. We compare it with the ADIMINE algorithm (Wang, Wang, & Pei, 2004). In the following sets of experiments, the parameter L is fixed at 200, and the parameter k is set to 2. The size of the memory is set to unlimited.

Effect of Partitioning Criteria

We first study the effect of using different partitioning criteria. There are three ways to partition graphs:

1. Isolate the updated vertices into the same sub-graphs, that is, $\lambda_1 = 1$, $\lambda_2 = 0$ (Partition 1);

2. Minimize connectivity between sub-graphs, that is, $\lambda_1 = 0$, $\lambda_2 = 1$ (Partition 2);

3. Isolate the updated vertices AND minimize the connectivity, that is, $\lambda_1 = 1$, $\lambda_2 = 1$ (Partition 3).

Figure 11.7. Effect of partitioning criteria

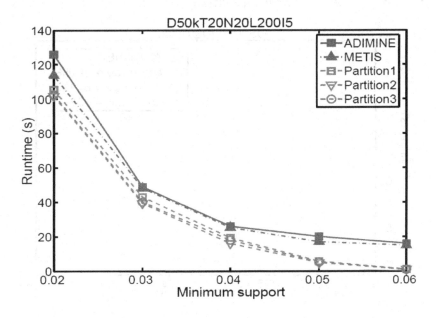

We also use METIS (Karpis & Kumar, 1998) to partition the graphs before mining the graphs in the database. The algorithms in METIS are based on multi-level graph partitioning. They reduce the size of the graph by collapsing vertices and edges, partition the smaller graphs, and then uncoarsen it to construct a partition for the original graph.

Figure 11.7 shows the results. The proposed graph partitioning algorithms perform better than METIS. Specifically, Partition2 gives the best performance. This is because Partition2 minimizes the number of connective edges between sub-graphs, which in turn reduces the number of joining graphs in the merge-join operations. This means that in the static dataset, the criteria to partition graphs based on frequency of updated vertices has minimal effect on the performance of PartMiner.

Varying Minimum Support

Next, we study the performance of PartMiner by varying minimum support from 1% to 6%. The results are shown in Figure 11.8. Compared to ADI-MINE, we observe that PartMiner needs less time to find the complete set of frequent sub-graphs when minimum support is greater than 1.5%. When

Figure 11.8. Runtime vs. parameter minsup

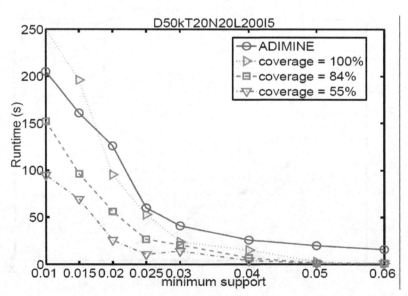

minimum support is less than 1.5%, we find that PartMiner needs more time than ADIMINE does to find the complete set of frequent graphs. This is because when minimum support decreases, more sub-graphs become frequent, and the sub-graphs also become more complex. As a result, PartMiner needs more time to count the frequency of the sub-graphs. In contrast, the index structure of the ADIMINE is advantageous at this time. However, if we only want to retrieve an approximate result of the frequent sub-graphs, for example, coverage = 84% or 55% (coverage indicates the percentage of the frequent sub-graphs found in the complete set), then PartMiner outperforms ADIMINE.

Effect of Number of Units k

We test the performance of the PartMiner by varying the number of units from 2 to 6. Recall that we have divided the database into units and these units can be processed in parallel. This implies that our PartMiner can be executed either in the serial mode or the parallel mode. In the serial mode, we measure aggregate time which is computed by adding the time spent in all the units together.

Figure 11.9. Runtime vs. parameter k

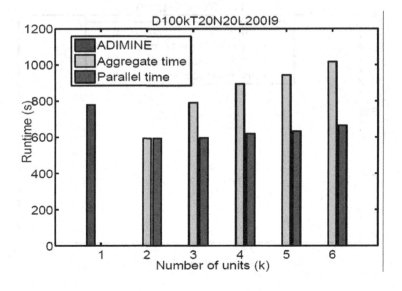

In the parallel mode (with 1 CPU), the units are executed concurrently and we simply take the maximum of the time spent in the units. From the results in Figure 11.9, we see that more time is needed to find the complete set of sub-graphs in the database as the parameter k increases. We also observe that the parallel running PartMiner is faster than ADIMINE in finding the complete set of frequent sub-graphs.

Scalability

In this set of the experiments, we evaluate the performance of PartMiner by varying the parameters T, I, and D of the synthetic data generator, which will affect the size of the graphs. Figure 11.10, Figure 11.11, and Figure 11.12 show that PartMiner scales linearly with the parameters T, I, and D, and is faster in finding the complete set (or approximate results) of the frequent sub-graphs compared to ADIMINE.

Figure 11.10 shows the results when the parameter T varies from 10 to 25. We observe that PartMiner needs more time to find the set of frequent graphs as T increases. This is to be expected since the frequent sub-graphs in the final results tend to be more complex with the growth of T.

Figure 11.10. Varying parameter T

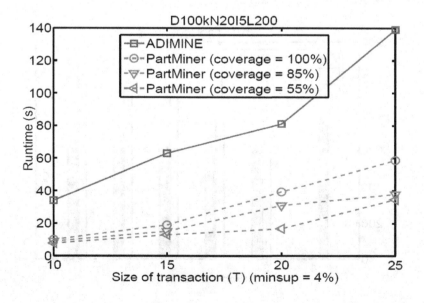

Figure 11.11. Varying parameter I

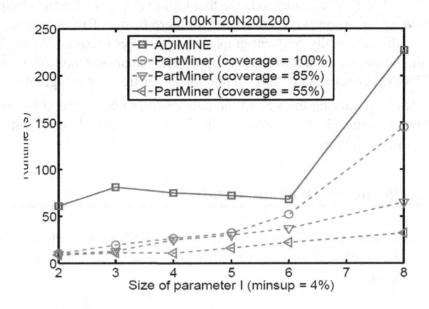

Figure 11.12. Varying parameter D

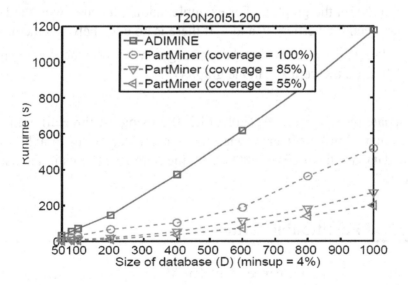

Figure 11.11 shows the performance of PartMiner when the parameter I varies from 2 to 8. The results indicate that to find the set of frequent graphs, Part-Miner is slower when I increases to more than 7. This is because the size of the potentially frequent graphs in the dataset becomes larger. As a result, the size of the frequent sub-graphs in the database tends to be larger, and PartMiner needs more time to find the larger frequent sub-graphs.

The effect of varying the size of the database from 50,000 to 1000,000 is shown in Figure 11.12. We observe that PartMiner scales linearly with the size of the database.

Experiments on Dynamic Datasets

In this section, we study the performance of IncPartMiner when updates occur. We implement a data generator which updates the database in three different ways:

1.   Updating the vertex/edge labels with existing or new labels. For example, updating the vertices/edges with label l in the graphs to the label l';

2.   Adding a new edge with an existing or a new label between two vertices v_i and v_j in the graph G. For example, adding an edge with the label l' between the vertices v_0 and v_1 if there is no edge between them;

3.   Adding a new vertex v, and a new edge $e(v, v_i)$ with the existing or new labels on the vertex v_i in the graph G.

We update the dataset D50kT20N20L200I5 using the three different ways, and evaluate IncPartMiner by varying the percentage of the graphs updated in the database from 20% to 80% with the number of units in the database fixed at 2.

Effect of Partitioning Criteria

We first test the performance of IncPartMiner by varying the partitioning criteria. Figure 11.13 shows the results. We observe Partition3, that is isolating the updated vertices AND minimizing the connective edges, yields the best performance in the dynamic dataset. This is because Partition3 not only

Figure 11.13. Effect of partitioning criteria

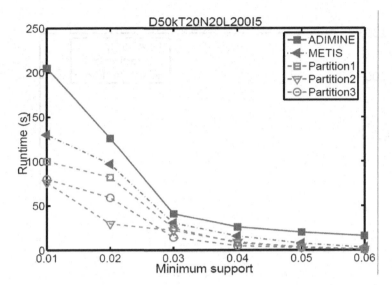

reduces connectivity among units, but also tries to isolate updated vertices into a minimum number of units, and minimizes the number of units needed to be re-mined and re-examined in the merge-join operation.

Varying Minimum Support

We evaluate the IncPartMiner algorithm by varying minimum support from 1% to 6%. Figure 11.14 shows the results of finding the complete set of graphs in the database. We note that IncPartMiner is more efficient in finding the new set of frequent graphs compared to ADIMINE and PartMiner.

This is because IncPartMiner makes use of the pruning results of the pre-updated database to prune those candidate graphs that remain unchanged. It also uses the differences between the pre-updated results and the updated results of the units to prune those sub-graphs that have become infrequent. This results in much savings.

In contrast, ADIMINE and PartMiner have to re-mine the database to find the sub-graphs that have been changed, and need to re-examine both the changed and unchanged sub-graphs.

Figure 11.14. Runtime vs. parameter minsup

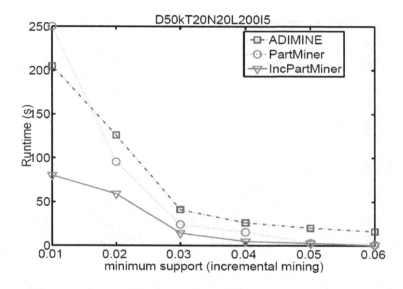

Effect of Number of Units k

Next, we test IncPartMiner with different number of units. We vary the parameter k from 2 to 6. Figure 11.15 indicates that IncPartMiner runs faster than ADIMINE when mining dynamic datasets both in serial mode and in

Figure 11.15. Runtime vs. parameter k

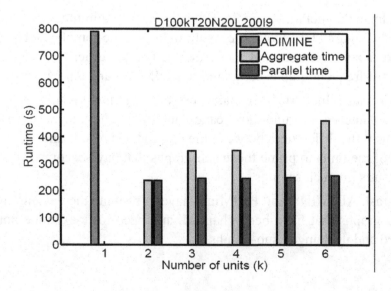

parallel mode. We believe this is due to the fact that IncPartMiner uses the pruned results of the pre-updated database to avoid generating candidate graphs that remain unchanged. This enables the IncPartMiner to check only those sub-graphs that were infrequent but have become frequent in the updated database.

In contrast, ADIMINE has to rebuild the ADI index structure and re-mine the sub-graphs, including changed sub-graphs and unchanged sub-graphs.

Effect of Various Types of Updates

Next, we evaluate the performance of IncPartMiner by varying the updating coverage in the database from 20% to 80%. Figure 11.16 shows the results of updating the labels of the vertices (or edges) to existing and new labels. Figure 11.17 and Figure 11.18 show the results of adding new edges/vertices to the existing/new labels. The results confirm that IncPartMiner outperforms ADIMINE in mining frequent graphs in dynamic datasets.

We observe that the updating coverage of the database has little effect on the performance of IncPartMiner. IncPartMiner scales linearly with the graph size and the number of labels in the database. IncPartMiner focuses

Figure 11.16. Update the node/edge labels

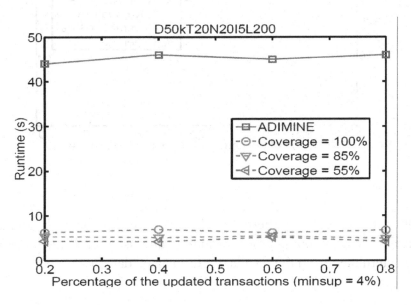

Figure 11.17. Add new edges between two vertices

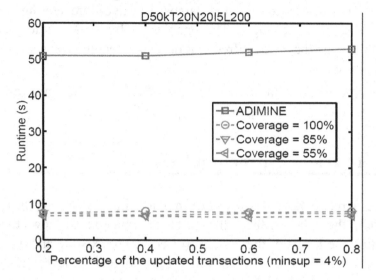

Figure 11.18. Add new vertex with an edge to existing vertices

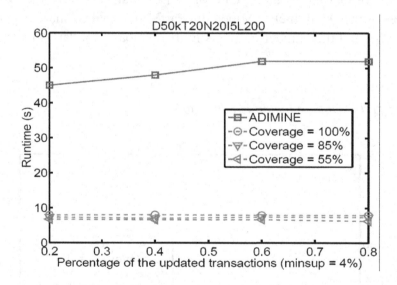

on patterns in the set IF (patterns which were infrequent but now tend to be frequent). The partitioning process handles patterns in UF while patterns in FI are determined from the results of pre-updated databases.

Summary

In this chapter, we have presented a partition-based algorithm PartMiner for discovering the set of frequent sub-graphs. Each graph in the database is partitioned into smaller sub-graphs. This enables PartMiner to avoid the thrashing problem typically experienced by most memory-based algorithms. Moreover, by exploring the cumulative information of units, PartMiner can effectively reduce the number of candidate graphs. Experimental results verify that PartMiner can find frequent sub-graphs efficiently and scalably.

We have also extended PartMiner to efficiently handle updates in graph databases. The algorithm IncPartMiner uses the pruning results of pre-updated databases to avoid generating candidate graphs that remain unchanged. It only checks those sub-graphs that were infrequent but tend to be frequent in updated databases, instead of re-examining both changed and unchanged sub-graphs as existing algorithms do. This leads to tremendous cost savings. The experimental results also demonstrate that IncPartMiner performs much better than ADIMINE and PartMiner in finding graphs when updates occur.

References

Bradley, P., Fayyad, U., & Reina, C. (1998). Scaling clustering algorithms to large databases. In *Proceedings of the ACM SIGKDD International Conference on Knowledge Discovery and Data Mining,* New York City, New York, USA, August 27-31 (pp. 9-15). Menlo Park, CA: AAAI Press.

Chi, Y., Yang, Y., & Muntz, R. R. (2003). Indexing and mining free trees. In *Proceedings of the 19th IEEE International Conference on Data Mining,* Melbourne, Florida, USA, December 19-22 (pp. 509-512). Los Alamitos, CA: IEEE Computer Society Press.

Faloutsos, C., McCurley, K. S., & Tomkins, A. (2004). Fast discovery of connection subgraphs. In *Proceedings of the ACM SIGKDD International Conference on Knowledge Discovery and Data Mining,* Seattle, Washington, USA, August 22-25 (pp. 118-127). New York: ACM Press.

Hall, L., Chawla, N., & Bowyer, K. W. (1998). Combining decision trees learned in parallel. In *ACM SIGKDD Workshop on Distributed Data*

Mining, New York City, New York, USA, August 27-31. Menlo Park, CA: AAAI Press.

Huan, J., Wang, W., & Prins, J. (2004). SPIN: Mining maximal frequent subgraphs from graph databases. In *Proceedings of the ACM SIGKDD International Conference on Knowledge Discovery and Data Mining,* Seattle, Washington, USA, August 22-25 (pp. 581-586). New York: ACM Press.

Inokuchi, A., Washio, T., & Nishimura, K. (2002). *A fast algorithm for mining frequent connected subgraphs.* IBM Research Report RT0448.

Karpis, G., & Kumar, V. (1998). Multilevel algorithms for multi-constraint graph partitioning. In *Proceedings of ACM/IEEE International Conference on Supercomputing,* Orlando, Florida, USA, November 7-13 (pp. 1-13). New York: ACM Press.

Kuramochi, M., & Karypis, G. (2004). An efficient algorithm for discovering frequent subgraphs. *IEEE Transactions on Knowledge and Data Engineering, 16*(9), 1038-1051.

Lee, C.-H., Lin, C.-R., & Chen, M.-S. (2001b). Sliding window filtering: An efficient algorithm for incremental mining. In *Proceedings of the International Conference on Information and Knowledge Management,* Atlanta, Georgia, USA, November 5-10 (pp. 263-270). New York: ACM Press.

Ng, R. T., & Han, J. (2002). CLARANS: A method for clustering objects for spatial data mining. *IEEE Transactions on Knowledge and Data Engineering, 14*(5), 1003-1016.

Nijssen, S., & Kok, J. N. (2004). A quickstart in frequent structure mining can make a difference. In *Proceedings of the ACM SIGKDD International Conference on Knowledge Discovery and Data Mining,* Seattle, Washington, USA, August 22-25 (pp. 647-652). New York: ACM Press.

Savasere, A., Omiecinski, E., & Navathe, S. (1995). An efficient algorithm for mining association rules in large databases. In *Proceedings of the International Conference on Very Large Data Bases,* Zurich, Switzerland, September 11-15 (pp. 432-444). San Francisco, CA: Morgan Kaufmann Publishers.

Shafer, J., Agrawal, R., & Mehta, M. (1996). SPRINT: A scalable parallel classifier for data mining. In *Proceedings of the International Conference on Very Large Data Bases,* Mumbai (Bombay), India, September 3-6 (pp. 544-555). San Francisco, CA: Morgan Kaufmann Publishers.

Shasha, D., Wang, J., & Zhang, S. (2004). Unordered tree mining with applications to phylogeny. In *IEEE International Conference on Data Engineering,* Boston, Massachusetts, USA, March 30-April 2 (pp. 708-719). Los Alamitos, CA: IEEE Computer Society Press.

Termier, A., Rousset, M.-C., & Sebag, M. (2004). Dryade: A new approach for discovering closed frequent trees in heterogeneous tree databases. In *Proceedings of the 4th IEEE International Conference on Data Mining,* Brighton, UK, November 1-4 (pp. 543-546). Los Alamitos, CA: IEEE Computer Society Press.

Wang, C., Wang, W., & Pei, J. (2004). Scalable mining of large disk-based graph databases. In *Proceedings of the ACM SIGKDD International Conference on Knowledge Discovery and Data Mining,* Seattle, Washington, USA, August 22-25 (pp. 316-325). New York: ACM Press.

Yan, X., & Han, J. (2002). gSpan: Graph-based substructure pattern mining. In *Proceedings of the IEEE International Conference on Data Mining,* Maebashi City, Japan, December 9-12 (pp. 721-724). Los Alamitos, CA: IEEE Computer Society Press.

Yan, X., & Han, J. (2003). CloseGraph: Mining closed frequent graph patterns. In *Proceedings of the ACM SIGKDD International Conference on Knowledge Discovery and Data Mining,* Washington, D.C., USA, August 24-27 (pp. 286-295). New York: ACM Press.

Yan, X., Yu, P. S., & Han, J. (2004). Graph indexing: A frequent structure-based approach. In *Proceedings of the ACM SIGMOD International Conference on Management of Data,* Paris, France, June 13-18 (pp. 335-346). New York: ACM Press.

Zaki, M. J. (2002). Efficiently mining frequent trees in a forest. In *Proceedings of the ACM SIGKDD International Conference on Knowledge Discovery and Data Mining,* Edmonton, Alberta, Canada, July 23-26 (pp. 71-80). New York: ACM Press.

Chapter XII

Conclusions and Future Work

Association rule mining in spatial databases and temporal databases have been studied extensively in data mining research. Most of the research studies have found interesting patterns in either spatial information or temporal information, however, few studies have handled both efficiently. Meanwhile, developments in spatio-temporal databases and spatio-temporal applications have prompted data analysts to turn their focus to spatio-temporal patterns that explore both spatial and temporal information.

In this book, we have examined some issues in temporal mining and suggested some improvements to existing sequence mining and periodic pattern mining algorithms. We introduced a class of patterns for temporal databases called dense periodic patterns, and described a periodicity detection algorithm to efficiently discover short period patterns that may exist in only a limited range of the time series. We discussed an I/O-efficient algorithm for mining frequent sequences as well as incremental update. We also described a new class of patterns called progressive confident rules that capture the state change of objects that leads to a certain end state with increasing confidence.

In addition, we have introduced new classes of spatio-temporal patterns and described efficient and effective algorithms for mining these spatio-temporal patterns. We presented techniques to discover topological patterns by imposing temporal constraints into the process for mining collocation patterns. We have designed an algorithm called TopologyMiner that finds topological patterns in a depth-first manner and follows the pattern-growth methodology.

We have studied the problem of discovering spatial sequence patterns. We presented two new classes of spatial sequence patterns, called flow patterns and generalized spatio-temporal patterns to describe the change of events over space and time, which are useful to the understanding of many real-life applications. We have designed two algorithms, FlowMiner and GenSTMiner, to find these two classes of spatial sequence patterns. FlowMiner is a disk-based algorithm and utilizes temporal relationships and spatial relationships amid events to generate flow patterns. GenSTMiner is based on the idea of the pattern growth approach and finds generalized spatio-temporal patterns in a depth-first manner. Our performance studies show that the proposed algorithms are both scalable and efficient. Experiments on real-life datasets also reveal some interesting flow patterns and generalized spatio-temporal patterns.

Finally, we have studied the problem of mining arbitrary spatio-temporal patterns by modeling spatio-temporal data as graphs. We have designed a partition-based approach called PartMiner for graph mining. PartMiner utilizes the cumulative information of partitions to effectively reduce the number of candidate graphs. We have also extended PartMiner to handle frequent updates in the database. The extended version called IncPartMiner uses the pruning results of pre-updated databases to avoid generating unchanged candidate graphs. IncPartMiner only checks those sub-graphs that were infrequent but tend to be frequent in updated databases, instead of re-examining both changed and unchanged sub-graphs as existing algorithms do. This leads to tremendous cost savings. The experimental results indicate that PartMiner is effective and scalable in finding frequent sub-graphs, outperforming existing algorithms in updated databases.

Future Research Directions

While this book has shown association rule mining to be a promising tool for spatio-temporal data analysis, there are a number of issues that need to be further investigated.

Data Integration and Data Classification

Real-world spatio-temporal data tends to be large and is obtained from heterogeneous data sources. How to integrate data from different data sources at different levels is an increasing problem that extends beyond spatio-temporal association rule mining and into many types of spatio-temporal statistical analyses. Hence, discovering knowledge from real-world spatio-temporal applications calls for data integration and data classification.

Representation and Computation of Spatial Relationships

In this book, we have focused on relationships of spatial coincidence and distance. However, there are other types of spatial relationships that may be used in spatio-temporal association rule mining, such as direction, topological relationships, and so forth. A structured study that is able to compare different spatial relationship types in association rule mining would illustrate the impact of choice of spatial relationship type on mining results.

Representation of Spatio-Temporal Data

Developing spatio-temporal mining methods should go hand in hand with efficient and effective spatio-temporal data mining. Each spatio-temporal representation approach and the corresponding data structures may impose some unique challenges on data mining algorithms.

Indexing Schemes for Spatio-Temporal Data

In order to ensure the efficiency and scalability of spatio-temporal mining algorithms, effective indexing schemes for spatio-temporal data are needed.

Efficient Trend Detection Algorithms

Trend is a powerful means of summarizing massive data into compact form. Current trend analysis algorithms are focused only on time series data. Extending trend analysis to spatio-temporal data will be a promising future research direction.

Discovering Changes in Data Distribution

Another meaningful description of spatio-temporal data is in terms of data distribution in an area over a specified time window. Recently, there have been some efforts to discover changes in data distribution in the form of time-space clusters. More efforts are needed to make the discovering process scalable.

Flow/Interaction Patterns Over Time

Closely related to the changes in data distribution is the discovery of complex flow/interaction patterns. Current efforts focus on direct and proximal interactions or influences. With the advances of real-time monitoring systems, intelligent transportation systems and "position-aware" devices such as cellular telephones, massive amount of movement, or interaction data are being captured. Complex interaction patterns require specially designed algorithm to discover them.

Spatio-temporal mining is still in its infancy. The challenges are great but the promises are greater still. As datasets and user numbers increases rapidly, a new era is upon us where the identification and mining of spatial and temporal data needs to be addressed efficiently and elegantly. It is our hope that this book will lead to a greater awareness of the issues and needs in spatio-temporal mining and encourage more researchers to join in exploring this exciting field of research.

About the Authors

Wynne Hsu is an associate professor at the Department of Computer Science and vice-dean (Graduate Studies), School of Computing, National University of Singapore (NUS). She received her BSc in computer science at National University of Singapore and her MSc and PhD in electrical engineering from Purdue University, West Lafayette, USA, in 1989 and 1994, respectively. She has published more than 100 technical research papers in various international journals, conference proceedings, and books. She has also served as a program committee member in numerous international conferences including VLDB, IEEE ICDE, SIGKDD, PAKDD, and DASFAA. Dr. Hsu is the principal investigator of a number of government-funded research projects. Her research interests include: knowledge discovery in databases with emphasis on data mining algorithms in relational databases, XML databases, image databases, and spatio-temporal databases.

Mong Li Lee is an associate professor and assistant dean (Undergraduate Studies) in the School of Computing at the National University of Singapore. She received her PhD, MSc, and BSc (Hons 1) degrees in computer science from the National University of Singapore in 1999, 1992, and 1989, respectively. Her research interests include data cleaning, data mining, data integration of heterogeneous and semistructured data, and performance database issues in dynamic environments. She has published more than 100 technical research papers in international journals and conferences such as

ACM SIGMOD, VLDB, ICDE, EDBT, and ACM SIGKDD. She has also served as a program committee member in various international conferences and is the editor of a number of books.

Junmei Wang is currently a research engineer at Siemens, Singapore. She graduated from the Department of Computer Science, School of Computing, National University of Singapore (NUS) in 2005 with a PhD in computer science. Dr. Wang received her BEng and MEng in electrical engineering from Xi'an Jiaotong University, China, in 1998 and 2000, respectively. Her research interests are focused on knowledge discovery in spatio-temporal databases.

*   *   *   *   *

David Cheung is a professor in computer science at the University of Hong Kong. He received his PhD from Simon Fraser University. Professor Cheung is the head of the Department of Computer Science and the director of the Center for E-Commerce Infrastructure Development (CECID). Professor Cheung's main research areas include databases, data mining, XML technologies, and bioinformatics. He has published extensively in international journals and conferences and was the recipient of the HKU Outstanding Researcher Award in 1998.

Ben Kao is an associate professor and deputy head in the Department of Computer Science at The University of Hong Kong. He received his BSc in computer science from the University of Hong Kong in 1989, and his PhD in computer science from Princeton University in 1995. Dr. Kao's research interests include database management systems, data mining, real-time systems, and information retrieval systems.

Chang Sheng is currently a graduate student at the Department of Computer Science, School of Computing, National University of Singapore (NUS). His research interests are spatio-temporal data mining, time series mining, and indexing spatio-temporal data. He received his MEng in electrical engineering from Xi'an Jiaotong University, China in 2003.

Chi-Lap Yip is an honorary assistant professor in the Department of Computer Science at The University of Hong Kong. He received his PhD in computer science from the University of Hong Kong. Dr. Yip's research interests include data mining, music retrieval, information retrieval, database, multi-lingual systems, and music typesetting systems.

Minghua Zhang is a research fellow in the School of Computing, National University of Singapore. She received her PhD in computer science from The University of Hong Kong in 2005. Her research interests include sequence mining, spatio-temporal mining, bioinformatics, and database. She has published papers in some top international conferences and journals, including SIGMOD, SIGKDD, and DAMI. She was a teaching assistant at The University of Hong Kong from 1999-2004.

Index